The Name of the Game

The Name of the Game

SPORT AND SOCIETY

Fred Inglis

HEINEMANN
LONDON

Heinemann Educational Books Ltd
LONDON   EDINBURGH   MELBOURNE
SINGAPORE   JOHANNESBURG
IBADAN   HONG KONG   NEW DELHI
TORONTO   AUCKLAND
KUALA LUMPUR   NAIROBI
KINGSTON

ISBN 0 435 18472 5

Published by
Heinemann Educational Books Ltd
48 Charles Street, London W1X 8AH
Filmset by Keyspools Ltd, Golborne, Lancs
Made and printed in Great Britain by
Cox & Wyman Ltd,
London, Fakenham and Reading

Contents

INTRODUCTION   IX

1 The memory of a people—let us now praise famous men   I

2 The forms of ceremony   34

3 Body and mind—thought and sport   49

4 Heroism and community—writing about sport   74

5 The idiom of the people—mythmaking and the media   90

6 Gesture as language—sport and its stories   133

7 Gentlemen, players and stars   153

8 Sport, cash and technology—the book of numbers   170

9 The world on the move   190

BIBLIOGRAPHY   203

LIST OF PHOTOGRAPHS   208

INDEX   210

Acknowledgements

The author and publishers wish to thank the following for permission to reprint copyright material: Laurence Pollinger Ltd and the Estate of the late Mrs Frieda Lawrence for 'What is He?' from *The Complete Poems of D. H. Lawrence;* Victor Gollancz Ltd for the extract from *The Hard Years* by Joe Brown; The *Daily Telegraph* for the extract from E. W. Swanton's article 28 August 1973; The *Guardian* for the extract from 7 September 1973; Frank Cass & Co for the extracts from *Readings in the Sociology of Sport* by E. Dunning; The *Daily Mirror* for extracts from the articles by Peter Laker and by Tim Richards (28 August 1973); Secker & Warburg for the extracts from *The King of Hackney Marshes* by Brian Glanville; Collins for the extract from *Autobiography* by Neville Cardus and for the extract from *The Barry John Story* by Barry John; Jonathan Cape and the Executors of the Ernest Hemingway Estate for the extract from *Death in the Afternoon* and the two extracts from *Fiesta* ('The Sun Also Rises') by Ernest Hemingway; Faber & Faber for the extracts from 'Marina' and 'The Waste Land' from *Collected Poems 1909–1962* by T. S. Eliot, and for the extracts from *George Mallory* by David Robertson; Penguin Books Ltd for the extracts from *This Sporting Life* by David Storey (Longman 1960) pp. 162, 228, 243, 245, 252, 255; Macmillan for the extract from *England, their England,* by A. G. MacDonell; The BBC for the extracts from *The Football Business* and for the extract from Alistaire Cooke's *Letter from America*; Allison & Busby for the extract from *The Sash He Never Wore* by Derek Dougan; Mrs M. Thomas for the extracts from 'The Manor Farm' by Edward Thomas from *Collected Poems*; the BBC General Advisory Council for the table from 'The Coverage of Sport on BBC Television'; A. D. Peters & Co Ltd for the extract from *The Flame* by Jim Hunter; The *Observer* for the extract from Michael Davie's article from the issue of 1 December 1956; London Express News and Feature Services for the extract from the article by George Whiting in the *Evening Standard*, 13 February 1977; Basil Blackwood for the extracts from *Philosophical Investigations* by L. L. Wittgenstein; and The Bodley Head for 'You, Andrew Marvell' by Andrew Macleish from *Collected Poems* (1955); Eyre & Spottiswoode for the extracts from *Fred: Portrait of a Fast Bowler* by John Arlott.

To my father

Introduction

This book, like any other book, goes out to an unknown audience. And yet, nobody as he writes can imagine that he speaks to nobody. You write with a changing vision, sometimes precise, sometimes vague, of a listening audience.

I start with and from my friends. I begin with my father, to whom this book is dedicated, and who has loved sport all his life, has taught me to do the same, and who has always understood the rich promise of happiness sport holds out, the mad exhilaration, the pointless, satisfying exhaustion, the beauty, the grass and sunshine, the growing images of friendships made and held in games. So I start by talking to my friends, in the hope of being recognized by them, of saying what *they* think and feel, but also in the hope that although they recognize what I say, they also see it for the first time, that they will say 'Yes, that's right, of course, but I'd never put it like that to myself before'. Partly, therefore, this book is a tribute to those friends, because, however unimportant rugby and cricket may be on the scale of eternity, I have never been happier than when running across thick, well-cut turf, with a ball in my hands and my friends around me. So the book is, further, a celebration of friendship itself, and this at a time when the way we live, our mobility and divisions, the deadliness of so much work, the desert places of so much public and social living, when these things do lethal harm to the very idea of friendship.

Saying so is at least an explanation of why the writing is at times so very full and ripe, and brightly, rather dewily coloured. It *intends* to strike strong chords in popular feeling; to try to give politics and metaphysics a ground in the lives people really lead, the landscape they imperfectly cherish, the passion for beauty always trying to find shape and voice. Trying for these things, I cannot have escaped vulgarity.

Better be vulgar and sentimental, than dried up and schematic. Nonetheless, this book has its determinedly intellectual bent. Indeed, it seeks to tie a knot between intellectual and popular life, of a kind placed under impossible and mostly breaking strain by the separatenesses of our giant social institutions – the great transit camps of the universities and schools, the blank unmeaning of everyday work. To put the intellect back in the fields is a great ambition, and only great men have really brought it off. William Morris, John Ruskin, T. H. Green, are the Victorian heroes I would copy in this.

With such schemes, there was little point in turning to the assured and mouth-filling emptiness of what little academic writing there is about sport. I suggest in the brief booklist those texts which seem to me to be written with some of the necessary vitality and searchingness required to think about the coincidence of body and soul made possible in sport. But the books have rarely been on the official shelves. I have had to start from where I have lived and where this introduction begins. Peter and Freda Inglis, Linda Benson, Lesley Aers, John Spragg, Colin Brain, Tim Mathias, Patrick Mills, David Perry, Laurie Drury, Tony Lewis, Quentin Skinner, David Hornbrook, Jonty Driver, Gordon Reddiford, have contributed more than they can ever know. It would indeed be a triumph if the book is worth what they have given to it.

While writing it, I have met other people to whom my thanks are due, who have given generously their time and help, particularly John Arlott, Christopher Chataway, Jack Charlton, Derek Dougan, Wilfred Wooller, Denis Howell, Virginia Wade, the Librarian of the Sport and General Press Agency and of the Sports Council, and the late Ed Lacey. I am grateful to Ann Nash, Denis Powers, and other students, whose unsung researches have been part of the work. Finally, the writings of John Berger are a deep and pervasive influence on all I say.

A portion of this book was written while I held a visiting Professorship at the University of Denver, Colorado. My thanks for its hospitality are also due and ready, particularly to John Williams, who made the visit possible, and proved, as ever, such a memorable host.

One last point: this book is conceived as part of a much larger enterprise, one of the sequence in which the predecessors I have written also stand. The conception is to imagine a human politics which will both reflect the faces of those who look into it, will name wrong and cruelty for what they are, and will hold out a vision of paradise. It would be the merest lunacy to suppose that one man could imagine this alone. This book and its siblings invite collaboration in the question 'What is live and what is dead in modern industrial society? What shall be cherished, and what put down?' I am looking for an answer where the lines cross between popular culture and the individual spirit, where the forms of society and people's feelings are lived as one. Sport is the point of one such intersection; there one finds the image of the people. Like any cultural scientist, I am practising both method and belief.

FRED INGLIS

1 The memory of a people—let us now praise famous men

I BEGIN WITH these photographs because they are the easiest, most straightforward way into all I want to say. The remarks they give rise to air the main themes of the book. Not every sport is here: it is not that sort of book. The photographs provide images which carry with them the ideas I want to talk about. There are photographs of active sports and contemplative ones. Of crowds and solitude. There are photographs of high drama, of beautiful movement, of great strain. The ideas they suggest I then go back to in more detail later on.

If things are said more than once, never mind. Most of all, this book is offered for *recognition*. All right, so it is just about games. Sport. A lot of men

running about in little boys' clothes. But sport is there, deep, deep in the experience of many men (and perhaps rather fewer women). It cuts across class, age, job, education. It is a scrapbook of memories which defines a life. It makes meetings possible through such scrapbooks.

Which returns me to the photographs. They begin as a sort of scrapbook. Pages from a national photograph album; the pictures put in for all sorts of reasons. They become the ground of an argument about sport and a people. About art and what it does for human experience.

If this book is true, a reader should say 'Yes. Yes, that's right. That's something of what sport *is*. And what it means to me, and to others. But, look here . . .' And then conversation with the book begins.

A photograph is many things in a household. It is a snapshot lying about the place.

Or it is the same kind of snapshot in an album. And then the context it needs is clearer. Someone who does not know the family can then understand it better.

It takes its place among memories. And memories are more than a sequence of snapshots:

> What images return
> O my daughter*

* 'Marina' by T. S. Eliot, *Collected Poems 1909–1962* (Faber, 1963).

What do we do with our memories? We not only summon them up as
phantoms from a lost past. We do not go through them, by turning over the
leaves of the album, in order to recover those lost scenes. Memories are
present now. They are part of who we are. In an album, we look at the
pictures, and laughing or half-crying, we turn to ourselves and others, and
say, 'Do you remember that?'

That day of all days. The exhilaration. The relief. That familiar mixture
of feelings in which the triumphant end you longed for has come, and yet
you wish it had not. Or at least you remember the moments which led up to
the triumphant curtain in a different way, so that those moments are now

part of the triumph, and you can wish them back again. At that time, of
course, watching *or* playing, all you wanted was for the whistle to go, and
the victory to be safe. Now, honour won, you can say, 'Wasn't it marvellous
when . . .' and taste with relish the bad moments. The moment, in this case,
when West Germany equalized on the stroke of full time to make it 2–2. At
the time it was utter and undeserved disaster. Now the goal can be
relocated in the memory of that perfect, blazing July afternoon. Re-
membering the agony of extra time makes the victory even more stirring
and more poignant.

And photographs may be poignant. The point of a photograph is that it is not special or mysterious or magnificent, like a great painting. Anyone can take photographs. And in the case of newsphotos, anyone can cut them out and keep them. Sporting photographs are like the snapshots of a national photograph album. They sharpen the poignant, salty memories of old heroes. They bring back memories of what has been lost, and is irrecoverable. And just because it *is* irrecoverable, the men and women who stir those lost hopes become special heroes, whose like we shall not look upon again. So it is that old men forever tell young boys, 'You ought to have seen Victor Trumper, or Bobby Jones.'

A queer use of 'ought' really; the boys could hardly have seen Victor Trumper or Bobby Jones. Yet the young boys in their turn will say the same sort of thing when they themselves become old men, and the young boys of the future will shuffle their feet, and yawn inwardly, and wonder when the old men will fall silent. This is how a society makes its history.

How its imagination continues and makes a tradition: an assembly of names and occasions, great victories and defeats, of ways of seeing and celebrating these things.

The next photograph might seem just a picture of an odd-looking tennis player.

But when you know it is Suzanne Lenglen and you know something of her, you see it differently. This was the first woman tennis player who wore short skirts (short then meant simply 'not full-length') and hit like a man. She hit very hard and angled her shots; she was fit. The Ladies' Tennis Clubs naturally associated her force, her Frenchness, and her victories with all sorts of allegations about her life. Well, that was the price of victory in

1921. You pay different costs now, and get more money back for it than anyone could ever have dreamed of fifty years ago.

The point of the picture is that Miss Lenglen remains who she was. We first understand the picture in terms of what it does not include. This is especially true about the photograph of a sportswoman now fifty years away from her triumphs. We complete the picture by referring to what is external to it.

Next there are two pictures of beautiful horses. For the pictures to be complete they must take their point from the time immediately preceding the moment when the news photographer took the picture immediately after each horse won. The first was at Ascot in 1973. The second in the same year in the champion stakes at Newmarket. Not only that. The second horse has just run his last race ever. Such knowledge also affects how we see the picture. Past defeats are extinguished; a great horse has gone out in such a way as to confirm his place in racing mythology. He won from short odds like the thoroughbred he was, confident, insouciant even

in middle age. And now he canters down the wings on the way to grass.

The eye can hardly pick them out
From the cold shade they shelter in,
Till wind distresses tail and mane;
Then one crops grass, and moves about
– The other seeming to look on –
And stands anonymous again.

Yet fifteen years ago, perhaps
Two dozen distances sufficed
To fable them: faint afternoons
Of Cups and Stakes and Handicaps,
Whereby their names were artificed
To inlay faded, classic Junes –

Silks at the start: against the sky
Numbers and parasols: outside,
Squadrons of empty cars, and heat,
And littered grass: then the long cry
Hanging unhushed till it subside
To stop-press columns on the street.

Do memories plague their ears like flies?
They shake their heads. Dusk brims the shadows,
Summer by summer, all stole away,
The starting-gates, the crowds and cries –
All but the unmolesting meadows.
Almanacked, their names live; they

Have slipped their names, and stand at ease,
Or gallop for what must be joy,
And not a fieldglass sees them home,
Or curious stop-watch prophesies:
Only the groom, and the groom's boy,
With bridles in the evening come.*

So the picture is complicated. This horse is a hero. And so much of England – the British Tourist Association and *New Yorker* view of England – is in the pictures with the horses. The hats, the uniforms, of commission-aires, of jockey, of owner and spectators. The faces: the ruling class faces on the right side of the gates; the sharp, knowing monkey face of the man on the wrong side. The jockey. The sunshine. The short, sweet grass.

All these details are sharpened by the knowledge of the situation. Without the knowledge, the horse might be any horse, the race-course anywhere. (Although someone who really knew the inside of racing would recognize more than the ordinary newspaper reader. But that is the point.)

Newsphotos are, sometimes at least, like the family albums of the nation. Members of the family who are not in the know, say, 'Who's that?' And the meaning of the newsphoto is then translated for them.

At the moment, there is hardly need to translate this newsphoto.

* Philip Larkin, 'At Grass' in *The Less Deceived* (Marvell Press, 1964).

This hero is near enough to the present for nearly all the family to know him. In a year or two the youngest members of the family will not know Bobby Charlton by sight; they will know the record. And the record will have become legendary, as has the picture.

Once the picture is part of the legend, it changes again. Charlton's amazing agility and lissomeness, the combination of power and grace in the picture then become a symbol not only of Charlton but also of football itself. You can buy posters like this.

By that stage, the picture has become a certain kind of art. But to say that clutters up the argument. The idea of art – what the word means to people – has become impossibly portentous. It comes at once too solemnly and too fancily into a conversation. People view it too reverentially or too contemptuously. They see it as to do with an unintelligible education; or else they *make* it into that, so that they have the key to the mystery which others cannot unlock. They turn art into a curriculum, or into a walk round a museum.

Say instead, that the picture of Charlton is an image. (It is not a painting.) It is not, however, an image *about* what Charlton did. It is an image *of* his action. Not only is the picture lovely, but Charlton's original action was also lovely. That is the great strength of photography. (Set aside elaborately posed and composed photographs, which are just like bad painting.) So the picture is an image in that it comes to stand in our imaginations for the possibility of all that unearthly orginzation of reflex, perception, judgement, and movement, which is what it is to act creatively.

The picture tells us that players of Charlton's specially remarkable sort can create utterly unthought-of actions out of the conventions of their game. And if such players can do this, than at least *any* player can imagine that he can do it as well.

And so the picture becomes an image of imaginable liberation. Football and photography being what they are, the image suggests all that follows and all that preceded it. In fact, Charlton scored from this kick. Against Southampton, at the Dell on 13 April 1968. The kick is both history and legend. It depends on our sense of the creativeness and productiveness of the relations which sport makes possible. Charlton was one focus of these relations, but he was so only because the team was what it was at the time. It was able to produce the moves which enabled Charlton to score the goals.

This is to make the words 'produce' and 'productive' much richer than their usually dismal wage-negotiation meanings. It also reminds us, though, of how the gap might close between art and work. All right, so Bobby Charlton plays golf or goes shooting 'after work'. Everyone needs a change. A market gardener's relaxation (as we say) is playing the piano. The concert pianist's re-creation (we might better put it) is to dig his garden. It is still possible to imagine work which would enable the finest relations on a football field or a running track to be lived at times by anyone.

There were such relations in the first four-minute mile. Roger Bannister ran it, but only because Chataway and Brasher paced him in the right way. It was a far less classic piece of miling than Bannister's great win over John Landy in the Vancouver Commonwealth Games a few weeks later. In this one, Bannister had an enormous, solitary run in home over the last 350 yards. The Iffley Road mile was a more casual occasion. (Look at the spectators.) It was also changed by being the first triumph and, like the Brigadier's last win, unchangeably a record. The friendship and dedication of these men to a set of arbitrary numbers on a watch created the relations I so admire. Like so much human endeavour, the target was in itself a chancy thing. It served to concentrate the intelligence, the friendship, the painful effort. It gave these things a context and a meaning in which to thrive. This thriving was not the point of the enterprise. The

point was to run a mile in a whisker under four minutes. The point of such an achievement blunts soon enough, and then what is remembered is the closeness of intimacy, the richness of high aspiration being fulfilled. The profound satisfaction of going to the limit of yourself in the interests, however arbitrary – you can shrug your shoulders for all you're worth about whether or not four minutes are worth killing youself for – in the interests, then, of something which is decidedly *not* yourself.

Even running, therefore, is not solitary. In a society which sets so much store by competitive, single, victory, the track runner can look like the ultimate expression of Darwin's principle. The fittest and the best win the great race for survival.

Kip Keino wasn't just the first international mile winner to come out of Africa. Nor was he just a beautiful runner to watch, though he certainly was that. Keino is also a hero because, again, he lives out the hope of so many Africans. He beat the white men at the games which, in a formalized context, they had brought to Africa.

Sport and politics don't mix? As soon keep the politics out of politics. (That of course is what all former winners – and rulers – would dearly like to do.) Given the inevitable and intense heat of track rivalry, Keino became the hero of free Africa, and became it because those countries were only recently their own people and anxious and aggressive about it, too. They had won their independence, and they would win their races too. They would, quite rightly, give their new athletic heroes plenty to eat and

a safe job in the army. And why not? The rich nations give their athletes safe homes and university running tracks and education grants and private

schools. The communist countries had learned the same lesson, hard and deep. Then their black runners would become more than their nation's heroes. They would become their nation's representatives.

The next picture is of the wonderful African steeplechase runner, Ben Jipko. There is a hero for you. Not in any footling sense – the idea of a hero as simply the empty bucket into which you can pour all your aspirations. The pop hero. Not the idea of the hero as a sort of pop-out or hard-edge 'personality', who has learned to present himself to his audience exclusively in the terms of his so-called popularity, terms which only require his audience to like him, terms indeed in which likability is the criterion of the mass hero or leader. (Allied strongly to notions of trust and trustworthiness.) A hero in another sense focuses and gives solid life to the hopes and desires of other people. That is, he is useful to them. Not in any trivial sense – they do not 'use' him and discard him. ('Use' in the market sense of consume.) He closes the gap between desire and actuality.

Jipko gave meaning to the term hero for thousands of his countrymen and his fellow blacks, and he did it with incomparable grace and worthiness. He did so quite without giving up his proper pride and the enormous dignity and authority with which he ran and with which he carried himself in ordinary social dealings. In this way, he was what a sportsman should be, in the ideal. Handsome, generous, courtly. He stood for – he was – certain manly virtues otherwise in disuse.

Zatopek, the great Czeck athlete who won three gold medals in the long-distance track events of the 1948 Olympic Games, was another such man. As only sportsmen can, he brought thousands of people wildly to their feet, shouting as hard as they could in a triple, plain, chant, each syllable equally stressed, 'Zat-o-pek, Zat-o-pek'. His combination of anguish and dashing beauty commanded the purest, most unselfinterested admiration. (Chataway's effortful, one-pace victory over Kutz in 1954 would be my purest experience of this kind. Quite pure. Lost in admiration, as the strong old saying goes.)

Sport registers these experiences for people. It expresses the deepest, most unspoken parts of their lives. It can give expression to life which otherwise would remain stifled or forgotten or put down.

It can shape great beauty in its conventions.

Each figure in the photographs of the boat or of girls diving draws a lovely, fluid line in the air.

Labour is blossoming or dancing where
The body is not bruised to pleasure soul,
Nor beauty born out of its own despair,
Nor blear eyed wisdom out of midnight oil.
O chestnut-tree, great rooted blossomer,
Are you the leaf, the blossom or the bole?
O body swayed to music, o brightening glance,
How we can know the dancer from the dance?*

* W. B. Yeats, 'Among School Children', *Collected Poems* (Macmillan, 1939).

That is what I meant earlier by saying of Bobby Charlton's incredible kick that it is creative work. His 'labour is blossoming', as Yeats put it in his noble rhetoric. In our games, 'our bodies are not bruised to pleasure soul'; that is, we do not suppress physical delight for the sake of the intellect. A great sport is always a dance.

Look at another heroine. Mary Peters who won an Olympic gold medal in the women's pentathlon in 1972 and topped off an amazing career at thirty-four by winning the Commonwealth gold in New Zealand in 1974. She is from Belfast: cheerful, homely, friendly, as they say, 'approachable'. She found a proper delight and gladness in her great wins. She cried and she laughed and, since British athletics are in a special position and free

from the grosser pressures of publicity, she was able to be a public heroine with complete success and quite unaffectedly. She did not have to be an entertainer, and though as intelligent about her varied and exacting event as was required for her to take on the international competition, she was not an athletic intellectual like Brasher.

Track and field athletes are supremely self-conscious. You might say that the most satisfying kind of individual expression – the kind after which you pull back and feel (or say), 'There! that's right. That's exactly how it ought to be!' – this kind of expression is a peculiar and intense awareness of yourself, a self-consciousness, in which the point of the awareness is to get something right which is quite outside yourself. A golf ball struck with absolute ease and sureness and (for you, or for him) perfect accuracy.

The important thing is that you've both hit it absolutely right. That is, you have said all you can say in the form of expression which the game opens to you. And then, this is important not only because an individual has been able to find free self-expression, but even more because he *is not* just free. He has to play by the rules. The form of the game is what he must bend to express what he has to say in it.

And that brings me back near, at least, to my starting point. For the word 'art', whatever else it means, denotes an activity which expresses and defines human value. It *signifies* something. The damnable thing about the idea of art over the last couple of hundred years (and especially since compulsory education was introduced) is that it has taken to itself special

kinds of holiness. And holiness and mystery in our society and its times being particularly suffused by cash, art has become stained in the sacred tints of those gold reserves which symbolize the inaccessible powers of our politics. Gold is dug out of deep holes in the ground, made into ingots, and put back in other deep holes with steel doors. And there the 'valuable' paintings join the gold ingots, guarded, mysteriously becoming with time even more valuable behind the guards in their uniforms. Novels, operas, poems, the technique of cello playing, electron microscopes, the statistical analysis of variance, all these may take on something of the same mystery and preciousness. They are guarded by walls. Access to them is limited. 'The highest intellectual productions are only recognized and accepted . . . because they are presented as direct producers of material wealth and wrongly shown to be such.'*

The great thing about photographs is that anyone can take them, read and understand them. There is nothing mysterious about a photograph. The same is true of sport. Though intimately bound up with great heaps of

* Karl Marx, *Critique of Political Economy* (Lawrence & Wishart, 1968), p. 202.

money it is not seen as a *producer* of material wealth. Sport is for itself, it is, so to speak, good-for-nothing, and because of that good-for-nothingness, its value is its own. It can be seen for itself. It is in this way that it is like art. Or what art should be like in a society where art and culture were open and equal.

Not that sport only embodies beautiful movement and rich relations. It can make for grotesques. Look at the photograph of the Russian shot-putter, Tamara Press. It is only natural to feel repelled when single-minded absorption in the drive for victory comes to this. Anabolic steroids put on

bulk in bone and muscle and subcutaneous fat, without detracting from performance. With more weight, you put the shot further. The deep tides of international politics come to a strange consummation in this woman's

sexless bulk, and her unprepossessing victory. Ideas of manliness and femininity are as strong and as changeable in sport as anywhere else. But it is human rather than doctrinaire to prefer Virginia Wade's sporting (and no less political) victory to the shot-putter's.

Well, sport is not only swift and graceful. It may be ugly, even at its most exciting. What brutal impulses pull us cheering from our seats, when a man goes solidly down like a tree? It gives us a kick, we say, to see him go over. And just before he does, there's a great crowd, thirsty for blood, cheering on the winner who will hit with all his power until his opponent cannot stand. Violence is never simple, and certainly not simply bad. It takes courage to stand up to violence. Boxing makes courage necessary within its conventions. It is a game, and you are playing the game. But the

convention of the game is that you hurt the other man until he is beaten. The one who is hurt more loses. Boxing can be frightening, both in action and effect.

Which is another expressive impulse – or rather, an idea which demands expression – in sport as in art. Fear, and facing fear.

Men and women climb because 'of the challenge'. The challenge is at least partly the challenge to overcome fear, to express courage. It is clear, however, as soon as I write that, that mountaineering does not begin from anything like so simple a tension as fear against courage (as though courage were just a matter of overcoming fear). Mountaineering, too, requires that

lovely absorption, poise, precision and creativeness of long-jumper or of bowls-player.

To say nothing of blind anger. But when you miss a putt, it is not so much that the sport expresses the image you are looking for – accuracy, the light, wristy tap which rolls the ball briskly against the back of the hole with a loud 'clop', and makes it rattle to the bottom. In this case, it is *missing* what you wanted to do which gives the moment its meaning. The anger is the direct experience. The anger expresses a direct need. But the act of putting is both experience – you really do the action – and the conventional gesture of the game. The gesture is like an idea. You have to perform it to play golf. Performing it is a necessity. You get it right, and the idea *is* necessity. The necessity of art which corresponds to the necessity of life. You get it wrong, and the correspondence is lost. That makes anyone angry, but the artist most of all. (Artist here, quite rightly, means someone who is very good at what he does, and aspiring always to do it better. An

artist thinks of the unchangeable consequence as being of greater importance than the action.)

Why write in this way of the great variety of pleasures offered and taken by millions of sportsmen every weekend?

Because I believe that we often misvalue our sports. We put too much and too little on them. This distortion is part of our history, a history which makes full, rich images of life very rarely available. A history which dams up and distorts the great energies of a people, and makes ugly what could be beautiful. Sports are the activities through which many people transfigure these distortions. To value our games rightly is to know better what makes our lives worth living.

For all that these pictures have stressed the solitary effort of individuals,
I believe and want to show that our life is more interesting and precious to
us when we, with the camera, pull back and see the whole scene in front of
us. The gladness, jubilation and excitement of all the men in the game, and
the thousands watching.

Sport as dance, indeed; and as great ceremony, as the shout goes up in
the air with the players.

Or even more moving, the great mass of runners breaking from the start
of a cross-country one bitter January day. The hard, clattering slap of
several hundred shoes, the slick slide of some feet hitting half-thawed,
lumpy mud. The little white puffs of breath gathering to a pall. The red

cheeks; the tight thighs, sinewy like an anatomy diagram, as they meet the slope, the muscles tucking and tightening at their knees, and the runners' cheeks hollowed to filter the cold air.

2 The forms of ceremony

I

SPORT IS AN ACTIVITY most men and a lot of women find it easy to talk about. There are easy things to say about it. You could say that a whole people shares its sport. In July 1966 when England won the World Cup at Wembley, thirty million people throughout the country were watching the match: half a nation.* And while people were thrilled by the game, by its simple technicality, they never doubted that their neighbours would know what was happening. They came out blinking into the hot July afternoon and grinned at each other over the garden fences. Quite large groups and knots of people elbowing amiably round the plateglass of television shop windows spilled away down the roads, suddenly and happily joined by a fraternity and an elation more certain and specific than any other voiceless companionship they were likely to know for the rest of their lives. Small boys threw themselves in delirious somersaults across the grass of their garden, their public park; they strained to imitate the controlled and fluid line of their heroes' movements. For a few hours a whole people knew by the victory of its football team that its sense of itself was confirmed in the outside world. And if a man does not see himself as confirmed by recognition from outside, he becomes closed in the sense of his own futility. In so far as many people live within a social world which they perceive as futile, then this pathology is both individual and social. Frustration and futility are more common conditions of life than satisfaction and a sense of meaning. You break out of the condition in so far as you can break out of loneliness. Either another person recognizes the condition, in which case you are no longer lonely (for example, you fall in love), or you transcend the condition under the impulse of a common aspiration – you go to war, or you win the World Cup. Either way, there are grounds for hope become visible. The aspirations or the recognition of other men make the idea of purpose real again. Then the examples of other men become images of possibility.

This is what it would be to live in a living culture. The culture of a people is its way of life. More particularly, it is those parts of a way of life which provide ceremonies of recognition and discovery; those areas which confirm and validate a man's sense of himself, a sense which itself can only

* Figures quoted in *The Coverage of Sport on BBC Television* (BBC, 1974).

be learned from a culture. If you were born and lived in a wilderness, you could have no part in a culture and consequently no identity. Many people in modern industrial countries live in a moral and cultural wilderness. Their culture provides small escape from the sense of unique personal futility which fractures human connexions and offers no images of fulfilment. A living culture provides men and women with an idea of purpose which gives meaning to the inevitable and hateful gap in daily living between values and aspirations. It makes connexion possible. It offers the chance of performing actions which may become examples. The examples of fine living by other men and women become images of social possibility. Our mythologies and our heroes give us the chance of recognizing our own best lives.

II

In a society which blocks, destroys or ignores the natural impulses of generosity, elation, heroism, grace, decorum, there are few corners of the culture which sponsor and cherish such impulses. Sport is one. Sports are of many kinds. You can watch them or you can perform them. Sometimes, as in fishing, or in cricket, you may do both. But playing games is a corner of the culture to which there is common and equal access. Sport fulfils the definition of a living culture in that it permits recognition of man by men: it is a liberation from an intolerable uniqueness and it holds out the possibility of fine living, the fulfilment of images which replenish the body and the spirit. In an often blank, divided, unregarding society, sports of all kinds offer an activity in which men can join happily with other men again. You could say that sport is the art of the people, and that the vast public ritual of the mass spectator sports is the last heroic drama of a community which has spent up its religious inheritance. You could say that sport is one of the great positive creations of an industrial culture, a lasting achievement of a kind to set beside the massive social novelties cast up by the surge of the industrial revolution. These activities are woven thickly together in the dense texture of what is called industrial culture. If we turn to football to symbolize most readily the presence of sport in our times, it is because the tremendous cast-iron stadiums are as solid, immovable a part of the industrial landscape at pitheads, steel rolling mills, the massive walls and windows and lintels of waterfront warehouses. The rollcall of the huge industrial townscapes built in the nineteenth century is the rollcall of the great football teams: Liverpool, Manchester, Sheffield, Leeds, Newcastle, Glasgow. So you could also say, at least of football, that it belongs to the industrial workers.

It belongs in the living-room as well as in the stadium. All over the country, at ten minutes past ten on a Saturday evening, seven, eight or nine million people are grouped appraisingly around the television screen, echoing in the conversation of the living-room the sudden clap of sound, the rhythmic surges of noise from a big football crowd. That sudden, splitting clap from such a crowd is instantly exhilarating and unmistakable; it is sunk deep in the folk memory of a whole people, and the memories which it evokes, heard now beside the great blind wall of a stadium, now muffled in a comfortable, overfull front-room, rise up and bind together hosts of men in cities and countries who could not speak to each other even if they saw each other.

Watch a crowd on the way to a big game. Then think of the same crowd going to work.

> Under the brown fog of a winter dawn,
> A crowd flowed over London Bridge, so many,
> I had not thought death had undone so many.
> Sighs, short and infrequent, were exhaled,
> And each man fixed his eyes before his feet.
> Flowed up the hill and down King William Street,
> To where Saint Mary Woolnoth kept the hours
> With a dead sound on the final stroke of nine.*

It is not simply that they are going to work and the spectators are at play, or rather, the trite difference takes the moral measure of the occasion. The working crowd in its huddled, trooping separateness can see no purpose in its journey. On the way to the match, the men and the few women walk quickly and uprightly. They bend their heads and talk earnestly. The gangs of lads roam the long parallel streets that lead down to the stadium, spread out in a long line from pavement to pavement, eyes bright, smacking the car bonnets, yaddering snatches of pop songs.

> – Goan to ther match, Wack?
> – Haddaway, Scouse.
> – On the Reds!

The older men, walking in twos and threes, grin a bit and unbutton their heavy, stiff overcoats so that they stand open like cupboards. They eye the girls, taken along by fiancés and got up for best, tight glossy boots and the long, glossy swathes of hair laid out carefully across their shoulders. The alertness they all are united in showing is, they would say, to do with the 'occasion'. But what does the 'occasion' do for them? Is it that going to the match is as unlike work as it is possible to be these days? Play versus work: two poles of being. Are the commonsense answers the right ones – that an occasion, by definition, cannot last? The excitement is a function of the occasion's being occasional. So a child looks forward to Christmas because it is a unique occasion; or rather on a child's timescale occurs at such interminable intervals as to seem unique. But this is not all, or even most of what there is to say about 'occasions', in this special sense. The occasion is defined by its being rare, by its being anticipated. Looking forward to it is in large part a matter of imagining an ideal version of the occasion; a

* T. S. Eliot, *The Waste Land – 1922*, (Faber, n.e. 1972), I, lines 61–8.

version against which the activity is subsequently measured. When actuality lives up to imagination – the play, the music, the football match is as good as we hoped it would be – then we feel fulfilled, satisfied. The success of an occasion therefore rests in its dissolving futility and frustration, in its enabling us to see the imagined best come true, and as a final and supreme consequence, making the experience of the present immediate, justified in its own terms.

The same thing happens in states of heightened anguish; they too are 'occasions'. They are occasions in which we perceive what has been lost, and we cannot ascribe sufficient meaning to it. But the occasion which satisfies us is an adventure in which the time that contains the occasion presents itself as irrecoverable. We are aware of the immediate; we live in it. 'We live where we are.' In so far as the occasion is something *other*, out there, then our attention directs itself away from the self and hence the experience of loss is not self-regarding but is the source of adventure, of the occasion's occasionality.

I believe that this experience of loss, the value of loss and its irreparability, and the paradoxical satisfaction which the lost occasion provides, is a key moral and formative experience, and of course sport is only a part of it. Each man and woman knows intuitively what this experience meant in childhood. As an eleven-year-old I went with my father to see the 1948 F.A. Cup Final, in which Manchester United beat Blackpool 4–2. With the arbitrary loyalties of a small boy, I had set my heart on a Manchester victory, and every detail of the afternoon was right. It was a beautiful day; the football was colourful and glamorous; the crowd was immense and the scene full of incident. The occasion took on for me the shape of an unrepeatable rite – a long train journey, a night in a London hotel, the packed, unprecedented ride to the stadium, and then the unbelievable numbers of people! After all this, the football: the goals and the sacred cup were the operatic climax of two days of the most intense, purposeful living I had known. All the time, my father's safe presence was there against which to measure the sprawling enormousness of the event; the sense of absolute and friendly safety which that presence ensured meant that the loss of this wonderful event, the sense I had throughout the game that I wanted to hold on to the special glory of this move, that goal, those colours, this amazing community of football fans, was given meaning. My power to retain the rich magnificence of the occasion was confirmed by his being there. He confirmed continuity. But of course the game could not continue. A football game is a metaphor as well as an example of the transience of experience. So what as a boy I took away from that great match was the clear perception that nothing could be the same again after the loss of the occasion, that its satisfaction was utterly unrepeatable; at the same time, the actuality of that ideal – the imagined became real and perfected in reality – confirmed my convictions of goodness and aspiration. The actuality made the idea of an opportunity

seem believable. Not in a Puritan sense, 'If these men can do it, so can I.'
More modesty is entailed. The object is worthy of attention in its own right,
and not because of me. Goodness, even goodness at football, is its own
reward. So what the child's imagination says (for children switch from
utter egocentricity to utter selflessness; the state of being is a function of
attention) is, 'How wonderful that men can perform these actions which
were in their excellence hardly imaginable even in the ideal.'

Obviously children do not think consciously like this. But the growth
consequent upon occasions such as I have described constitutes an
experiential rejection of meaninglessness. The concept of meaninglessness,
of utter contingency, is simply unavailable to a child. Faced the whole time
by loss, it does not despair. A child rediscovers meaning insistently.
Adventure for a child is the vivid recognition that what is precious which is
happening will be lost beyond recall. Adventure for an adult is the
recovery of this perception in such a way as to hold on to your identity
while admitting the exhilarating (and panicstricken) possibility of limitless
contingency. The blanking out of identity is a world without shape.
Excitement is the perception of both possibilities at once: the momentary
and uncontrollable abandonment of identity to the intense assault of time
tensed against the certain indestructability of the self. Such an excitement
is more, no doubt, than sensuous: it is a rite of passage, and it is an
experience passed and repassed at various degrees of intensity as a man
becomes a man, and matures. Each re-entry into the experience is a
confirmation of himself and the ultimate loss of himself, and a main
function of the imagination, working within the necessary constraints of his
history and his culture, will be to make such experiences authentic, rich,
and available.

Every great painting, or piece of music, or poem, intensifies and judges
this central human experience: life crumbling, mobile and evanescent; but
life endlessly renewing itself.

> When I have seen the hungry ocean gain
> Advantage on the kingdom of the shore,
> And the firm soil win of the watery main,
> Increasing store with loss and loss with store;
> When I have seen such interchange of state,
> Or state itself confounded to decay;
> Ruin hath taught me thus to ruminate,
> That Time will come and take my love away.*

The painting catches the movement at which the main figure turns and
looks at us. In another moment she will look away. Or turn back. The piece
of music of its nature depends upon its movement. You can play it again.
But it will not stand still. Its elusiveness is a necessity of its magic, such that
the efforts to catch and retain and re-experience it are endlessly thwarted

* William Shakespeare, *Sonnet 64*.

while yet the continued possibility of the music guaranteed by the notes on the page means that the work of art contains and expresses the tension I have tried to describe – between transience and fixity, between form and chaos, between shared meaning and personal anarchy.

III

A rich culture gives this experience many forms, and gives them continuously throughout its public and its private domains. The power of sport in our culture is that it embodies and gives significance to this experience at a time when other forms of this expression, for whatever causes, have dwindled or withered away. To say this is to give meaning to the cheery platitude that sport is a religion for some people. In so far as religious liturgy and ritual expressed for a people its perception of its own worth to itself and its own morality, than it is a simple truth to say that sport discharges something of this function for a secularized people.*

Going to the match is the pleasure it is because football gives the grace and fury of physical movement a structure; the structure gives moral meaning to transitory action; the meaning permeates the whole social ritual surrounding the football. Then what is passing and irrevocably lost – that pass, that goal, that match, that player – can be regretted because it has meaning. It is not dissolved into the impassivity of the vast inane. Denied this expression in whole areas of its public life, the football crowds and the football players of Britain, of indeed the world, use the game as a receptacle for the aspirations towards form, beauty, order and meaning which define their essential humanity and are absent from so much of their shared social institutions. The finest moments on a football pitch or a running track, or in many sporting arenas, as the sportsmen and spectators of different games all know, are among the few beautiful things our society has to offer. It is a radical deficiency that it should be so. That the moments are so often contaminated by cheap nationalism and a bitter, rancorous brutality is to the point but, the brawling apart, football is one of the areas of our lives in which we nourish and admire images of elation, grace, decorum, co-operation and vividness, and it is the living significance of these images that they are mobile and changeful. The confusions of attention which surround football, the vulgarity, cruelty, acquisitiveness, snobbery, meanness, all go to emphasize the diversity of its participants, and their reasons for being on the ground at all. The thirty-, forty-, fifty-odd thousand people at the big grounds – Anfield, Old Trafford, White Hart Lane, St James's Park, Maine Road, Highbury – there to watch the super-leagues of Britain and Europe, are not always there because they'll enjoy

---

* Just how secularized is a matter for debate: nothing like completely, of course, as witness the numbers of people who spend their lives in a half-atheistic and superstitious limbo, rising to religious participation for baptism, marriage and funeral.

it. Going to the match is such a rich social ritual because it contains and
expresses such diverse social meanings. Many of the dolly girls, jigging up
and down by the railings, will be bored. For them the match is the ante-
room to the festival of Saturday. Tea at home with the family after the
game, the drive to the pub to meet the crowd, on to the dancing and the
music, and the friendly easy hour after midnight in the back of the car high
in the dark above the lights of the town. The small boys at the front of the
terraces will be cold by halftime and only sporadically attentive before
then. The gangs, packed against their rivals on the narrow shelves will
chant and sing and sway as much to their private, anarchic rhythms as to
those of the game, shoving one another across the crush barriers, poking
elbows into friends' stomachs, shouting with hoarse laughs, and breaking
into sudden wild pleasure at a piece of pretty footwork on the pitch. For
them, Saturday is the time to state their loyalties and their defiances;
allegiance to each other, to their manhood and their team, allegiance
against all other gangs and other ages. And for the older men, heavy
treading, heavily built, standing shabby and powerful as old buses, the
Saturday match is for them as for others an act of conviviality. The ground,
the game, the friends they go with, are dense with history, with the
associations of other games and players, and dense with a lifetime also
whose natural impulses towards gladness, eloquence and power have
found only this vocabulary in watching football.

I have been speaking as though all sport were football. But it is surely
true that if you ask anyone in Britain what he thinks of when he hears the
word 'sport', most people will say 'football'. These images – the stadium,
the towering spindly floodlights, the crowds hurrying in the roads below
the vast blank brick of the stands, and the great shout as the teams spill out
of the tunnel – these are what sport first signifies in the imagination of the
people. And then, tied to the network of football power and its glittering
élites, are rank upon rank of small league clubs, hiring a handful of men
fulltime, paying the rest a few quid, turning out every Saturday in front of
four hundred people in grounds that would hold eight thousand. And after
that, the one million amateur footballers* sprinkled over Hackney
Marshes and the public parks, the tussocks and cowpats of wired-in fields
all across the country. In the gaps of this colossal network, the small boys
skin their knees in a million more backstreets, grim tarmac playgrounds,
and brown, beaten waste lots.

This brief, airborne view gives on its plane some sense of what it means to
have a common and equal culture. Perhaps with football the democratic
dream condenses momentarily as fact. To say this is not to pretend that
football and footballers are always lovely to watch, that they are not often
petulant, ugly, or simply dull in action; it is not to slide over the wilful

---

* Figure estimated by the Football League Secretary, and quoted in *Radio Times*,
4 September 1971.

destructiveness of the game and its spectators, its waste, its desolation, and indeed on any adequate moral scale, its comparative triviality.

But our moral scale is not adequate, and the place occupied on it by football (and football as symbolizing the rich culture of sport) is potent in the lives of men and women as few other convivial activities can be at the present time. That place is a portion of our national culture which is common and equal in the sense not that all men are equally good at it (which would be obviously false) but that football provides a vocabulary which many men may speak. That vocabulary permits those who share it to recognize and express the beauty and resourcefulness of human movement, both individually and in concert. Such general terms – 'beauty', 'grace', 'power' can only have meaning in so far as they have a context. The game is the context which defines 'beauty' and 'grace' and so on: within that structure, the terms mean what they mean. But 'beauty' and 'grace', 'power', 'ugliness', 'clumsiness', are not only descriptions of how men and women may move, they are also evaluations. A powerful shot at goal is not a difficult thing to recognize: we know what power in that context looks like. But power is not just a matter then of describing the shot; it is also, and quite unavoidably, a matter of evaluation. A powerful shot exhibits some at least of the characteristics we admire in a piece of football. And our capacity to agree that a particular move is well-judged or beautifully executed not only pivots on our definitions of the term 'well' and 'beautifully', but also on what actually took place, on the facts of the matter. So in judging football, as in judging any human behaviour, our descriptions entail an expression of our values. You cannot have the fact of a powerful shot at goal without the idea of the *value* of power. Or at least you cannot think the fact or describe it. To call a shot powerful or a pass delicate or a save marvellous is both to describe and to judge it, and the one *is* the other. Sport is an activity in which it is peculiarly difficult to get away from the condition of our language which enforces the identity of facts with values. Judging sport, like judging art, is controversial nearly always. You have only to hear the partisans arguing after the game to know that. All sorts of views are possible of the same goal. They are possible because of different physical standpoints (stand or terraces); because of different loyalties (Reds or Blues); because of different personalities (cheerful or glum). To those very complicated degrees, controversy cannot be settled. The whole thing is a matter of opinion. And yet. Yet the nature of the ideas of beauty or force, or simply of success, is such that to have the idea is to have the notion – some notion – of the value; and to agree about its application is to acknowledge that beauty is somewhere *out there*, somewhere other than in the eye of the beholder. Finally it is to agree that in any case the *fact* of the move in the game entailed its also carrying a value.

This is an argument to go back to time and again. But it is central to people's lives. After all, we learn as we grow up a commonplace view of the world in which nothing is held to be finally true which is not defensible by a regular method of counting. And what is held to be true in this way is fact and what you think of it – what human value you set upon the fact – is held to be quite separate and to be attached to the fact by a personal act of choice. But it is not always a matter of choice. Without the idea, as I have said, which the words express, we would not have the fact; but the idea itself expresses a value. Think of words such as 'victory', 'defeat', 'triumph', 'punishment', as well as those words I have suggested like 'power' or 'beauty' or 'efficiency'.

I am saying, I suppose, that a shared culture, like the shared language and gesture which are its medium, expresses, shapes and imperceptibly changes our language. To say this returns us to seeing sport as an area of cultural life in which the great and moving dream of a democratic society comes alive in our times. This minor human ceremony, in other ages an instrument of military training or merely a riot on holy days, helps to keep alive in the imagination of a largely sedentary and isolated society, essential, wholesome moral images. It provides a ritual framework for the precept that we should aspire after all things good and beautiful, and that we shall surely lose them in our lives, even while we keep glowing and irreducible in our ageless imaginations. This verse from a poem describing the writer reflecting on his memory of a jazz record sounds more defeated than the experience it describes may make a man feel, but what it says generalizes that experience of a shared culture which I have explored.

> Truly, though our element is time,
> We are not suited to the long perspectives
> Open at each instant of our lives.
> They link us to our losses: worse,
> They show us what we have as it once was,
> Blindingly undiminished, just as though
> By acting differently we could have kept it so.*

It is the great public rituals of the spectator sports which most obviously do this, which 'show us what we have as it once was' and show it in that bright and dazzling light, 'blindingly undiminished' so that old men, fat men, small boys, watching the long muscles of a runner's brown thighs sliding smoothly into place, feel their imaginations swell to encompass the retrieval of their inevitable losses, long past or still to come, 'just as though/By acting differently we could have kept it so'. The contexts of sport allow for those long perspectives to open before us; allow us to see and understand not only the loss registered in the gap between our trivial incompetences as footballers and the unbelievable reflexes of the man we are watching, but also the loss we experience as this game we have been part of fades, as the light fades, on a winter afternoon. The greatest games,

* Philip Larkin, 'Reference Back' in *The Less Deceived* (Marvell Press, 1964).

like the greatest art, are at once a fulfilment and an intolerable poignancy. They satisfy all that we had hoped for of this high adventure, so that we experience what we so insatiably looked for as children from every experience – that high-pitched, intense absorption in which aspiration and activity become one. But then the poignancy, because at the close the loss of such fulfilment is absolute.

A living culture moves according to such rhythms; makes the rhythms tolerable to us, and gives every man access to them. Such a culture is a map which a man can use to interpret the bewildering diversity of signals which assault his senses. A blank and broken culture, such as we have now, will leave large areas of human purpose unfulfilled and essential human rhythms discordant. A rich and common culture will provide a symbolism which holds dynamic tension between restlessness and satisfaction, a tension kept in free, electric play across a whole plurality of human activities.

'Play': That is the word. We come back to that. The 'play' of a culture is a condition of its adequacy, of permission of access granted to, and taken for granted by, all the members of a history. So a common and equal culture will be a playful one, one which expresses, defines, and symbolizes glee, delight, gaiety. If it must be playful, it must be severe as well. For his cultural life symbolizes a man's striving, his restless dissatisfactions with his condition, his strenuous, uncertain labour to attain the best. Riven by his contradictions, by desire and its frustration, he struggles into articulation, into language, or into the language of gesture.

So the strong, dedicated vision of the distance runner is set upon a private vision of attainment which in our times finds perhaps an inevitable symbolism in the tiny variations of a stopwatch, the miniscule calculations of statistical difference. The grim heroism of such running against the clock is surely tied to the demand we make of achievement. It is part of the puritan spirit and its awful exaltation of the stiff, insensuate will. The endeavours of any man or woman draw their energy from the stretched contradictions of his spirit, but they find their shape in the contours of the culture. Thus long-distance running is the sporting triumph of the ethic of individualism just as, in another dimension, competitive football is foremost the sporting symbolization of the industrial workers – the inter-city rivalry, the group effort, the containment and economy of movement and equipment (it is the cheapest game in the world – all you need are a ball and two feet), the swank and boisterousness of success, the crowds, the grounds – but I have said this. The point is this: your culture symbolizes the power you have to realize yourself. It provides a language for expression and for definition and for judgment as to value. 'Self-expression' – the old battle-cry of infant teachers – is not enough. You express yourself if you roll yourself up in a ball and refuse expression. But expression in language is expression for others, and in exchange with others the expression is redefined, and changes; your understanding of it changes and consequently your estimate of where it comes in the scheme of your language, its expressions and values. The symbolic languages of a culture, among which sport takes its place, make it possible for a man or a woman to be a person at all. They embody the act of recognition.

IV

We make our bonds with the world and with others as a consequence of being recognized. A mother chucks her baby under the chin, or claps her hands at it, plays peep-bo behind her apron, and gives it back the rattle it throws persistently out of the pram. All these familiar, loving acts of attention confirm the otherness of the world and its relation to the baby. This 'other' person, the mother, seen at first as simply an extension of the baby's own being, gradually takes on separateness and connectedness through the constant evidence she provides of her social bond with the baby. It is society and history that the baby learns from the start, and these abstractions take on vivid and concrete life with every contribution the mother makes. Without these contributions the baby could not feel itself recognized at all; it would drift, catching such glimpses of itself as caught its eye and constructing a world of terrifying blankness whose only meaning was itself and a handful of signs from a moral wilderness. We only learn what part of our selves we can call our own as we recognize what is not our own – what is the world-out-there and how far, in turn, the world-out-there looms over us and penetrates us, invading what we think of as our own. A psychoanalyst describes the process in his own terms:

> What would we consider to be the earliest and most undifferentiated 'sense of identity'? I would suggest that it arises out of the encounter of maternal person and small infant, an encounter which is one of mutual trustworthiness and mutual recognition. This, in all its infantile simplicity, is the first experience of what in later reoccurrences in love and admiration can only be called a sense of 'hallowed presence', the need for which remains basic in man. Its absence or impairment can dangerously limit the capacity to feel 'identical' when adolescent growth makes it incumbent on the person to abandon his childhood and to trust adulthood and with it, the search for self-chosen loves and incentives . . . *

We offer ourselves to someone else, with all our imperfections upon us, and in accepting us as we are, the other person (parent or lover or friend) extends that human recognition which is necessary to a human being in order that he shall feel his identity to be his own. This is the paradox. What we feel to be our true selves needs the constant endorsement of others in order for us to continue to esteem that self. Living at a time in which the endorsements of themselves offered by society are scattered, incomplete, and often crippling, the participation in sport which I have been describing casts on a corner of people's lives that steady light by which they

* Erik Erikson, *Identity: Youth and Crisis*, (Faber, 1968), p. 105.

are able to see and understand themselves in relation to their aspirations for themselves, and for others.

> When religion loses its actual power of presence . . . an age must find other forms of joint reverence for life which derive vitality from a shared world image. For only a reasonably coherent world provides the faith which is transmitted by the mothers to the infants in a way conducive to the vital strength of *hope*, that is, the enduring predisposition to believe in the attainability of primal wishes in spite of the anarchic urges and rages of dependency. The shortest formulation of earliest childhood may well be: I am what hope I have and give.*

In its local way, now greatly distorted by the hateful absences elsewhere, sport sheds that light and, as a whole culture should, makes common recognitions possible. That is, there are experiences so organized in the structure of a sport that our feelings are vindicated by the activity. And not only our feelings. Our ideas and purposes as well. It is a common failing of industrial culture that we split ourselves into bits and pieces which are then quite separately nourished by diverse activities. Thus, music and art for 'feeling', business for 'practical' thinking, philosophy for 'abstract' thinking, sport for the 'physical side'. *Mens sana in corpore sano* was the Latin tag which neatly expressed this whole world view. The old dualism of body and soul looks increasingly less credible these days, not so much because the religious beliefs which litanized it have declined, as that our whole picture of the individual and the relation of his self to society has changed. To say it again: we make and are made by our culture and our society. It is a main purpose of this book to explore that making in both its directions. Inevitably, this is to talk about who we think we are – the idea we have of ourselves. When we do this it is quickly clear that – playing games being the example – physical action, pleasure in that action, and the very rapid processes of selection and judgment involved in performing it, can only be separated in a metaphorical sort of way.

Think of a first-class tennis player playing a match at full stretch and on his best form. All the time he has to make and execute an unbelievably rapid sequence of decisions: taking each decision involves discarding a multiplicity of other possible decisions. Simply to speak of this behaviour is to see that traditional dualism will not work, even though it is useful and important at times to be able to think of someone as having this or that sort of spirit. To do this the whole time – to underwrite the split and fragmentary account of men – is to misunderstand the connexions between all the pieces which compose a man. Until you have a linguistic hold upon certain concepts in playing a game, you have no game. The idea of a rule is itself intellectual. Then within the rules, the player produces a whole series of unprecedented 'transformations' – that is, newly-created structures which could only exist because the rules (the grammar) exist, but which constitute wholly new arrangements of the structure of rules. Without

* ibid., p. 107.

linguistic and intellectual organization a player cannot imagine what it is to play a cross-court backhand to the base-line or a top-spun ace service. His perception of these physical incidents – this dropshot, that return – is at the same time a function of his intellectual deployment of language. And as the perceptions give rise to admiration, amazement, excitement, horror, relief, then the coincidence of feeling with perception and understanding make it impossible to return to linear notions of experience in which perception comes first, followed by understanding, followed by feelings. It is indeed sporting activities which make us see the interpenetration of what our traditions teach us to call body, mind, and soul. Or to put it another way, in our culture it is sport which gives rise to the experience and recognition of this interpenetration most vividly.

Any account of sport in terms of its culture (or indeed of a culture in terms of its components) must, to be adequately human, provide a moral scale for the test of its own justifications. Thus the quotation from the psychoanalyst on the need in times of secularization for 'other forms of reverence for life' came to rest upon the noble formulation that a child define itself like this: 'I am what hope I have and give'. I have suggested that the great convivialities of the mass sports permit some of their members to make this affirmation. But it is naturally the case that we should ask of a sport that it justify itself not only in relation to childhood or youthfulness but also in terms of old age.

> An aged man is but a paltry thing,
> A tattered coat upon a stock, unless
> Soul clap its hands and sing, and louder sing
> For every tatter in its mortal dress . . .*

For too much of the time we all of us live, deep in our lives there is the conviction that the materially productive years – the years of the increased output of wealth or acquisition of property, the years of childbearing – are those which count highest on the moral scale. Before that, children are preparing for that rich, fulfilled state of affairs; after that, old people are waiting to die. It is a conceited and nasty view of the world, the only satisfaction to be derived from which is that it catches up in the end with absolutely everyone. On a different scale, just as the experience of childhood is itself to the child, and the *hope* towards which maternal recognition is so validating and productive an encouragement is not in the long run but in the immediate future, so the experience of old age should be *itself*, of its own nature. The function of the pastimes of old age should be to give meaning and value to experiences beyond those of productivity. The moral scale of our community is too often one which deprives the old of a sense of still participating in serious and social affairs. It is a failure which means that those values freed of productive and competitive overtones

* W. B. Yeats, 'Sailing to Byzantium', *Collected Poems* (Macmillan, 1939).

which might develop through the prime and middle age and support old age are given very little recognition. Faced with this blankness and dissonant with those dominant values, old people, so long as their fantasy life has not gone dead, turn to nostalgia as a key means of support in their solitude. 'Once upon a time I shared a community of values, not thrusting and aggressive like these, but stable, affectionate, jolly . . .' Once again, it seems to me that the experiences offered by sport, both the sports of old age like bowls, darts, fishing, together with the continued access of the old as spectators and archivists of younger men's games, ensures a continuing meaning in their lives for some fortunate old people. They can enjoy for the sake of the activity itself, their sports; those sports confirm them in their membership of a community of the old; the sports further keep open for the old a way of entry into the community of younger men and women.

V

Any theory, any chart of sport as a significant corner of our culture must make some sort of fit with these ideas and these stubborn facts. I have spoken much of the time as though the only sport which counted in a theory of culture was football. No doubt it is the most present in the national imagination. No doubt it is the most astonishing sporting product of British industrial culture. But a comprehensive account of why sport matters to us so much must include the dozens of less known, less practised or, for whatever reasons, less publicized sports, if the account is to meet the measure of a proper anthropology: that is, so to explain a part of a man's life to him that he recognizes more clearly where he stands.

Anthropology? But that is an academic study. Very well. It is more than time that academic study took itself into the real world in an effort to help that world live better. These strictures have special point when making general theories about an activity as diverse and contradictory as games playing. The parody title (avoided for this chapter) 'Towards a theory of games' has about it that special air of bankrupt nullity reserved for its products by certain shrivelled forms of social science. Yet everyday usage recognizes something in common between all sports and games in giving them just that characterization. To set aside for a moment the distinction between a sport and a game – if playing is in some sense a unique dimension of our lives, what does it in all its endless variety *do* for us? What spaces in our social identity would be left unfilled if we had no sports or if we took no part in them?

This chapter has looked at the relations between the cultural life of a society and its sport. It has opened up the idea of social identity, of growth and ageing. Of continuity. But there are difficulties. Not least is the difficulty of writing about the forms of experience which though endlessly discussed in society – in ordinary conversation, in newspapers and all forms of broadcasting – is not often written about in more theoretic ways.

It is, supremely, the intention of this book to provide some sort of theory of games. A theory not in any dead academic sense, but in what may be more importantly thought of as a political sense. To say that this book is about the politics of sport in no way commits me to discuss the rights and wrongs of black sportsmen like Basil D'Oliveira or Arthur Ashe not being allowed to play cricket or tennis in South Africa against white South Africans. Such issues are undoubtedly political in the most sharp and vivid sense. The problem is so to draw the lines out from these much-headlined incidents, and others like them, that we see how they prefigure the lines of many more private lives. Caught in the obscure definitions of their playing are many of the public meanings of men's and women's lives. Long debarred from South African tennis courts, Arthur Ashe was both more and less than an international sportsman. He was the representative, the quiet spokesman for an imprisoned people. He was a man out of a job.

To put the matter either way is perhaps to extend the meaning of the word 'politics'. The politics of sport is then the public meanings of games. And, in spite of cash and noise and hatred and triviality, one source of the enduring power of sport in the national imagination is that it is within those confines that men still dream the old dream of a unity of culture, the re-establishment of the old, confident, joyous world. A world which relived, in Yeats' words, 'a gusty energy that would put all straight if it came out of the right heart', a world of a popular art which was filled with 'the colours of one's own climate and scenery in their right proportion', a condition richly met by the English cricket, the American ball game, the Brazilian football, which so precisely and vividly render the colours and contours of their own landscape and history. Tangled and inarticulate in the ritual grammar and theological vocabulary of modern sport is a remote vision of men joined in an activity at once happy and combative, strong in both friendship and rivalry, beautiful and strenuous. An activity rich in creative pointlessness. Many of these powerful social needs have been attributed to art, and others to the non-productive sections of domestic life. But that characteristic of industrial society which is designated by sociologists as the divisions of labour, and by psychologists as 'splitting-off', whatever its origins, serves to mark off men from men, and to set them against one another.

It is the strength of different games that they serve to rejoin men and to overcome such divisions.

The difficulty is then to talk about this possibility. For we are talking about that delicate and mobile area of social experience at the point at which it becomes permissible intellectual inquiry. Such an area makes nonsense of the conventional divisions of social and intellectual labour. It is the point at which experience and the intellect cross over. What can we do to prevent those two roads moving inexorably away from one another? How do you talk about sport without aridly intellectualizing?

3 Body and mind—thought and sport

WE ASK OURSELVES therefore what good it is to us to have a theory about anything. The word 'theory' can mean many things, and almost all of them are regarded suspiciously in the English mind. Probably the most respectable is the meaning signified by 'scientific theory' when what is referred to is a theory in the sense of a testable hypothesis. But we are thinking here of the word 'theory' in both a more general and a more reach-me-down sense. Not theory as when a friend tells us that old so-and-so has a new theory about taking a number two iron from the tee at the sixteenth. That sort of theory is in a rough way scientific; it depends upon the sequence hypothesis–experiment–verification. No, the theory meant here is what it is that we appeal to when asked, 'Why do you play rugby?' or, 'Why do you like to go sailing?'

Sailing. Touch, unwarily, a sailor upon his sensibility, and prepare to take your deserts like a man. Go along the banks of the Dart, the Hamble, the Fal, the Blackwater, the Crouch; call in at the pubs of Dartmouth, Burnham, Cowes, Poole, Falmouth, Chichester, Dereham, Tenby. In these places you will find, as an outsider, a dense, traditional community from which you are, more or less, excluded. You find a complex association of lives and sport, of systems of production and ways of living, of status and respect and ritual, of trivial snobberies and profound human meaning. What will you do to understand these things? Why should you try in the first place?

You try because there you will find some of the deeper meanings, the 'deep play' in Bentham's phrase, of a whole society. Imagine. You, a non-sailing man or woman with a close friend who is a sailor, are in Dartmouth in late August. The river flows down between the deep, tree-lined slopes of the valley, to a hopelessly picturesque headland topped with a folly and an observation tower, and sloping down to the tumbled, broken rocks and the changeful sea. The town lies along the western bank of the river, and is defined by its waterfront, by the strong square coping blocks and the intermittent, black iron capstans, and the square-cut steps worn to a slight dip by many feet passing down to the water's edge. Stone and water is the loveliest and most emblematic of the unities of townscape, of the places where men live: permanence and change hold their place peaceably beside each other, the mass of the wall at once single and awful and at the same time infinitely varied by the grains, the infinite lines and petrifactions of its surface. The stone is solid and fixed, but it absorbs heat and reflects the sunlight, itself reflected by the water. The play of light on its faces is picked up as much from the restless water as from the sun and rain. Counterposed one against the other, stone and water also penetrate each other; beneath the tide the stone staggers and waves, is bent and elongated and compressed by the movement of the waves, on the tranquil blue day the level sea is as smooth as obsidian.

The stone and water of Dartmouth harbour provide more than just a pretty setting for the boats. They mark the point which divides culture from the impassive inane. Even at sailing's most commonplace, in a graceless boat on a millpond, a tyro sailor feels a grain of frightened excitement leak into his blood as he leaves the shore. Hence the scorn which the self-styled proper sailors feel for anyone who sacrifices certain mysterious, unspecifiable but well understood aspects of sailing to modern technology in the interests of mere speed. But to say this returns us to the busy quays and the amazing variety of boats which crowd the wide water. They are of course lovely to look at, 'picturesque' as they say. But consider that particularly fine topsail sloop anchored in midstream: carvel-built, a hundred years old, three-masted, slender and fleet when seen across a hundred yards of water, solid, braced and startlingly bulky when you are close up to her. She is the *Charlotte Rhodes*, presently leased by Coca-Cola, heroine of the internationally best-selling TV serial 'The Onedin Line', still in the flood tide of private enterprise. She is in utterly perfect condition, she recalls what the hero of Conrad's short novel *The Shadow Line* says of his new mercantile command as he sees her for the first time – his first, thrillingly unlooked-for command:

> I knew that, like some rare woman, she was one of those creatures whose mere existence is enough to awaken an unselfish delight. One feels that it is good to be in the world in which she has her being . . . that illusion of life and character which charms one in men's finest handiwork radiated from her . . .*

Conrad's hero makes appeals to certain master-meanings which all real sailors would recognize. The captain boards his ship. 'Half an hour later, putting my foot on her deck for the first time, I received the feeling of deep physical satisfaction. Nothing could equal the fullness of that moment . . .' And he goes on up to the poop, past the gleaming brass fittings and polished rails – the trimness and high polish themselves expressive of antique mysteries and symbols – down to the captain's cabin.

> Deep within the tarnished ormolu frame, in the hot half-light sifted through the awning, I saw my own face propped between my hands. And I stared back at myself with the perfect detachment of distance, rather with curiosity than with any other feeling, except of some sympathy for this latest representative of what for

*Joseph Conrad, *The Shadow Line*, Dent 1917.

all intents and purposes was a dynasty; continuous not in blood, indeed, but in its experience, in its training, in its conception of duty, and in the blessed simplicity of its traditional point of view on life.

It struck me that this quietly staring man whom I was watching, both as if he were myself and somebody else, was not exactly a lonely figure. He had his place in a line of men whom he did not know, of whom he had never heard; but who were fashioned by the same influences, whose souls in relation to their humble life's work had no secrets for him.

It is a beautiful passage. It is a fine novel. I take a novel as I do so often later in this book because in our picture of the intellectual world, novels (and sometimes poems and plays) are given pride of place as the most direct transcriptions of personal experience as it is immediately perceived and lived. In the general view of things, novels – like, perhaps, film and television – are much less records of right conduct and judgement, than they are of felt life. A novel is life standing still to be looked at. By the same token, but in contrast, a science is a way of observing that life from a distance, 'objectively' as we say, and recording its incessant facts without any preference as to which you set down. Finally, a theory, distinct in this reach-me-down philosophy of mind from both experience and science, is pictured as an arbitrary frame set intellectually and hence unfeelingly down upon the warm motion of the living. For my purposes, however, a novel (and a sport) is science, theory, and experience all at once. This is true because a novel is a metaphor, a way of catching and fixing the unstoppable current of life–as–experience.

Is this to speak in riddles? No. It is to speak in language, and language is stronger than we know. Our minds use language regularly as magic. Life bursts upon us as sudden, arbitrary and total. We turn the tenor of life into experience by giving it names. Language is not just names-for-things; it is a frame made by the mind and put down upon the meaningless torrent of life. Before life is named, it is vast, potential, and inane. When we name it, we seek to command it. We utter spells to tame it and bring it under the reach and grip of our imagination. Language is a gesture which seeks to order chaos and command vacancy. Gesture defines and gives meaning to space. But gesture is not impromptu; it takes its meanings from the dense, compacted rituals of a long history – in some cases, the longer the history, the more sacred the ritual, simply because of its length, and that deep atavism of our blood which insists on the presence of the past as a necessary condition of social order, of the nature of holiness, of making sense of the future.

II

Sport is intensely ritual and in some cases sanctified gesture. It is a sort of magic. I mean that quite seriously, but I have to insist on the word 'magic' because it is now of course dishonoured, or at least misunderstood.

Remember what sudden terror is like. It is our response to the utterly
abrupt and total irruption of the outside world into our whole selves. Not
into our consciousness, nor upon our bodies; but *into* our whole self. Terror
is not a reaction of body, mind, or soul in distinction from the others. It is
total, because the assault of the world upon the self in such a case is total. So
we cast back at this event a total gesture which seeks to subjugate it, to put
it down and hold it in a place where we can see and understand it. There is
a long, strong history behind the tales of wizards who move boulders and
secret doors in the rock with magic gestures and words and spells. They are
symbols of the self which seeks to control the world in and by the creative
projections of body and mind together. Sporting lives have an always
traditional and central place in these endless and essential constructions.
In a book we shall return to, *Homo Ludens*, the Dutch historian of culture,
Johann Huizinga, identifies the play-element in society as being of the
utmost necessity to its meanings and continuity – indeed, as distinguish-
ingly *human*.

> Play is an activity which proceeds within certain limits of time and space, in a
> visible order according to rules freely accepted, and outside the sphere of
> necessity or material utility. The play-mood is one of rapture and enthusiasm
> and is sacred or festive in accordance with the occasion. A feeling of exaltation
> and tension accompanies the action, mirth and relaxation follow.*

These remarks take us back first to Conrad and then by way of *The Shadow
Line* to Dartmouth and the holiday sailors.

Conrad's captain looked back over the men who had sat in that same
chair. He could see no faces in the mirror but his own, and now his own was
only important in so far as it extended but did not complete the line of men
whose faces counted for less (*meant* less) than their representativeness in a
dynasty.

Turn to the man walking into the public bar of 'The Castle' in
Dartmouth. It is a handsome bar which cherishes its seagoing and nautical
connexions. The floor is solid, stained wood; the long oak counter curves
slightly for almost the full length of the room with an echo of a sailing ship's
rail and bow in its bulk and shape, the rubbed surface polished by
generations of rough woollen elbows and chests leaning over it in that most
familiar and natural of seagoing poses, a knee bent slightly so that one
seaboot is cocked up on the low, first rail. And above the navy blue denim
and wool, the tanned brown face with the eyes crinkled deeply at the
corners from looking into spray and great winds and the white, intolerable
sun. The brasses, the lamps, the plain, pretty, stylized prints on the walls,
the brass chronometer screwed above the bar, the neat wooden nooks – all
these nicely calculate and express the meaning of Dartmouth to the sailor's

---

* Johann Huizinga, *Homo Ludens: a Study of the Play Elements in Culture*
(Routledge, 1949; Paladin, 1970), p. 31.

satisfaction and, no doubt, to the landlord's greater profits. Well, sailing is nothing if not trade. But then, as the sailor who has come in and is now drinking beer in slow, gigantic draughts, his upper lip sunk well into the slight foamy head and his hand, ignoring the handle, grasping the chunky, square-panelled tankard rounds the stoutest part of its belly – as he would tell us, sailing is nothing if it is only trade. And Conrad, in *The Shadow Line*, tells us the same:

> The reward of faithful service. Well, faithful service was all right. One would naturally give that for one's own sake, for the sake of the ship, for the love of the life of one's choice; not for the sake of the reward.
>
> There is something distasteful in the notion of a reward.

'There is something distasteful in the notion of a reward.' Yes, indeed; so there is in an activity whose *only* consummation is successful trade or plentiful production, hence the profound, unnamed, pervasive hatred so many men feel for that work which is supposed to offer one of the central meanings of their life. My contention is that sport is a main alleviation of and escape from that condition of estrangement from what is one of the central values of industrial society: a man's relationship to his work. And indeed that relationship itself defines a range of meanings, so that in so far as his view of work becomes ambiguous, problematic, or contested, his life plunges into a disorder and at worst meaninglessness, from which his sport may temporarily rescue him, especially if he is good at it. There, holding squash racket, golf club, a hunter's bridle, or fastening skis, or, with more completeness, hearing the waves beneath the keel smarten to a regular, clopping crackle as the mainsail fills and hardens before the wind, there the frustrations of tomorrow's fatstock prices, or of the assembly line in the paintshop, or of bloodyminded schoolchildren, clear away. The immediate intractability focuses clearly on questions of timing, economy, purity, technique. There is a right and wrong way to perform the realized move in the game which is selected from the range of possibilities before him by the player; and it must be done right. There are no doubt moments in many men's work when this may be true, but the ubiquity and passion of sportsmen take the measure of what are the far larger absences and desert places of the work.

For the meanings that are breaking down so vastly in industrial culture are threefold, and all turn on the hinge of man's work (and man means men, not women; hence the man-centred nature of sport). First, the meaning of work in the past which (seen from the present) is significant because it has made possible a prosperous entry into the present. Second, that present is defined as the society of free, productive men, in benevolent competition one with another. Third, present competitive work (and its entailment, bargaining production) though at times boring transforms a man's work into his children's guarantee of a future; temporary estrangement now is purified by its becoming a 'monument' in the lives of prosperous children.* But all these meanings concentrated in work are coming to look less and less plausible: the vast labour of the past has mortgaged rather than liberated the present, the present rate of production cannot sustain itself and despoils the earth; time lours, and the future holds few guarantees cashable on present work for our children. The values of industrial work, which have been sustained in Europe and North America for most of the century, and which indeed impelled the amazing recovery of Europe after the Second World War, are clearly breaking down. The social order which they define and secure is therefore liable to transformation. Now that is not to say that our world is about to cave in; upheaval is more likely to be submarine and intangible, though none the less tremendous for that. And of course the changes in sporting life themselves reflect and carry forward the same revolutions. But they do so in special ways, and what most directly concerns us in this book is that with the displacement of work as the central, meaning-bearing activity in society, other more marginal forms of life proffer their meanings – or, more likely, are quarried for support – instead. There are plenty of men whose golf, football, dahlias, roses, pigeons, motorcars or bikes, piano-playing or astronomy, provide for them the confirmation and forgetfulness of self which is the experience of value. Value or meaning, that is, is the ultimate justification of activity.

To say so puts us into an infinite regress. If we say that hard work confirms our sense of *worth* to ourselves and to our society, we have vaguely asserted something about the importance of a sense of identity being given by the endorsement of society, which still leaves us with the difficulty of understanding why society should think that work is worth doing, and why it gives purpose to life. One clear value does emerge as we come to talk about sport, and that is pleasure: pleasure is an intelligible justification for action, though not by any means an absolutely straightforward one.† Its intelligibility is indeed one of its most attractive aspects, and makes hedonism, the philosophy of life which makes the experiencing of pleasure the main point of life, a very possible morality. But once said, the doctrine rings false: it is not conditioning but necessity, the mere facts of our life and our psychology, which insist on the claims not only of asceticism (the opposite of hedonism) but of altruism, selflessness, goodness, duty.

III

This is hardly the place to begin a theory of ethics. It *is* however the place to point out that sport is for many people an experience within which they

---

* I have used Charles Taylor's paper, 'Interpretation and the sciences of man', *Review of Metaphysics* (January 1971), in these remarks.

† As Alasdaire MacIntyre points out in 'Pleasure as a reason for action' in *Against the Self Images of the Age* (Duckworth, 1971).

may sort out the claims upon both their emotions and their morality of the contradictory meanings and values within which they live. Beauty, says Plato, is the one true form which we love naturally and by instinct. If Plato is right, and I believe he is, amazing though his claim may be, then the pleasure we take in a beautiful piece of sporting action (whether we perform it ourselves or not) is rightly taken to be a central meaning in men's lives. And the more rightly, the more the labour culture fails, and work and production fail to have a bearing upon your past, present, and your own and your children's future.

The present strangeness of things is this: that so much of what Conrad describes in his mercantile marine captain's mind now thrives for men in contexts which are moral and political light years away from the necessary, bustling ply of ships between Newcastle and Bangkok, San Francisco and Genoa. The continuity of sailing goes beyond, far beyond, the systems of production and distribution, the enormous intricacies of trade which are part of the world chronicled by its novelists, reflected in its folklore, and mythologies. Its heroes have been traders and naval officers in the warlike protection of trade; or, if you prefer, buccaneers and explorers and swordsmen. Drake and Frobisher; Raleigh and Hawkins; Cabot and Pym. Then Cook and Nelson and Collingwood, Hawkins again, and in the world wars, Jellicoe, Beatty, and Evans, Mountbatten and Cunningham. These names, like those of their discoveries and ships and victories, resonate in the mythology of seafaring, which is woven so densely into our national imagination and identity, and is proving so unable to interpret the hugely changed reality of a brave new world that hath no such creatures in it.

Sailors, like any group defined by the exclusive intensity of devotions and mysteries, have built up a vast structure of ritual and mythology. The Dartmouth sailors would not go much on the old-fashioned history book names I have mentioned. But those names are part of the strange totemism of sailing. The special continuity of tradition, the training and conception of duty named by Conrad are sustained in the symbols of 'The Castle's' bar and the special signs displayed by the beer-drinker we saw there, commander of the ketch, older and less a product of the antique restorers and the wardrobe nostalgia of the glossy advertisements than the *Charlotte Rhodes*, which now rocks at anchor in midstream. The particular tilt of his peaked cap, its salt and sun-bleached age, the worn durability of his clothes, the quality of his stance and confidence contain their special meanings only in a society, or rather a group within a society, confined and deepened by long traditions and rituals. Indeed, the point of ritual is to reaffirm the social order for its members and to penetrate the heart and soul of novices and newcomers and make them accept and obey that order.

The social order of the sailing community renews itself in relation to traditions and rituals which are at least partly independent of the trade which the captain in *The Shadow Line* is there to further.

All the nice girls love a sailor,
And you know what sailors are . . .

And again, 'there is something distasteful in the notion of a reward'. Nice
girls love sailors because they are manly men, manliness being imagined as
composed of physical courage, the endurance of hardship, the survival of
long distances, the return laden with the spoils and trophies of victory. To
this, in the romantic picture of heroism (and not at all necessarily the worse
for being romantic) are added certain qualities of personality and
behaviour such as taciturnity; strong feeling (especially the capacity for
romantic sexual love) held under tight rein; the capacity to bear pain
without complaint; forcefulness and decisiveness in the face of danger or
ambiguity; resolution; and supremely, strength of will in some rather
narrow definition related to stamina and the determination to overcome
inner resistance and weaknesses.

These are the traditional attributes and marks of a manly man,
particularly a hero. They have been deeply confirmed by the politics and
history of both the country and the continent. They were forged to meet
the exigencies of a country expanding its economy, its technology and its
empire under the pressure of a particular version of individualist theodicy.
These forces coincided to make such a man necessary, and the forms of
European moral thought provided plenty of precedents for such a man in
the doctrines of Greek ethics and Christian metaphysics and politics after
Luther, Machiavelli, and King Charles's head. Such a man is written
down in the annals of sailing, and kept alive in half a million* small boats of
which we have gazed at two or three hundred on the Dartmouth
waterfront. Those sailors and their womenfolk would themselves hardly
confess to such a picture, but the irresistible force of its continued, historical
momentum is there in the idiom, the styles, the rituals and techniques of
sailing itself. The sailing community, for instance, sets great store by
authenticity and the correctness with which tradition is kept sacred.

It is difficult to speak precisely. When a group watches a stranger move
up the Dart, the community notes with critical eyes just how far he holds
way on his sail, and scorns the use of the (of course inferior) engine. The
boat threads past a big motor cruiser, all glass deckhouse, the property of a
rank outsider and barbarian, past the ketch and the schooner, past a tall
cutter, past dozens of trivial minnows on the wide water; the engine,
necessary now, chugs harder and runs quicker, slows as it is thrown out of
gear, and the neat little vessel, barely moving by this point, slides trimly up
to the buoy and the oilskinned figure holding the forestay in the bows picks
up the moorings with a boathook and hauls them inboard. The group on
the quayside sigh a little with critical admiration; whoever he is has made a
beautiful job of coming to anchor. All fast. The engine coughs and stops.

* Figures estimated from *S. W. England: Survey of Water Resources and Leisure,
Devon and Cornwall C. C. S., 1976*.

The vessel is home. Its owner has proved his mastery of the mystery. He has ensured his inclusion in the group, and has provided for introduction. In 'The Castle', a stranger can say to him, another stranger, 'You made a lovely job of picking up your moorings.'

By that moment much is known about him. The style of his sailing, the appointments of his boat, its traditionality, the way he wears his uniform and arranges his visage and gestures, all these bespeak his loyalty to a particular version of sailing life and its meanings.* Within that continuity, as he confirms his membership of it and its community, he may even be allowed to make quite bad mistakes. The mistakes then become written into the mythology of the community and confirm its continuity through time. Friends return to that confirmation by rehearsing the mythology across the warm beer and full bellies, the muddy eye-watering haze of cigarette and pipe smoke – 'Remember when Bimbo bet that he could get up river against the tide, and stuck on the mud and sat on the mainmast parallel with the mud, pissed as a newt, singing filthy songs. Then the mast tipped and in he slid, into the mud up to his waist . . .' And so on. Tears of laughter running down each other's faces, the two or three friends renew their fealties to their brotherhood in these solemn, necessary ceremonies, five, six pints sunk to bind the oaths tight. And the story binds the absent friend in even closer to the community, because not only is he a member, he is also part of the mythology which defines membership. His experience is no longer his own. The comic disaster on the flats places him just as surely as the round-the-world sailors who have followed the redoubtable Francis Chichester in the traditions so richly evoked by Conrad.

Conrad, of course, is not in the least dewy-eyed about his community. The indulgence which it extends to its brotherhood is not larger or smaller than men in concert need anywhere, and includes in its slipshod morality, the base, necessary fantasies of all men. The kind of conversation we overheard is the small change and hard currency of the Royal Yacht Club, Harlequins RFC, Leander Rowing Club, the MCC, the Royal and Ancient Golf Club and the Jockey Club, every bit as much as those nobler songs of honour and fraternity whose chords I have already touched.

> They were attuned to the eternal peace of Eastern sky and sea. They loved short passages, good deck-chairs, large native crews, and the distinction of being white. They shuddered at the thought of hard work, and led precariously easy lives, always on the verge of dismissal, always on the verge of engagement, serving Chinamen, Arabs, half-castes – would have served the devil himself had he made it easy enough. They talked everlastingly of turns of luck; how So-and-so got charge of a boat on the coast of China – a soft thing; how this one had an easy billet in Japan somewhere, and that one was doing well in the Siamese

* I take some points here from Erving Goffman's books, *Encounters: Two Studies in the Sociology of Interaction* (Allen Lane, 1973) and *The Presentation of Self in Everyday Life* (Penguin, 1969), while remaining worried by the lack of *people* as (opposed to personae) in his world.

navy; and in all they said – in their actions, in their looks, in their persons – could
be detected the soft spot, the place of decay, the determination to lounge safely
through existence.*

Sailing, hunting, shooting, riding, fishing: the ruling-class sports are
touched with special grandeurs by virtue of their longevity. Nor is
understanding such meanings narrowly a matter of the class-struggle, or
at least not in so far as that misty concept purports to explain all social
phenomena. Indeed, what is intended throughout the pages of this book,
but particularly in this chapter, is to identify the unique ways in which
sport carries meanings which, as I have suggested, have been driven out of
their more central embodiments and realizations. Sailing is a case in point.
It is intricately mythologized *and* realized in its relation to the livelihood of
the nation: no ships, no trade. It connects with the great and gone names of
national history and identity. Moreover, the universal attributions of that
history weigh its technology in very loaded scales wherever ships put to sea.
For the greater honour is always paid by sailors, and by a national
imagination with a host of sailing images in its memory, to ships under
canvas as opposed to those under motor-power.
   Such homage is an archaism of a sort familiar to anyone in the West, but
perhaps especially in England. The honour paid to archaism derives from
more than simple longevity; a clinker-built sailing boat is thought of as true
to certain essences of sailing and of sailing as somehow *natural*. The shaping
and planing of the timbers to just those curves, to that lovely relation of
horizontal and perpendicular which make the lines of a boat, these are
perhaps loved for the human presence and continuity they speak of. The
varnished wood, the much polished brass absorb the feel of hands; the
rubbed finish is always deepening under men's hands. Not only that. The
wood and metal speak, so to say, of absorbed experience, but they are, in
the mythology and in fact, still near enough to their origins in nature to be
recognized. A timber was once a tree in a builder's yard; the glinting brass
was ore in rock. And even though modern technology will have climbed far
enough into the proper boat to change hairy hemp and stiff canvas into
terylene fibre, the advance thus far of progress is noted by a true sailor, and
he regrets it, and swears it will get no further on such a boat.
   This dense web of meanings lives in, gives life *to*, this sailing community.
Its members' contempt for sailors obsessed with racing and speed, with the
latest refinements for shaving invisible metal specks off their smooth steel
hulls, stems from the family of meanings I have described. Tradition,
continuity, friendship, ritual, style, grace, courage, these and many other
meanings are gathered into this web, this form of life. It is this delicate
membrane I wish to touch. Sport is important because the meanings live in
its forms of life as nowhere else in industrial society. They are peculiarly

* *Lord Jim* (Dent 1900; Penguin 1957), p. 16.

visible among sailors; sailing is no doubt a sport but, because of such complex origins, one which stretches into many non-sporting corners of the national identity. Its connexions with work and production, with the necessity of *transport*, mean that its force and place in any description of sport are unique. And yet its inclusiveness makes it an ideal type; it may signify far more than sport, and more than other sports, but what those other sports mean is mostly to be found prefigured in sailing.

IV

Imagine. Imagine a scene of such familiarity in the national imagination as a lovely cricket ground. The wide space of grass is like the water of the estuary, and the spectators who watch the movements of the cricketers note the details with something of the fellow-sailors' eyes. The ground is bounded by huge and splendid beeches and chestnuts; it is late August again, and already there is beech mast and the green, pulpy chestnut shucks to crunch underfoot on the boundary, like flotsam at a quayside. The shadows of the trees dapple the grass like water and the ritual movements of the players are as tall, compact and significant as those of boats. It is a relatively static game, and intricate. It is purely formal. (The players stop for tea.) The lissom, wiry fast bowler with the brown baked features, bowling from the far end, has bowled teens of overs already; it is a lot for a weekend cricketer. The shadows slant long from the trees; the ground lies in the shadows of the Pennines, and the orange haze of the sun already presages Autumn. Two black men are batting, not to score runs, but to reach full time. The fast bowler is tired, dead tired, and his shirt sticks to his back. He takes his long, bending run in to another stunning, stopped shot played with a dead bat. In the batsman's invincible tenacity, in the bowler's tiredness which he will only allow to sweep over him when the last ball is bowled, there is for them an honour and virtue which in turn causes deep wellbeing. Honour, virtue and wellbeing are the experiences and qualities which the tradition of the game permits the players to share as they walk off the field. The tradition requires them to observe rules and conventions which deepen and extend the community of the game. The right way to remove his gloves as the batsman walks in, the gesture of acknowledgement with his bat to the applause (for the rules also and centrally deal with how to be watched and how to watch), the gesture of virtuous exhaustion with which the fast bowler has flung his sweater across his hot, sodden shoulders, these maintain the tradition as they invite the admiration and envy of the spectators.

It will not do to speak of that scene simply as the vestiges of a nostalgia for a golden past, even though the nature of tradition is such that this element is certainly present in it. The tradition also contains those other, transcendental meanings I have named. Heroic exhaustion; honourable wounds and mud; the perfection of gesture; the maintenance of continuity; friends. In cricket as in sailing, men make the ideal shapes out of these meanings and present them as invisible works of art to the spectators, especially to those who are women and who love or admire the players. The lean fast bowler presents his 6 for 47 to his sweetheart as a trophy brought back from the tournament. He enters his sport's annals with his figures. That is why sportsmen always look themselves up in the record books. It is not conceit. It is a reassurance that they have acted in a known history, and that they are themselves.

Think of a huntsman. In important ways he is like a sailor. Nowadays, he will see himself with many of those associations. The 'contact with Nature'. The contact with a history in which those who rode were those who ruled. The sense of exaltation (literal and spiritual) and of nobility. The noble man rides. The sense of being watched, and of commanding. The pride which is akin to, and may become, courage. The recklessness which may transform itself into a purity of being and of freedom, like being in love.

Are these merely the qualities and experiences of a feudal society? If so, what is it which is so unkillable within these dying traces?

It is not so. The deep-chested rugby player who runs powerfully out before his home crowd, wearing his club's famous colours, is also like the huntsman. He too rejoins meanings of friendship, creativeness, truthfulness, courage, which no other activity can provide in so convincing and generous a way. Similarly the fisherman who comes home, chilled, soaked through to the bone, very tired below the first stars twinkling in a yellow and blue twilight, he too brings back a few small trout as works of art which confirm the value of physical exhaustion, personal creativeness, the experience of beauty and the display of courage. Sailor, huntsman, footballer, fisherman, hurdler, bowls player – all reanimate in their actions values and human meanings which are unkillable, not in spite of the failing symbols of industrial society, the master symbols of work and free productivity and prosperity, but precisely because of these failures.

Sporting lives do not, however, transcend their history. These virtues are as I have named them; they are not weird ghosts of feudalism, nor are they trappings of a bourgeois or proletarian culture. They come, as they must, out of a present history, now and in England. It is perfectly possible to attach particular versions of sporting friendship or sporting arrogance to certain kinds of class consciousness. Looking at the class structure of England shown in the photograph from the racecourse (page 8), listening to public-school rugby players at Twickenham, to the deathly bray of those arrogant voices, watching the thin, lank jaws and heavy spectacles of bowls players conferring above the gently knocking, clacking woods, is, as always in this country, to watch class differences so obvious you wonder amazedly at the continuing calm of it all. How on earth can each tolerate the other?

But they do. And they do at least partly because of the dream which sport always holds out. As I said before, sport in almost all its manifestations promises an ideal politics: a world in which access is common and equal but in which distinction is clearly acknowledged, understood, and honoured; a world untainted by vulgar gain and reward; a world in which natural rivalry and competition is vigorous and gentlemanly, in which style matters more than victory; a world in which social structure is fixed, hierarchic, and quite unjealous and unoppressive. Men in industrial societies found the grim purchase of the systems of production gripped them with a cold and killing grip. They spent decades of struggle in prising open that grip, and clearing a space between private and public life and its morality. All classes joined in clearing that space, a space in which, for once, politics and the moral life coincide. It is perhaps one of the more notable achievements of British society since, say, the 1867 Trade Disputes Act; it is what is meant in popular usage when people speak of 'the gift for compromise' which marks our institutions.

Sport lives in that space, neither public nor private, not work, certainly, but affirming some of the old working values, the labour culture. But while men seek at times to make sport free itself from itself (and the more they try, the more it is pinned down by history), at other occasions it is more than ever open to the movements and trends of the times precisely because it is placed in such structural ambiguity and vacancy beside the main poles of being in the world we live in. The space between public and private living is just that, a space; heaven knows what demons may fill it.

It is this position it holds between public and private living, there in the space men have fought to create for themselves in the name of their personal freedom, which makes sport so accessible *and* so puzzling. For in a paradoxical inversion, it is often the case in British society that it is so-called public life which holds the greatest mysteries for most people, and our private lives which are paraded and examined and symbolized in public. Politics, the domain of public living, takes place behind closed doors; its main figures are those for whom we open the doors of big, black saloon cars and whose well-dressed figures we watch over the shoulders of the crowd and the photographers and the police as they mount sweeps of steps to disappear through grand portals. Private lives, in this strange substitution of sacred and profane, are then the main subject of public debate: in newspapers, gossip, television, in literature and in intellectual inquiry. Far more is known in both folklore and fact about breast-feeding, sexuality, the treatment of very old relatives, or numbers of lavatories, than is known about who runs British oil in whose interests, how and by whom cheques are written to pay for hospitals or schools, how men are appointed to the most powerful jobs in the country, and what they do when they take them on. And then what we most learn from the relentlessly insistent representation of private life, especially in television's most familiar images, is that private life is uncreatable or is falling apart or is exposed to such an intolerable bright light, through such magnifying lenses, that its ordinary, decent, humdrum connexions and relations begin to soften and melt away. The gripped values – home, families, children, pub-time, creativeness in garden, workshed, sport or motorcar – begin to slip through people's fingers.

V

Why does this happen? Is it really happening at all? A sufficient reply can only point to the lives we all lead, interpret them, and then ask whether or not the interpretation is a true one. Trying to answer such questions is an argument in social science; the sportsman may skim these last sections of the chapter. The book, after all, intends an answer by its example: to talk about sport as I do *is* to do the kind of social science necessary if intellectual life is to help men understand themselves, and live better. Let it do to say that the exploration of the values and meanings which a society cherishes or changes or tears down can only exist in the languages it has which are commonly understood. Such understanding is no slight thing. The plural 'languages' is well advised, because this book treats of systems of stylizations, gestures and rule-governed movements which partake of language forms, which have a grammar, a syntax, and an aesthetic. This is not the place to press home a teasing philosophical point, it is a difficult, perhaps impossible business to establish an *identity* of structure in systematic gesture as in language. For these purposes, analogy will do: we understand the meanings of sport because we understand our common language. We not only understand that language, we live in it. If there were no language, there could be no community. Sport is not (obviously) the same thing as language, not least because its signs do not immediately refer to objects outside themselves. A right cross in boxing is itself. It does not refer to a particular object. It would be more accurate to understand the blow in the boxing ring as more like a metaphor *within* language, than a distinct form of language itself.

These theoretic details return us to the question of understanding and valuing the social life we live in. Understanding the curiously in-between essence of sport turns upon accepting the interpretation or placing of its social significance as between public and private lives, together with the substitution of sacred for profane, open for closed in what one would think of as their natural domains in a democratic society; public power is become sacred, private meanings profane. Both tendencies, however, turn upon a much more pivotal change in social identity, and that is the shift from institutional loyalties and responsibilities to personal sincerity and authenticity as the focus of allegiance. The forms of imaginative and actual relationships more and more express *individuality* (rather than membership) as the core of being. You might say that ideals of honour and loyalty have been supplanted by those of integrity and dignity.* At the same time,

---

* A point I take from Peter Berger et al., *The Homeless Mind: Modernization and Consciousness* (Penguin, 1974).

the new emphasis on 'individuality' came up hard against the blocks and blankness of public life as I have described it. The vindication of personal life is increasingly difficult in a world which denies individual responsibility and whose giant networks make it easy to do so. The old clichés about giant size, impersonality, facelessness, 'them' and 'us', bureaucracy, and so on, are perfectly sound as far as they go. Language is, as ever, the key to the new class system. The rich nations have the managements and the managed; the technical study of their relation is systems analysis. Individualist doctrines, whether ethical or political, have no purchase on such a state of affairs.

Consequently, individuality is forced to assert itself as spectacle. And it is here that my two subjects coincide, and sport becomes politics. For sport is the readiest expression of individuality lived as spectacle, and its position in the space between public and private life makes it an especially suitable stage for that spectacle. You can argue, as people have,* that under modern conditions of production all life appears as an immense accumulation of *spectacles*. All that was once directly lived, is now transformed into representation. It is a view which emphasizes the enormous presence in the rich, industrial nations of the mass media, particularly as manifest in the symbolism of advertising and in the texture of consumer culture. It is with the detail of consumerism that the circle of the argument completes itself. For changing politics into dramatic spectacle may be said to coincide with the consolidations of the big industrial cities. The Great Exhibition at the Crystal Palace in 1851, and the arcades of glass and slender steel piers built in Paris a little before by Fourier, initiate the city as spectacle. Window shopping, with its profound consequences for experience, became universally possible; became the urban pastime.

The uncertainty of knowing whether or not a man is an agent or an actor in society, a spectator or a participant, was compounded by the transformation of so much ruling class life into political pageant. The hunt, the regatta, the race meeting, the tennis party, became centrepieces of spectacle, and the reality of the occasion was by spectators and participants alike felt to reside in the *visibility* with which the ritual was correctly performed. The unique emphasis on the spectacular nature of ruling class ritual which begins to be evident from about the end of the nineteenth century, found and finds a peculiarly rich set of forms in the mass sports which emerge at the same time. Since that time, the notion of the self as an image has strengthened a great deal, but more than that, we have placed these images in a dramatized context. That context confirms the ambiguous sense any audience has that it owns the performers but is powerless to affect their actions. The performers in turn act always as those conscious of being watched by those whose admiration they must retain, while also feeling themselves godlike and superior. (The state of mind is

* Gary Dubord, *La Société du Spectacle* (Le Seuil, Paris, 1967).

well presented in the novel and film, *This Sporting Life*, which I look at later.) These are the conditions which make that important section of the power élite, the celebrities,* and thus it is that we begin to think about the star system, and its central place in our moral and political economy.

Mentioning the stars is simply the easiest way in to any discussion of the human meanings of sport. The relation of star to spectator, of action to spectacle, swims into focus only when we place sporting life, as I have done, between public and private life. And the key question we then bring to each of its manifestations is, how much of what we see and love in sport is real expression? How much *is* the creative, genuine expression of people's feelings and ideas? And how much, on the contrary, is the result of the deep manipulation of their beings by the dark forces of modern production, the heavy, dead penetration of body and soul hidden in the reach-me-down cliché, 'conspicuous consumption'?

VI

'In the midst of life we are in death.' The only way to come at answers to these large, momentous questions, is to watch and wonder with all the delicacy and impertinence of a great anthropologist. Some men have started to write of sport out of that tradition of inquiry which insists on classification along a grid of typical features. The traditional social scientist's form of classification, however neat and tidy, gives us little leverage on the rich, messy life which is at the heart of the mystery. Consider. Roger Caillois devises a typology of games: a system of the typical features of *all* games.† What sort of theory will he be able to generate? What shall we do with it?

There is one important difference between Caillois' ideas and the general account of sport which emerges from these pages. It is that Caillois is interested in *anything* which counts as play or as game. He is classifying all forms of playful, non-productive behaviour. Our interests in the book are narrower and more concrete. They concentrate entirely on the physical sports of modern industrial countries. They occupy therefore only one small sector of Caillois' scheme of things, and they are far more manifold than he allows.

He identifies four key elements in every game or every play situation. These are: competition, chance, mimicry and vertigo. Thus, football is dominated by the idea of competition – of *winning* (his special term for this element comes from Greek drama, the *agon*, or ritual contest; hence, protagonist/antagonist); but of course competition and rivalry is written fundamentally into the conditions of almost all play involving more than

---

* The argument is developed in C. Wright Mills, *The Power Elite*, (Oxford University Press, 1955).

† R. Caillois, *Man, Play and Games*, (Paris, Plon 1960; London, Thames & Hudson, 1962).

one person. It is then a condition of competition that as far as possible both teams or individuals play on equal terms, and serious inequalities of ability are allowed for by handicap (carrying weights, giving away strokes, etc.) or stratification (divisions of ability), and the legislation of the game is constantly renewed according to key notions of fairness. Advantages such as batting first or running on the inside lane are put to 'fair' chance by tossing a coin. The element of chance typifies all games such as dice and roulette which consciously eradicate individual gifts, skills and experience. Men gamble on games of chance precisely because they can do nothing about the outcome. The game of chance is, if you like, a parody of that view which sees men as the blind, helpless and absurd objects of directionless fate. To play dice or poker is to enter that view of the universe and bet on the chance of luck. This is the expression of absolute equality; the elimination of personality and behaviour. Competitive games turn on the reality of human consciousness become action. Chance games deride this idea as delusion.

The other two elements are much less usable for our purposes. By mimicry, Caillois means simply acting, playing at being someone else, dressing up and so forth. That this is an important part of children's behaviour we all know at first hand. Just in what relation this impersonation stands to the daydreams of boys and men who while playing their own games at their own level of ineptitude, pretend to *be* their Saturday heroes, their Bjorn Borg, Bobby Jones, or Denis Compton (according to age), is not at all clear, and will perhaps only come out when we look at one or two of the stories written about sports in Chapter 6. The experience of vertigo which Caillois selects as the fourth criterion of a game has an arbitrary look about it. He sees this as the pleasure which feelings of dizziness, 'voluptuous panic', headlong descent (as in tobogganing or skiing) bring about or the wild confusion of balance and perception induced by rides on various funfair machines. (I think I would prefer to say that qualities answering to this description but going well beyond it are to be found in many types of games and provide for that momentary, exhilarating, and terrific loss of identity, experiment with which is a main experience of both art and sport.)

Caillois classifies games according to the preponderance of one or other of these elements. So team sports come under competition (*agon*), fruit-machines or counting-out games under chance (*alea*), dressing-up under mimicry, skiing or parachuting under vertigo. He also arranges the sports and games in each column along a scale from *paidia* (the Greek word whose root means 'child') to *ludus*, the Latin for game. Roughly speaking, this is a scale running from improvised, largely spontaneous and ruleless play to organized, skilful, technical and rule-governed games.

Caillois' scheme gives us a frame of sorts, but in so far as this book centres upon modern, organized sport, all our interest falls in the segment marked out by competition and rules, skills, craft. Yet to say this is at once to feel dissatisfied. Is it really the case that the pleasures provided by tennis or fishing are accounted for according to this very general frame? It is immediately clear that pointless spontaneity and improvisation are richly a part of playing football and cricket, that skiing may be competitive, and that most of the more lonely, contemplative, sedentary, or geriatric games such as fishing, bowls, dressage on horse-back, kite-flying or dancing, speak to desires and provide experiences not at all accounted for by this scheme.

Such a scheme of classification purports to be, as they say, 'value-free'. That is, the principles which organize the scheme derive from the nature of the activities studied, and are not brought into the scheme from outside. There is one brief but in its way celebrated attempt to identify play as a key component in the good society. Such an insight comes near the main premises of this book, which is that organized sport is an essential experience in industrial society if men are not entirely to go without the experiences of beauty, joy, exhaustion and friendship. I have already quoted from the book; in it, Huizinga looks back with a certain wistfulness at a Renaissance aristocracy whose tourneys and riding, fencing and dressage were of a piece with a complete image of the educated courtier: soldier, scholar, athlete, gentleman. It is a noble image, and it has never been lost within that European tradition of education which appealed to the image of a complete man. The dream has haunted, for good and evil, many of the major spectator sports of modern times and, if it perpetuated tired snobberies between amateurs and professionals, this was at least partly because without the idea of an amateur nobody could quite imagine how to keep alive this necessary angel, the fictive but important gentleman-athlete. The professional artist – whether a painter or a cricketer – may be said to do things for the things' sake; the amateur does things for his own sake, for the sake of doing them. The antique image was aristocratic. It partook of an ethic in which display and courtesy and magnificence lay close together in the moral positives of the society. Though such positives are not much honoured in explicit celebration today – nobody actually confesses to liking swagger, swashbuckle, elaborate manners or munificence – it is probable that one place where they are at once expressed and contained is in the sports arena. In so far as we live with not one but a number of well-integrated moralities, the diversity of sports and their diversity of values reflect this state of affairs. It remains to be seen whether an individual sport can reconcile the claims of both aristocratic and democratic values within its touchlines.

Huizinga detects some diminution of true playfulness as modern sport emerged from the British industrial revolution. He writes mournfully:

> In modern social life sport occupies a place alongside and apart from the cultural process. The great competitions in archaic cultures had always formed part of the sacred festivals and were indispensable as health-and-happiness-bringing activities. This ritual tie has now been completely severed; sport has become profane, 'unholy' in every way and has no organic connection whatever with the

structure of society, least of all when prescribed by the government. The ability of modern social techniques to stage mass demonstrations with the maximum of outward show in the field of athletics does not alter the fact that neither the Olympiads nor the organized sports of American universities nor the loudly trumpeted international contests have, in the smallest degree, raised sport to the level of a culture-creating activity. However important it may be for the players or spectators, it remains sterile. The old play-factor has undergone almost complete atrophy.

This view will probably run counter to the popular feeling of today, according to which sport is the apotheosis of the play-element in our civilization. Nevertheless popular feeling is wrong.*

Now that declaration, no less baldly, seems wrong. It posits an unreal clarity about the terms of play (that is, not 'in earnest'). And it is not hard to show from everyday experience that sports remain 'indispensable as health-and-happiness-bringing activities'. The whole enormous testimony of the next three chapters establishes that, and you will only disbelieve them if you hold some view of health and happiness as only really being credible at another time and paradisal place before the industrial Fall. What we hold sacred is certainly important, and no less certainly sport may be trivial. But it is simply false to say that sport is rudely 'profane' and inorganically related to the whole society. Good heavens, the nature of sporting economy intimately reflects the whole structure of modern capitalism, at the same time as it keeps in being a queer, unofficial inversion of market theory which implies the ever-present possibility of radically different and revolutionary criteria of economic success. There is no doubt that, as according to Huizinga and those rather odd bedfellows in whose hearts his words about play, overseriousness and the genuine amateur would sound an echo – the older members of the MCC, the Royal and Ancient Golf Club, the committee of the Leander Rowing Club – as they would in their different accents say, 'These boys play too seriously today. It's all technique and no fun. It's too dull and workaday. They're only interested in winning. None of the old gaiety and recklessness. There's so much statistics. Ah, remember when . . .' And so on. Well, they're partly right. There are losses, heartfelt losses to count. And gladiators were always mightier than now. Victor Trumper, W. G. Grace, Eddie Hapgood, Adrian Stoop, Suzanne Lenglen. No matter that the New Zealander John Walker would have beaten Paavlo Nurmi in the mile by nearly twenty seconds. Those were the days, and such the heroes.

But no record of the present will do which simply pencils in a steep downward gradient. Culture as diminution? Rats. The theory of sport offered here for the use of all sportsmen and women is more particular and more loose-textured than the two glanced at earlier. We can best start from the way Ludwig Wittgenstein talked about games in order that he could find a more satisfactory way of talking about and understanding the

* Johann Huizinga, *Homo Ludens*, p. 224.

meaning and structure of language. He wanted to break down the idea that there was a single structure to language of which the simple sentence was the molecular composition. Instead, he demanded:

> Consider for example the proceedings that we call 'games'. I mean board-games, card-games, ball-games, Olympic games, and so on. What is common to them all? – Don't say: 'There *must* be something common, or they would not all be called "games"' – but *look and see* whether there is anything common to all. For if you look at them you will not see something that is common to *all*, but similarities, relationships, and a whole series of them at that. To repeat: don't think, but look! Look for example at board-games, with their multifarious relationships. Now pass to card-games; here you find many correspondences with the first group, but many common features drop out, and others appear. When we pass next to ball-games, much that is common is retained, but much is lost. Are they all 'amusing'? Compare chess with noughts and crosses. Or is there always winning and losing, or competition between players? Think of patience. In ball games there is winning and losing; but when a child throws his ball at the wall and catches it again, this feature has disappeared. Look at the parts played by skill and luck; and at the difference between skill in chess and skill in tennis. Think now of games like ring-a-ring-a-roses; here is the element of amusement, but how many other characteristic features have disappeared! And we can go through the many, many other groups of games in the same way; can see how similarities crop up and disappear.
>
> And the result of this examination is: we see a complicated network of similarities overlapping and criss-crossing: sometimes overall similarities, sometimes similarities of detail.
>
> I can think of no better expression to characterize these similarities than 'family resemblances'; for the various resemblances between members of a family: build, features, colour of eyes, gait, temperament, etc. etc. overlap and criss-cross in the same way. And I shall say: 'games' form a family.
>
> And for instance the kinds of number form a family in the same way. Why do we call something a 'number'? Well, perhaps because it has a – direct – relationship with several things that have hitherto been called number; and this can be said to give it an indirect relationship to other things we call the same name. And we extend our concept of number as in spinning a thread we twist fibre on fibre. And the strength of the thread does not reside in the fact that some one fibre runs through its whole length, but in the overlapping of many fibres.*

Wittgenstein wanted to establish that the ideal type of sentence was more than simply a statement, and that you could not get at the meaning of meaning by stripping language down to its component parts and their barest essentials. The word 'red' only means what it does in a whole series of contexts. And then we relate the word and the experience it signifies to the other words and experiences gathered under the heading 'colour'; in this way, our concept of colour – as Wittgenstein describes the extension of the concept of number – extends, 'as in spinning a thread we twist fibre on

---

* L. L. Wittgenstein, *Philosophical Investigations*, I, trans. G. E. M. Anscombe (Blackwell, 1953), paras. 66–7.

fibre'. We twist, so to speak, usage upon usage until the rope which we have woven depends for its strength not on any reducible essence but upon long, tested strain in a diversity of use and strain.

We shall find out far more about the meanings of games if we do not insist on a watertight scheme of classification, and look instead for 'a complicated network of similarities overlapping and criss-crossing: sometimes overall similarities, sometimes similarities of detail'. And so, with Wittgenstein, we shall say 'games form a family'. This will permit us to identify a variety of different purposes in games: a game does not by this method have to be *all* competitive or *all* spontaneous. This way we can work from people's everyday valuations in order to see how the concepts of 'sport' and 'games' come to have their meanings. We can see that the precision and co-ordination of hopscotch is related (by family, as it were) to those same virtues in squash. We don't have to rule out childishness from what look like very rule-governed sports.

So the theory of games advanced here is one which tries to take its valuations from the shared, if often unspoken, meanings of its society. We shall count as sport what generally counts as sport for modern industrial society. But students of culture and of the expressive arts have also come to see the arrival of leisure as the central theoretical question in the study of culture and to identify that leisure as the really lived social experience.

VII

All of which brings me back to anthropology. For in so far as this book treats of an intellectual discipline in the human sciences, it is anthropology I am practising.

What do I mean? I mean the careful and systematic study of cultural ecology, of the human conditions under which people make the meanings and values by which they live. And when I write 'meanings', as I do so often in these pages, I intend those shared concentrations of value in life which people naturally understand in the language they share, and this sharing is identical with the entirely unassuming encounter implicit in meaning anything at all by the words we use.* The same goes for the common meanings of formal gestures. And to recognize the meanings those carry – in sport, of course, as our immediate example – is to interpret a central core of human symbolization with such inevitability and immediacy that it would seem gratuitous to think of 'encountering' as being involved in meaning, or of conventions at all. (Even though in such gratuitousness, it is an agreed convention that symbols mean what they do.)

This kind of anthropology therefore seeks out the intended meanings of social life, and tries to interpret the value they have in the structures of that

* I take much here, as everywhere, from F. R. Leavis, especially in his most recent book, *The Living Principle* (Chatto & Windus, 1975), especially pp. 57–8.

life. Such a quest is not the same as those undertaken by different sorts of cultural scientist who may on the one hand pile up the useful, over-powering heaps of brute facts about society – there are columns of them in the last chapter – and on the other, record the assorted behaviours of a society with an eye on deciding what their *function* is in the maintenance of the social structure (which is itself only there as a way of providing a metaphor for the amazing fact of social continuity through time and space). The school of sociologists and anthropologists calling itself functionalism starts out from the premiss that social actions either conduce to, 'reinforce', or enact social structure. In so far as they do not, they become anomalies, and are put down. I would rather say that social behaviour is vastly more manifold than any such explanation presupposes. Either way, explanation as the point of social science is better translated as the giving of reasons and *not* causes for people acting as they do. In other words, everything turns on the precise, intelligent, interpretation of what has been accurately described. The justification either for the functionalist, who has to have accurate, checkable descriptions to work with, or even more for the anthropology I profess here, is to be found in these remarks of Wittgenstein:

> In order to get clear about aesthetic words, you have to describe ways of living . . . Judgement is a gesture accompanying a vast structure of actions not expressed by one judgement . . . giving reasons for admiration of a poem etc. is like providing further descriptions of what it is like . . .*

He is telling us that when we interpret systematic or regulated human behaviour, we do so by adjusting and extending our descriptions of what we say. At the same time, these descriptions take in judgements of value, as our description implies approval or criticism. The more we try our description for accuracy and agreement, the more we give the behaviour an interpretation. As we say, we 'try to make sense of what is going on'. 'Making sense' *means* something like 'discovering the coherence of', the process whereby in the name of pattern and order, we interpret the life around us.

This interpretation is not so much a matter of uncovering the reasonableness, the rational grounds for a set of actions. Football, or the sort of fishing after which you throw the fish back when you have caught it, hardly answer tests for rationality. 'Making sense', as I say, is something we all do all the time. Think of trying to interpret a children's playground game which you are watching for the first time. We work not for the larger rationality of the game, but for its rules and conventions, and the way in which these shape and order some queer corner of playground experience. Within the rules and conventions, as we umpire them, we find the

* In L. L. Wittgenstein, *Conversations About Aesthetics*, ed. C. Barratt (Blackwell, 1967), pp. 11–16.

coherence of the game, its satisfactory shapes. But nothing will come of nothing. The children's game, in all its oddity (such as that odd game of 'French skipping', a strange agility test involving ritual jumping on elastic loops) relates to the society round about it. In oblique and non-social forms, the game symbolizes, makes a metaphor of, essential social themes.

I take it that these remarks are true of any game or sport. Sport in all its strange forms prefigures the shape of social life. It is not quite enough to say it is a 'metaphor' for social life; narrowly taken, metaphor signifies a linguistic gesture in which properties not usually ascribed to certain things are so ascribed either in order to give concrete life to what is normally abstract (an idea or a feeling, for instance) or in order to change our perception of something whose special details we would never have seen without the metaphor. Well, by this token, boxing is a metaphor for the reality of aggression, a realization of the master-symbols of courage, endurance, quickness, grace, victoriousness. Tennis is a metaphor for many of the same values. But both games also *enact* in their gestures these values. They give them *real* life, and hence move from metaphor to immediate experience. Muhammed Ali really does fight Foreman, but in ways which make really hurting one another very difficult (special gloves, no hitting below the belt, etc., etc.). So sport has both dramatic and metaphoric content. Lastly, of course, it has a social context – the heavyweight championship of the world is at once these two real men, a symbolic fight to the death, and the meeting of two nations, or two classes, or two societies of rival negroes. In Clifford Geertz's words, in an anthropological essay on the ancient sport of Balinese cockfighting, the sport is

> a cultural figure against a social ground, . . . and its aesthetic power derives from its capacity to force together these diverse realities . . . Its function, if you want to call it that, is interpretive: it is a Balinese reading of Balinese experience, a story they tell themselves about themselves.*

And as we return from the circumscribed commotion of a cockfight to the manifold and broadcast life of sailing with which I began this chapter, then it is perhaps clear that sports indeed tell us many and different stories about ourselves.

'Telling stories' and 'making sense' are the homely, intelligible epigraphs to this disquisition. Sports tell us stories; they make sense of the world.

> In the case at hand, to treat the cockfight as a text is to bring out a feature of it (in my opinion, the central feature of it) that treating it as a rite or a pastime, the two most obvious alternatives, would tend to obscure: its use of emotion for cognitive ends. What a cockfight says it says in a vocabulary of sentiment – the thrill of risk, the despair of loss, the pleasure of triumph. Yet what it says is not merely that risk

---

* *Interpretation of Cultures*, (Hutchinson, 1975), pp. 444 and 448.

is exciting, loss depressing, or triumph gratifying, banal tautologies of affect, but that it is of these emotions, thus exampled, that society is built and individuals are put together. Attending cockfights and participating in them is, for the Balinese, a kind of sentimental education. What he learns there is what his culture's ethos and his private sensibility (or, anyway, certain aspects of them) look like when spelled out externally in a collective text; and – the disquieting part – that the text in which this revelation is accomplished consists of a chicken hacking another mindlessly to bits.*

Geertz goes on to say that Balinese life expresses itself very differently elsewhere, but that the cockfight is essential to part of it. Similarly, the sheer *range* of our sporting lives in Britain reminds us just how diverse and rich is the experience for which the sports are the conjunction of dramatic reality, of a metaphor for values, and of social context. And, in his phrase, the 'use of emotion for cognitive ends', providing a way of thinking for a people to whom practical action and feeling comes more easily than intellection, sports and art become versions of the same thing. Each of them formally enacts – dances, if you like – some of its society's attitudes. Interpreting the dance means attending closely to what it says.

There are no statistical tests of this attention. All we can do is to look closely at the reports we have, and those I recreate, of the sports around us. The natural material to attend to is people's conversation about sport wherever it occurs: in books, newspapers, on television.

What this means in practice should emerge as we look first at the languages of sport as we tell ourselves about it: on television, in the newspapers, in the flood of good and bad books, biographies, memoirs, novels, about sport. And then it will come out in the attempt to see what the lived experience of the sport is like – the patterns of participation, the cash, the way we initiate our children into playing.

Speaking with this generality, it becomes easy to sentimentalize the way sport features in our lives. Authenticity and sincerity are such powerful words for good in our experience, that we may suppose that they refer only to 'good' feelings. But of course ugly, hateful or simply childish feelings may be perfectly authentic, and we shall certainly see such feelings expressing themselves through sport. So it is not that sport works only for redemption. Equally, the argument put throughout this book is that, so far from being as Huizinga says, a non-organic and unrelated area of culture, as things are, sport is one of the main cultural experiences. It bodies forth some of the main meanings available to us, and at a time of deep moral confusion, it may, at its best, permit the clash of moralities, the contradiction of moral imperatives, to be known and understood and balanced. The old, bitter opposition – between democracy and excellence, between the individual and the group, between heart and mind, between aristocrat and worker – these irreconcilables, rather than being at each

* Clifford Geertz, *Interpretation of Cultures*, p. 449.

other's throats, can live in the spontaneous ebb and flow, the high tension, of creative play. When this happens – and it can only happen momentarily – then a man becomes whole, to himself and to his times. He rediscovers purity.

4 Heroism and community—writing about sport

So WE DREAM OF PURITY. We dream, that is, of a state of fortune in which by our actions we discover an absolute integrity of being, a sense of at-one-ness with the world in which what we do vindicates the person we think we are. In this state, the gap between social experience – how we generally are and feel about our lives – and the forms of expression closes up, and the society together with our feelings about the society are lived as one.

The dream lives within many private lives in the social mythology about love. Now 'myths' do not imply falsehood. They simply mean the images – the pictures, visions and ideals – which a whole society makes up for itself as guides to and illusions about conduct. There is a living tension between theory and experience. There always has been, of course, but different ages experience the tension differently. You could put it like this (simplifying very bluntly). All men and women spend their lives trying to pull together, or to reconcile themselves somehow to the split between, what is actual and what they desire. How they do this depends on their picture of the world. That picture reflects (among other things) a greater or lesser confidence about the world. A confidence, that is, that they *can* bring the actual into line with what they desire. The great peaks of European experience have risen from a combination of assurance and profound change. Men have been riding the crest of a new wave. So when the great buildings of Renaissance Florence were built, its paintings and music completed, its enormous wealth flowing in and out of the banks in the earliest recognition that it is liquid capital which increases fastest – all these events fitted a picture of the world in which men were the centre but not the measure of all creation. The greatness of their churches – say, the famous church of Santa Maria degli Angeli begun in Florence in 1434 – was best seen inside from the very centre of the Cruciform below the dome. The spectator therefore was given the centre of things from which to see creation. And his creation, the church, was itself a part of the larger Creation. Men were not gods; they were confident of a place next to God.

As the changing movements of Protestantism and the Galilean astrology which pulled man out of the centre of things came to press harder and harder on this central position, it broke up, and was replaced by a much more provisional, isolated and subjective point of view. Perhaps it is clear enough that within such an unrivalled combination of wealth, creative-

74

ness, cocksureness and modesty, it is possible for art and expression to come together, for popular and educated culture to be one. But when the Florentine Renaissance was over, the theories men made about themselves – their social mythologies – turned about a very much more fragmentary and individual position. There had been a sort of Fall, and the Garden of Eden was no longer a place which could be reflected on earth. Creation became something out there, a man was separated from it. Then he only has his arts to tell him what the Garden may be like. The arts become his only vision. Where painting or poetry or architecture had been for the Florentines forms of the natural sciences, they now became forms of the moral sciences.*

It is then possible to see all subsequent peaks of cultural and social experience as the result of renewals of confidence and excitement. The English Renaissance – the time of Shakespeare, William Byrd, Ben Jonson and Inigo Jones – grew essentially out of the same conditions as the Florentine. It took nearly a century for the cold Northern island to absorb via the Dutch all that drifted across from Europe. The next renewal of confidence on such a scale sprang from the changes of thought and of production which issued in the French and American Revolutions. The philosophers of the Enlightenment, the revolutionaries, the ideas of Hegel, of Blake, the music of Mozart and Beethoven, all declared an unprecedented faith in the rediscovery of reason, happiness, and freedom. I speak here as though the work of a handful of men tells us everything about the vast, slow changes of a continent. But the point is that these men fill to the limits a certain consciousness which was emerging from changes in perception, in social relations, in economics, in manufacture. At the same time, thousands of people still died in the most desperate conditions, and thousands of others were killed trying to change those conditions.

But the leaders of the time showed what was possible. They brought to mind – in the fullest sense of the phrase – new potentialities. And at times, these potentialities became real in the lived experience of the time. The actual and the desired came together.

The dream of purity of action combined with integrity of being which lives most strongly in the popular imagination is fulfilled when you fall in love. To be in love is to recover the lost Eden: to be whole within the personal meanings available in the society. The mystic ideal lives in every popular magazine, in innumerable films and novels. Of course it is women who make most regular appeal to the myths; the magazines and the romantic movies are thought of as being women's stuff: men largely see themselves as debarred from the public expression of tenderness. *Their* satisfactions, their best definitions of identity lie elsewhere, particularly in sport. But the important point is not that being in love is womanly; it is that

---

* The epigram is taken from John Berger, in *The Moment of Cubism and other Essays*, Weidenfeld and Nicolson, 1969. I have broadly adapted his views above.

being in love is personal. The intensity of individual feeling – its sincerity and its truthfulness-to-yourself – is a main standard by which to judge the value of experience. Its value lies in its testability. In a situation in which what is valid is deeply confused and obscure, at the least one can test one's most intimate feelings for validity. And so being in love has become an ideal type experience. It has been so since the heroines of nineteenth-century fiction. It supplies a test for truth – personal truth. At that time, even the public heroes and men whose success was given public award, they too were held to vindicate much of the same view of experience. They were mythologized into ideal types. They saw themselves as such types – as Heroes, Lovers, Leaders. The vast honour and acclaim given to men as different as Mungo Park, Cecil Rhodes, George Gordon, was alike in that each man was acclaimed for his *solitary* contributions to human welfare. Each achievement was defined as the result of inspiration and lonely virtue. Men in their role as heroes provided the structural antithesis of women in their role as goddesses.

This public myth about the personal value of heroes and goddesses is still sunk deep in our national folklore. It is not clear in what ways it survives but there is an argument to be made that it *should* survive and that, however démodé it sounds, a society without heroes is not simply without moral bearings, it is unimaginable.

It is more to the point, however, to show that with these changes towards the exaltation of personal life, and particularly of personal feeling, the artist came also to see his experience as not only what defined him, in Wordsworth's words, 'as a man speaking to men', but also as

> a man, it is true, endued with more lively sensibility, more enthusiasm and tenderness, who has a greater knowledge of human nature, and a more comprehensive soul, than are supposed to be common among mankind; a man pleased with his own passions and volitions, and who rejoices more than other men in the spirit of life that is in him . . .*

The poet, painter, or musician, that is, becomes the saint of subjectivity. The vividness with which he can present himself is the test of the power of nature and of true sincerity in him. In so far as he is sublime, he is crazy. This was, and is, the most popular view of Van Gogh, Picasso, Frank Lloyd Wright, Einstein, Pasteur, W. B. Yeats; the artist becomes identified with a singleminded vision so that even when apparently normal and con-ventionally dressed, what gives him his uniqueness and his *explanation* as an artist is his vision, true in one sense, crazy in another. He is thought of as living on a different plane from that of ordinary life, the comparative (though reassuring) poverty of that life but as measuring an emotional intensity intolerable to most people. By this token, robustly everyday figures like Vaughan Williams or Henry Moore, perhaps Rutherford or Niels Bohr, can be assimilated to the extra-social group of 'geniuses', and

* William Wordsworth, Preface to *The Lyrical Ballads*, 2nd edn. (London, 1800).

placed not according to what they can do, but by what they can *see*.

What has been the point of this long digression into the way in which English society has seen artists? It is that repeated premiss of this book that, at least since about 1880, the meanings and functions of art and sport in industrial society have lain very close together, and that at the very least something of what sport means to us will be revealed by a consideration of how we see our artists. And we will see *them* clearer, as measured against how they have been seen within different frames of European consciousness.

Since about the turn of the First World War, art, almost irrespective of its conclusions, has been thought of as pointing towards the irrationalism and beastliness of humanity in public and, at best, the strenuous difficulty of winning some redemption in private. Those who have taken any notice of art have expected it to tell them of the hollowness of triumph, the illusions of beauty, the universality of pain, the fraudulence of hope and gladness. There has been much in the times to justify the view; the writers, painters and musicians have hurried to fulfil such expectations with an unselfconsciousness whose vanity might have been salutarily cut back had they realized just how much the impulse to tell the dreadful truth was the product of the expectations of a self-lacerating audience. The sociology of expectation and its determining force is too subtle and strong to measure. It is enough to say that those who once looked for art to supply declarations of hope and aspiration, images of gladness, celebration, and beauty, looked elsewhere.

Beauty, though. The gentle, great British and American publics have never made much of beauty. When they want beauty, they have preferred it to be quiet and familiar rather than surprising, and they have come to expect it in only limited parts of their experience and surroundings. One such place, since towns became such dirty and noisy places, has been the countryside. A day in the country has become an amiable ritual for spiritual refreshment. You go to the country to look at beautiful views and villages. Naturally enough, when things have been hard and bad, people have looked to the countryside and its associations to provide some peace and quiet – a stay against the rest of life. And in this essential refuge certain sports – particularly cricket and fishing – have come to figure at its very heart.

Consider. After the First World War, the popular imagination made strong efforts to take up where it had left off in the long, hot summer which ended in August 1914. To reach back to the other side of the slaughter, now apparently pointless, and to recreate a pastoral picture of the England destroyed by the terrible changes of the war. By the early part of this century cricket had come to play an integral part in that strange, powerful formation of ideas about the English countryside and its history which swims at large through the national imagination. Observation, myth, record, and half-history are so deeply entwined that it can no longer be

made clear which elements are strongest in that imagination. The effect
comes through in countless poems, good and bad, about the English
landscape. It comes through in countless more advertisements when, in
625 lines and with the most expensive television techniques, cricketers and
unforgettable girls are photographed into the sun in the interests of the
greatest profits of the smallest number.

> . . . The church and yew
> And farmhouse slept in a Sunday silentness.
> The air raised not a straw. The steep farm roof,
> With tiles duskily glowing, entertained
> The mid-day sun; and up and down the roof
> White pigeons nestled. There was no sound but one.

These, here beautifully noted and ordered, are the stage properties of the
unkillable rural idyll:

> . . . a season of bliss unchangeable
> Awakened from farm and church where it had lain
> Safe under tile and thatch for ages since
> This England, Old already, was called Merry.*

'This England'; that phrase itself is resonant with unnumbered public
quotings of John of Gaunt's speech in *Richard II*. And in myth,
'unchangeable' is right. This picture of the landscape is lifted out of history
and lives in the mythology of the nation's mind to be evoked for a dozen
different purposes: for this man's stirring speech to the local Round Table,
for that one's advertisement for orange juice or summer holidays, for a
girl's letter to her mother-in-law about a day in the country. It is
completely wrong to say blankly, for instance as Brian Glanville and
George Orwell both do,† that cricket is an upper-class sport, and the
pastoral idyll in which cricket is the centrepiece is the product of the
mandarinate which dreams up in cadenced prose social fantasies for its
class. What has actually happened, as always, is much more complicated.

For it is true to say that the official ideologies of the people who ran and
still run the country produced – in the magazines, newspapers and novels –
pictures of the countryside whose ordered, changeless, rhythmic beauties
somehow were supposed to endorse a just as ordered and changeless social
world. The ritual which combined and expressed most richly and
politically the harmony of nature and society was cricket. The problem is
that many men who did not at all accept the changeless view of things saw
cricket as one of many sports which express and celebrate men at home
with themselves, men joining in a gleefully pointless game, a game in
which as much as anything the pleasure is that the sun shines on your back,

---

* Edward Thomas, 'The Manor Farm' in *Collected Poems* (Faber, 1949).
† Glanville in the essay quoted below reprinted in *People in Sport* (Collins, 1970),
p. 48.

the grass is freshly cut, and you can take your time. *That* feeling, strong and important as it is, is not one which is necessarily trapped in the class war.

Class in sport in Britain is a funny mixture: in some circles, it is so obvious an element, the unexamined assumption of its presence everywhere becomes one sort of crass cliché; in other circles – generally of the sportsmen themselves – to mention class is like making a rude noise. And what we actually mean by 'class' will perhaps only come out when we try to take the measure, to weigh up the distinct, manifold pressures of a society which come out when we listen, in fact or in books, to people talking about sports which they love.

If we stay with cricket we can read some of the changes that have occurred in the work of the most remarkable cricketing journalists of the past half century, Neville Cardus and John Arlott. The names choose themselves, for both men brought to sporting journalism (in Arlott's case, mostly for the first decade of his fame on the radio) a much more widely read experience, a more fluent and graceful tongue and a keen critical sense, than was usual with sportswriters. Cardus, in his bestselling *Autobiography,** gently derides the preciousness of his early reporting: it went, after all, with that post-war literary nostalgia in which the genteel, plaintive tableaux of snobbishness provided by novelists like Hugh Walpole, R. F. Delderfield and Warwick Deeping set the tone for conventionally fine writing.

Cardus was the first man to write with this gusto and energy about cricket:

At Kennington Oval in 1902, Jessop played the most wonderful innings in all the annals of Test matches. On a bad wicket England were trapped – they needed 263 to win. Three men were out for 10, and five for 48 – the cream of English batsmanship; Maclaren, Palairet, J. T. Tyldesley, Hayward and Braund. Nothing apparently could be done against the Australian attack on the vicious turf. F. S. Jackson played a watchful game while the pitch was at its worst, but in the circumstances science was out of the question. For science demands some foundation of logic and order; and how was it possible for mortal batsmen to apply known principles to bowling which on an insane wicket performed illogicalities of spin, and behaved like something in a Walt Disney film? Jessop came forth, and he at once took the game out of the prison of cause and effect; he plunged it into the realms of melodrama, where virtue is always triumphant. Before he came to the wicket on this lurid afternoon, the Australian team had been a ruthless machine – the unplayable ball and the clutching hand in the slips. In a short period this same Australian team was reduced to a rabble. Jessop scored 50 in 55 minutes; and then another 54 in ten minutes; that is, he made 104 in 65 minutes, in a Test match, on a bowler's pitch, after his team had lost five wickets for 48. Kennington Oval that day went crazy. People had been leaving the ground in thousands. Jessop caused delirium; perfect strangers embraced. The ball was a dangerous missile all over the ground and out of it.

* Collins, 1947.

Fieldsmen went in danger of decapitation. The windows of Kennington were threatened, and the neighbouring streets were noisy with an excited mob who could hear, if they could not see, what was going on inside the Oval.*

The delight in the spectacle Cardus catches here is exactly right: that chokey glee with which we watch not only absolute accomplishment but also, incredulously, the triumph of 'your' team, when it was certain of defeat, rescued by the hero at the very last minute. The rich satisfaction in the voice at 'reduced to a rabble', the hilarious extravagance of 'Fieldsmen went in danger of decapitation' – this is the sort of narrative which Cardus made possible. And he had a lovely ear for an anecdote – a really good *journalist's* ear, the point at which the journalist is most alive to the details which count most, details which carry whole areas of meaning. To have such an ear is to be something like Henry James describes a good novelist as being:

> . . . blessed with the faculty which when you give it an inch takes an ell, and which for the artist is a much greater source of strength than any accident of residence or of place in the social scale. The power to guess the unseen from the seen, to trace the implication of things, to judge the whole piece by the pattern, the condition of feeling life in general so completely that you are well on your way to knowing any particular corner of it – this cluster of gifts may almost be said to constitute experience, and they occur in country and in town, and in the most differing stages of education.†

At his best, Cardus could do this. At the same time he contributed towards a new social mythology – he helped to register its arrival. This was the mythology of the sporting hero, the popular idol. Cardus's first hero was the England and Lancashire captain, Archie Maclaren.

> Once in a Test Match at Sydney, Maclaren won the toss and went in first with Tom Hayward. Arrived at the wicket, Archie took guard in his customary lord-of-creation manner; a vast crowd waited while Maclaren stretched his shoulders, reviewed the fieldsmen in front of him, then looked round to the leg-side. Joe Darling had placed three men near Maclaren's legs in a close semi-circle. Maclaren addressed himself to Darling:
> 'Joe,' he said, 'what's the meaning of this?'
> 'What's the meaning of what, Archie?'
> 'Why,' said Maclaren, indicating with a sweep of his bat the crouching leg-side fieldsmen, 'why – what are these people doing here, Joe?'
> 'That's my field for you, Archie,' replied Darling. Maclaren waved his bat at them again. 'Joe,' he said, 'take them away.'
> 'Take who away?' inquired Darling.
> 'You know what I mean, Joe,' said Maclaren, 'please take them away.'
> And Darling persisted: 'But, Archie, I can set my field as I choose, get on with the game.'

* Neville Cardus, p. 181.
† Henry James in *The Art of Fiction and other Essays*, ed. M. Roberts (Oxford University Press, 1948), p. 14.

'Take them away, Joe,' said Archie with undisturbed patience, 'how do you expect me to make my celebrated hook-stroke if these damned silly people get in my way?'

Darling declined to change his field, so Ernest Jones bowled and the match at last began. Maclaren drove Jones twice or thrice for straight fours, then Darling removed a man from the leg-trap and sent him to the deep, behind the bowler. 'Thank you, Joe,' said Maclaren, 'now we may proceed with the match like gentlemen.'*

The tale is very funny and excellently told. Maclaren is seen with a touch of irony ('lord-of-creation manner', 'stretched his shoulders') and a great deal of proper affection. He's made a touch more self-aware than he probably was – 'my celebrated hook-stroke' – and the story-teller's timing, for comic effect, as a man would tell a story really well in a pub, is masterly. The affronted Olympian imperturbability caught in the paragraph beginning, 'Why,' said Maclaren . . . 'why – what are these people doing here, Joe?' ('these people'! That most English of disdainful phrases).

These examples are the best of Cardus. The pleasure in the public drama of cricket, the comedy always latent in taking such a weird activity so seriously, are both nicely judged. But always the style is liable, even at its best and most affecting, to be stained by the old, nostalgic structure of feeling which twists for so many the shape of their lives and how they learn to see them even at play. On what the writer feels is the positive, celebratory side of this feeling, it comes through as this:

> I was only twelve years old when I saw Trumper at Old Trafford on this deathless morning of July 24, 1902. His cricket burns always in my memory with the glow and fiery hazard of the actual occurrence, the wonderful and consuming ignition. He was the most gallant and handsome batsman of them all – he possessed a certain chivalrous manner, a generous and courtly poise. †

This is one of those shining images, caught and fixed in childhood, of absolute human perfection towards which all subsequent experience aspires. It is of such memories that I wrote in Chapter 2. Cardus, in writing of Trumper and Maclaren and others, not only went a long way to form the idea of a sporting hero – he also formed such heroes according to two rich, memorable but, as always, reductive stereotypes. And then, as we all do, he used the stereotypes of the past to tell lies about the present. It is character-istic that he does this most tastelessly after anecdotes about his other kind of stereotype, the rough, blunt, honest and dour, Yorkshire-and-Lancashire working-class cricket professional.

> Following a wet morning at Leeds, with burning sun at two o'clock, Emmott and Rhodes went forth on the field of Headingley to inspect the wicket. I was allowed to go with them. Rhodes pressed the turf with a forefinger, 'Emmott', he announced, 'it'll be "sticky" at four o'clock.' And Emmott bent down and, with thumb and forefinger, fondled the moist but drying turf. 'No, Wilfred,' he said,

* Neville Cardus, p. 175.

† 'Cricket of Vintage' in *Full Score* (Cassell, 1970), p. 95.

'half-past'. Dedication, shrewdness, caution, extended to godlike humour. These were 'county' characters, from mill and factory or pit, having horse sense and no more education than was needed in their condition of life. I have for years believed that a man should be thoroughly educated, or not at all. The middle way, 'O' levels and all that, produces anonymous competent mediocrity, enslaved to technology and efficiency. The salt of the county nurture is eliminated.*

And, like the Thurber cartoon, here it comes again: the old, grisly story of a past in which, though he sees so much that is strong and good, Cardus with so many others from the social class which he pulled himself into by his own efforts, his talent, his conceit, makes an insolent parody of these men's lives. You look at cricket as you look at anything else, out of a certain view of history. Cardus's view is seamlessly of a piece with a whole ideology carried and perpetuated into the twenty-first century. The ideology holds that, at the same time as its subscribers removed their dividends from its processes, the Industrial Revolution broke up the tranquil, self-explanatory order of rural community, its work and play, and placed its members in the meaningless abstractions of urban life. When Cardus, in an invincibly snobbish passage† laments the supersession of the Emmott Robinsons and George Hirsts in Yorkshire cricket teams by Herbert Sutcliffes '[their] hair resplendent with brilliantine', 'their tailors obviously in Savile Row', he goes on to this nasty view of modern townscape, where

> . . . the last rays from the summer evening sunshine fell like naphtha on pavements full of pimply youths in thirty-shilling suits and suede shoes, with their girl friends, nearly all bad of tooth, either going into or coming out of a Palais de Danse or Plaza.‡

If you see the modern world in these rancorous accents, the satisfaction you take in Wilfred Rhodes is going to be that he, at any rate, knew his place and for all his sturdy independence could be counted on to act as a docile bucolic, to bowl all afternoon on a plumb wicket or to be fatuously slaughtered by German machine-guns. The strength, the best side of what Cardus makes out of cricket is, as he says, his belief 'in hero-worship and the Great Man'.

> A. C. Maclaren, as I have told you, lighted a fire in me never to be put out. He had an aristocratic face; he walked the grass as though he lorded it . . . When a snick sped to him from a fast bowler, Maclaren descended on it and the ball was thrown high in the air, with the same action which had scooped it up, an eighth of an inch from the turf – a great swift circling action, momentous and thrilling.

Cardus, as few other journalists do, brings out how thrilling his sport is,

---

* *Full Score*, p. 104.
† *Autobiography*, pp. 158–9.
‡ p. 164.

and he names the virtues which make the heroes of the game what they are.
He confirms and circulates a strong tradition in British sport which
upholds the aristocratic and feudal line. His heroes are courtier-
gentlemen, autocratic and proud as well as gracious, and yeomen peasants,
good sound British stock, the salt, of course, of the earth. I have already
suggested that the moral collision we all live with between (among other
rivals) the gentleman and the democrat, may be held in a lively but
manageable balance in sports. Supporters of the aristocrat (to call him
that) tend to suppose that he has disappeared, but that what he stood for is
indispensable. Different sportswriters write their threnodies on different
time-scales. I make the point to emphasize that the image of the courtier-
gentlemen retains a lot of life in our times, and the sports arena is one place
where he is still invoked. In a very recent radio talk Alistair Cooke spoke in
these genuinely touching terms of the great golfer, Bobby Jones. For
Cooke, Jones's kind of style vanished in the late twenties – for Cardus it was
in 1914. The difference precisely reflects their ages (Cardus was born in
1890; Alistair Cooke in 1905). Cooke notes that each age makes it own
kind of hero; then he says,

> We can see now that the twenties were the last decade when the idea of style was
> essential to the conception of a sporting hero . . .*

Roger Bannister? Edmund Hillary? Peter May? – there's a 'fifties list for
him; my list.

Cooke says that in the path of 'the enormous slugger Dempsey' or Babe
Ruth in baseball, the idea of style was shrinking to nothing.

> But in golf certainly there was a great yearning in every duffer to develop the
> swing of Bobby Jones, whom the most celebrated of English golf writers
> [Bernard Darwin in fact] compared 'to the drowsy beauty of a summer's day'. In
> our own time we could say that the swing of Arnold Palmer or Jack Nicklaus has
> all the drowsy beauty of a hydraulic drill. The effect of Jones's mastery of the
> game, by means of the most effortless grace, transformed golf from a minority
> sport for the rich and aged into a young man's game.*

It is Cardus's view of history; it is indeed the Englishman and his history.
Well, Cooke's reminiscence and obituary of Jones has its grace. For the
moment we need not worry in what relation his view of history stands to
real history. He sees truths, economic truths which have their bearing, bear
heavily upon, styles of 'style'.

> Long before he did something that had never been done, and it's safe to say will
> never be done again – to win the British Open Championship, the American
> Open Championship, the British Amateur and the American Amateur in one
> year – long before that, I doubt there was a man, woman or child in America
> and Britain who did not know about Bobby Jones, the easy, debonair modest
> Southerner with the virile good looks who came to have no more worlds to

* In one of his *Letters from America*, sent for broadcast in 1972.

conquer and retired at 28, still an amateur. I make bold to say his feat of the so-called Grand Slam will not happen again because today golf too has turned into a money-making industry, and the smart young amateurs go at it like navvies.

So there was the unique combination of two attributes that are now dated: Jones had great grace and he remained an amateur. And Cooke underlines the attractiveness of this golfing master, with a cultivated taste in literature, a Harvard degree in engineering, and a successful law career. But what counts is the goodness and the grace of the Jones who Cooke presents to us. The peroration, simple and moving as it is, is worth quoting at length.

All this is very rousing, and very attractive to people, to the English especially, who like – or used to like – the idea of the casual hero, the master who beats everybody with one hand, while the other hand plays the piano or follows a profession. But it does not explain the charm of Bobby Jones, the hero as human being. I will give you one example. Once, during the last holes of an American championship, he pushed his ball into the woods and went in alone after it. A moment or two later, he came out of the woods and signalled to the marshal. In addressing the ball, he had accidentally barely touched it. He said so, penalised himself two strokes and lost the championship by a stroke. I told this story later to a young gorilla of a golf hero, who said: 'What was he? Some kind of a nut?'

In his 46th year, Jones was suddenly afflicted with a backache. In an exploratory operation, it was found that he had a rare and paralysing disease, a neurological nightmare: syringomyelia – a growth of fibrous, horn-shaped tissues in the spinal cord. So first he went on sticks and then into a wheel-chair, and the last time I saw him, three years ago, he was down to less than six stone, had arms like bones out of Belsen, and could not wear even a dressing-gown because it felt as if it pressed against his nerve ends. You had to learn this from his wife or son, for he maintained, till he could hardly breathe, his gentleness, and unwavering courtesy, and rare Southern irony . . .

Until he could no longer even bear to read, he answered every letter, and his mail was enormous. When an old golf writer lost his house in a hurricane and wrote to say that his greatest loss was a hundred-odd letters received down the years from the great man, Jones went through 20 years of files, had all letters copied and signed them again with his pitiable scrawl.

Well, the word 'gentleman' is by now very much an anachronism. It got worn out by covering too often what William Empson once called 'utter grossness of soul tempered by a desire to behave nicely'. But in an older and better sense, that of a man who unfailingly combines goodness and grace, it fitted Bobby Jones like no man I have known.

Well, in his turn, someone could report that Arnold Palmer has *his* claim to be called gentlemanly. And others. The elegant cadences of a Cooke and a Cardus are in unhurried retreat before the times they do not like much and understand less. But the moral point is true. When there is no agreement about what a concept – perhaps the concept of a gentleman – means, then there can be no way for the idea to be translated into an action. Indeed, it would be impossible to define the idea without describing actions. Hence, a concept (in this example, a way of behaving) may slowly grow pale, and spectre-thin, and finally die, and the moral language is to that extent the poorer. Sport keeps alive a number of concepts which have been central to our morality and without which an already diminished moral vocabulary would go properly bankrupt.

To talk like this should not be taken as any easy endorsement of what Cardus and Cooke say. Take an incomparably finer book than Cardus's *Autobiography*, John Arlott's *Fred – Portrait of a Fast Bowler*.* Cardus makes his Yorkshiremen talk like a music-hall act – full of apostrophe aitches, and Emmott Robinson saying 'Hey, dear, dear, dear; what's t'matter, what's t'matter.' The condescension is as relentless as the picturesqueness. 'I gently strolled over the grass, under the trees and their brown early autumn leaves, behind the little wooden benches that ringed the playing-field.' John Arlott stands much, much closer to the real history, and stands there, too, quite without admiring the arc of his own gestures.

Arlott is writing about Fred Trueman, the remarkable English fast bowler who became, as a few sporting heroes like Bobby Jones do, famous even to people who knew and cared little about golf or cricket. One marked difference from Cardus's way of presenting heroes is that Trueman is not simply hero-worshipped – as is the case with Cardus's two stereotypes, comic-yeoman and proud artist-aristocrat. There is a remark of John Berger's much to this point:

> Bourgeois culture is no longer capable of producing heroes. On the highbrow level it only produces characters who are embodied consolations for defeat, and on the lowbrow level it produces idols – stars, T.V. 'personalities', pin-ups. The function of the idol is the exact opposite to that of the hero. The idol is self-sufficient; the hero never is.†

John Arlott's Fred Trueman lives in Time: he grows and changes, renews and fades according to the real, intangible rhythms of a real man's life. The prettified country idyll has gone from this geography.

> Fred Trueman was not a level bowler. He could always be a good one; at times he was lit by the fire of greatness: and the most stirring memories of him recall days when, in face of completely discouraging opposition, conditions and state of the game, over-bowled and ill-supported, he tried harder than any captain could fairly ask, and sometimes succeeded beyond the bounds of reasonable possibility. On the other hand, there were occasions – rare, but undeniable – when he turned it in.‡

That is a very different voice – easy, conversational, authoritative. The subject is the subject; Trueman is not, in other words, object for the writer's decoration. The writer's interest is deliberately historical, and

---

* Eyre & Spottiswoode, 1971.

† John Berger, in a lecture at the ICA once; I don't know if it's in print.

‡ John Arlott, p. 106.

writing history is a matter both of fidelity to the facts and of recreating – so far as it can be done – the meaning that actions had for the actors involved. Finally, it is a matter of the historian coming at some judgement of what the meaning of the history is for him and his audience. Seeing his subject like this is not a matter of neatly separating the three perspectives: in good history they are all there, all the time. But the changes involved in such writing are something like the changes you feel when you read a novel after reading an old epic. Cardus's figures are epic heroes – Trumper, W. G. Grace, Spooner, Harry Makepiece, Wilfred Rhodes; Arlott's Fred is a much more alive, close, often anguished figure.

> During the tea interval Fred was in some discomfort with an attack of the squitters. Some of the Hampshire players were unwise enough to laugh at him. He went out in awful anger, which was unusual, for, despite impressions to the contrary, he was not an angry man – most of his fierce expressions and gestures were more dramatic than profound – took the new ball, rolled his sleeve and bowled out Hampshire twice. In ten overs he took six wickets for 11 runs and hacked them down from 166 for two to 191 all out. They followed on that evening and with a night's rest in the middle he tore apart their second innings with six for 28 in 19.3 overs. His match-figures were twelve for 62: consider those of the other seam bowlers in the match – Cowan one for 70; Heath three for 125; Shackleton two for 98; Baldry none for 5.
>
> No one, however, knows what kindled the fires when, at Edgbaston in 1963, on a pitch which had proved useless to Hall and Griffith, he rose up in splendour and bowled out West Indies with a final explosive five for none in nineteen balls, and brought England their only win of the series.
>
> The kindling could be sudden and unexpected. All that anyone knew was that suddenly he was going eagerly back to his mark; there was a belligerent spring in his run, he came over like a storm-wave breaking on a beach, and followed through with so mighty a heave that the knuckles of his right hand swept the ground. Where previously the ball had curved off the pitch calf-high, it now spat to the hips or ribs: wicket-keeper and slips moved deeper; the batsman, who had seemed established, was late on his stroke; and the whole match was transformed. (also p. 106).

Well, in some ways this is duller writing than Cardus's; or rather it is penny-plain to his twopence-coloured. But the language has a zip and succinctness which gives the figures life. Arlott is much more interested in the statistics than Cardus, and that too is part of a more general change; and if there is no doubt that the statistics can be boring – one generally skips them when reading – there is also no doubt that, like numbers in other sorts of history, they pin the book down to the countable facts. They keep it real. What Arlott never does is lift his memorable moments out of a match and transform them into a sort of non-historical or epic vision. Cardus's description of Trumper's wonderful innings which I quoted, somewhere takes off from any earthly cricket match and becomes celestial. Arlott places these high, unforgettable moments deep in the match, and then the sequence of matches to which they belonged. He is not a leisurely reporter:

the narrative is crisp and rapid and technically very sure and observant. He sees the inward rhythms of a match – and in the end these are much more interesting than the celebration of the celebrities which, as we shall see, fills so much everyday journalism – and he sees, too, the completely unpredictable chances of things which renew exhausted or uninterested men and change the whole movement of events.

May preferred the spinners and it was originally only to allow them to change ends that he brought on Trueman. The Australians in the pavilion, who could not know his purpose, observed the entry of Trueman with unease; they feared, justifiably, that in these conditions the cutter bowled at speed might turn the game. They were relieved when he bowled off his full run. Harvey, batting with all his natural grace and sensitivity went to drive the third ball of the over; it did not turn, it simply held up; the stroke was too early and Dexter made the catch at cover. That single delivery and catch tilted the match; it filled the rest of the Australian batsmen with misgivings. Trueman, with his unfailing acumen in matters relating to cricket, perceived the situation. He cut his run and, without much reduction in pace, aimed at the dust patches on and outside the right-hander's off stump. O'Neill edged an inswinger and Cowdrey caught him at short-leg. Simpson moved across but not far enough and was bowled. Benaud, groping, was bowled through the gate by an acute off-cutter for his second duck of the match; and the left-handed Mackay edged a catch to John Murray. In the course of twenty-seven balls Trueman had taken five wickets for no runs: Australia had collapsed from 99 for two to 109 for eight; and, as the other players stood back for him to walk in first, the Yorkshire crowd threw off its incredulity and cheered Trueman into the pavilion as they had done nine years earlier, when he struck his first destroying blow at the Indians. (pp. 141–2.)

It would be hard to describe cricket better than this. Arlott gives us the events and the meaning of the events. The style is plain and almost completely without metaphor; but here as everywhere Arlott's writing is rich with insight, and intellectually pure and honest. Some of the best writing in the biography describes Trueman's career as that of a colt and as an amazingly fast but immature Test Match prodigy. Arlott recounts, with both irony and relish, the anecdotes about Trueman which classed him for run-of-the-mill journalists as a 'character', but which Arlott uses to place Trueman as precisely *not* that kind of battle-scarred pro who in prewar days was content to soldier on towards pensionless retirement, and coaching the upper-class to make an elegant 27 in the multi-coloured caps of the Sussex Martlets C.C. Trueman was one of cricket's New Men: and all the better for it. This is one of the implied lessons of Arlott's book. On tour with the MCC under the (strange-to-say) managership of the Duke of Norfolk, Trueman, Arlott says, 'struggled past some rebukes by His Grace – "call me Dukie" – for occurrences he did not even recognise', and when later he reports the 'fine' of £50 mysteriously docked from Trueman's (and Illingworth's) tour play, Arlott objects that

neither ever received any satisfaction as to why they had been fined. MCC made a statement that the decision had been taken by a committee of MCC acting on reports and advice from Ted Dexter, the captain, and the Duke of Norfolk, manager of the touring team. Demands for a hearing or a discussion were refused: the Duke proved extremely evasive and the punishment – without a hearing – rankled with both men for many years. (p. 152.)

Arlott presents the sporting hero as man. Trueman is not fixed in a cricketing never-never land of the reminiscences in which he never grows older and never gets tired. As witness:

It was one of his shaggy days; the humidity that made his outswinger 'go' so late also pumped the sweat through his heavy undervest to darken his shirt with the ancient stain of labour. His forelock jerked forward by the delivery-heave, clung moistly to his forehead: he crouched at short leg with a trouser leg rucked damply on his calf and, when the other players stood back for him to walk in first at the close of play, his face was sheeny grey with exhaustion: and he dragged his head back to return a friendly jeer with the effort of a drained man, getting back to his seat in the dressing room on will-power. (pp. 159–60.)

I would like to quote, simply as evidence of Arlott's powers of storytelling, his fine account of the 1963 Test Match between England and the West Indies when, as he says,

. . . at the highest level of performance and with much at stake, the competitive elements of cricket – runs, wickets and time – fused into a dramatic unity. (p. 161)

But my interest for the moment is the way – the strong and memorable way – in which Arlott in writing a biography, also catches much of the new and important life which began to flow through cricket, after some lean years, during Trueman's career. Even so, Trueman in his turn becomes one of the great, gone heroes, and in a stirring elegy, Arlott lets him go:

On the way down from greatness, this was the last year of prosperity. He could not accept that he was no longer a great bowler: and at moments he was: but they were moments. He was thirty-four years old; he had been given some long and heavy stints and now it was apparent that they were too long and too heavy. He did not believe he had had enough. He could still, when stirred to it, make good county players look like second raters but he had used up his borrowed strength. He could no longer come back after a burst – not because he did not want to, there was nothing he wanted more – but the machinery now simply took the rest it had so long been denied. (p. 173.)

There is far too much truth in this book for Arlott to leave some timeless Trueman still bowling down the years. He draws in both growth and ageing, and he makes the man do both with dignity. He does not claim that Trueman was always dignified; but he writes without impudence (unlike most sportswriters). He names Trueman's complex faults and virtues, and never lets him off lightly, but does all this with a light, affectionate and serious pen. Arlott has a right sense of privacy, which is what it is to leave a man his dignity.

The last page opens a paradox which transpires just because the biography closes when Fred Trueman stops being a fast bowler.

> When he ceased to be a fast bowler a life ended. No doubt there was, is, and will be a life of a person by the name of Frederick Sewards Trueman who is not a fast bowler; but that is a separate man, almost a stranger to Fred the fast bowler. This other man will not roll truculently up from short-leg, cap crumpled on head, to snatch a thrown cricket ball out of the air. He will not, having now caught his audience, set off, shoulders and arms heavy with threat, thick legs unhurriedly purposeful, to a distant mark. He will not, ringed by a tensely silent crowd, come rocking aggressively in to bowl faster – in his faith – than anyone else in the world. He will not make a threateningly propelled cricket ball cut curves in the air and angles from the pitch almost as sharp as those of his reminiscence. He will not blast out the finest batsmen of his time to a figure beyond all others. He will not lard the earth with his sweat, nor curse flukers and edgers with lurid oaths, nor damn authority. He will not shock the cricket world into half-delighted, half-awed repetition of his ribaldry. Fred did that : Fred, the fast bowler who is now cricket history – a complete chapter of it. (p. 183.)

The paradox is one briefly referred to by Scott Fitzgerald when he mentions a character in a novel as 'one of the most powerful ends that ever played football at New Ham, a national figure in a way, one of those men who reach such an acute limited excellence at twenty-one that everything afterwards savours of anticlimax.'* The Trueman Arlott has drawn seems to have the strength of character not to be 'forever seeking, a little wistfully, for the dramatic turbulence of some irrecoverable football game'; Trueman, in other words, will not simply feed on his past. Yet what identity does a man have when the grounds for that identity pass away with the years? And when the identity has been so intensely public, and to a real extent the product of what the spokesmen for public expectations, in the newspapers and broadcasting, have assigned to a person as the broad, simplified outlines of his or her personality, who shall he be, when he is a private man once again?

It is a main part of the distinction of John Arlott's book and a benefit of the best mind yet to write and talk about sport, that Arlott provides so many insights into this experience. Trueman as he shows lived his cricketing life intensely and in public. Yet, partly because cricket is less subject to the fatuous inflations of show business PR than, say, football, partly because Trueman was and is his own man, and a strong man at that, the mediations between 'self' and public 'image' were less difficult – or if not less difficult, then more successfully resolved – than in the cases, the symptomatic cases, of many other sporting heroes.

---

* *The Great Gatsby* (Scribners, 1925; Penguin, 1969).

5 The idiom of the people—mythmaking and the media

IT WOULD BE HARD, now, to find better writing about any sport than that of John Arlott. I have named and demonstrated the virtues from the one biography. The differences implied between Cardus's prose and Arlott's are, as I have said, more than personal. They are historical. They signify changes of taste which in turn could not have taken place without much deeper changes in how people saw and valued the game of cricket. But this seeing and valuing is not often done through books. The regular language of public sporting discussion is that of television, radio and newspapers. To turn to them raises again one of the central questions of this book: what are the contrary pulls of mass expression and mass manipulation? And when do they pull in the same direction? To put it less compactly: how much of popular culture is, in a commercial society, the product of narrowly exploitative intentions on the part of a small group, and how much of that culture is genuinely expressive of popular feeling and ideas? Does the gap matter very much in any case? It is a question to go back to several times later, but of course it presents itself regularly when we read the sporting sections of the papers and watch the telecasts. The pressures then which need measuring come from the conflicting, uncomfortable mixture of a particular sport, the 'house style' of a particular newspaper or broadcast programme, and the quality of mind and spirit in a given human being. At the right time and place, when subject, sport and style coincide – as generally in Arlott's writing and talking – we find the best possible way to talk about sport. More often, one or other of the pressures – the demands of a given style, a given sport, or of that curious, inhuman artifice of mass communications, 'personality' – distort the plainness, density and warmth of speech which should be possible in talking of activities in which so much is shared by so many people.

It is more complicated a matter than 'looking for an idiom',* though Brian Glanville is briskly intelligent on that subject. He writes of a 'split between mandarin indulgence and stylised stridency, this itself a valid reflection of the class structure', which will hardly do as a picture of English styles of speech, and contrasts a USA in which Roosevelt could clown

* The title of an essay by Brian Glanville first published in *New York Times Book Review* 18 July 1965, reprinted in his *People in Sport*.

about with a baseball at a match which opened the season with a Britain in which Harold Wilson, discreetly suited, stood in for royalty by shaking hands with the two Cup Final teams. He cites as explanation of the poverty of English sportswriting the hoary chestnut of the extension of educational opportunity, the products of which want nothing to do with a way of working and writing which is locked in such a dismal vocabulary and a fake rhetoric. He instances the paradox posed by Cardus and Arlott, working-class boys who have made good and built for themselves a high mandarin style, as compared with Peter Wilson, sports columnist of the *Daily Mirror*, an Old Harrovian from whom this was a typical piece of demagogy:

> What is courage? I give you the answer, fellow Englishmen, in two words – Don Cockell . . . this was the kind of extra courage which makes you proud to belong to the same race as the boy who grew up in the back streets of Battersea . . . And that is why the high and the mighty, the men with riches and the men with power, the women with beauty and vast possessions are rising in a kind of primaeval mass . . . [with] sympathy and acclamation for a man from thousands of miles away, whose tongue they can hardly understand.

Cockell was an overweight, honest slugger who like many English heavyweights before him was ground to defeat by an incomparably stronger American (in this case Rocky Marciano), but bore up against terrible punishment gallantly. What is wrong with this passage is not that Wilson lacks an idiom, but that the *Daily Mirror* at that stage had cast itself as needing, scattered through its pages, just this queer combination of populism and chauvinism. The Cockell–Marciano fight was staged in 1956; the house style of the *Mirror* then as for many years rested upon sustained doses of that grisly mixture of jumped-up patriotism and the strident insistence that its most typical readers – the English people it really spoke for – were the 'boys who grew up in the back streets of Battersea'. Appeals to their pride of country of this sort – the sub-Churchillian cadences: 'proud to belong to the same race', 'the men with riches and the men with power' – have had little place in the ordinary language of the English working class since the old jingo days before the 1914 to 1918 war. That war itself, and the assorted class betrayals which followed it, rendered most of the old-style rhetoric incredible. Not many of Churchill's admirers in the Second World War were private soldiers or munitions workers,* and when he *did* get through to them, and there is no doubt that happened, it was much more because he offered a dogged, tenacious, enduring image of courage in the face of quite impossible odds, than because of any more high-flown appeals to God, Harry and St George. A journalist like Peter Wilson is enough of a genuinely demotic figure to know this: the appeal of

---

* Some of the evidence for this appears in Angus Calder's *The People's War: Britain 1939–45* (Cape, 1969).

Don Cockell's defeat is exactly that he hung on so bravely. But the puffed-up inanities about 'the men with power, the women with beauty', the shoddy mouth-filling of 'a kind of primaeval mass', these were of a piece with the *Mirror*'s house-style and have little place in popular rhetoric.

Yet there is something important to say of such writing – and of all Peter Wilson's famous series in the *Mirror*, 'Sport with the lid off – Peter Wilson Exposes'. One main historical movement of this century has been the growth of mass communications. Notoriously, the unrepentent Lord North-cliffe saw his newspapers as crudely manipulative: the version of the *Daily Mail* he wanted was one which would serve the most banal, vulgar and irreflective characteristics of a mass society of which he provided a ruling class stereotype. Well, many of the newspapers reflected and deepened just that stereotype. All that Collingwood said in 1938 of that press can be amply justified. That patrician scorn is not simply the product of an uncomprehendingly severe intellectual faced with an alien language. The evasions, the sentimental tarradiddle, about Spain and Germany, were real enough.

> In the first respect, I became conscious of a change for the worse during the eighteen-nineties. The newspapers of the Victorian age made it their first business to give their readers full and accurate information about matters of public concern. Then came the *Daily Mail*, the first English newspaper for which the word 'news' lost its old meaning of facts which a reader ought to know if he was to vote intelligently, and acquired the new meaning of facts, or fictions, which it might amuse him to read. By reading such a paper, he was no longer teaching himself to vote. He was teaching himself not to vote; for he was teaching himself to think of 'the news' not as the situation in which he was to act, but as a mere spectacle for idle moments.*

But the making of a human institution is rarely along a single line. Lord Northcliffe will certainly do for the villain of this story, but the newspapers were not only made in his simple-minded images. The claims that later editors made that they were the spokesmen of their readers grew through, and grows yet towards, some moments of truth. To see the spread of mass communications in this way gives Peter Wilson's efforts and intentions rather more point. Put together his peer-group of sports journalists, Frank McGhee also in the *Mirror*, Desmond Hackett, Peter O'Sullivan, Clive Graham, Crawford White (a notable team) in the *Express*, E. M. Wellings in the *Evening Standard*, Alan Hoby in the *Sunday Express*, Reg Drury and Frank Butler in *News of the World*, who are with Peter Wilson the most vigorous and independent of all, and Eddie Waring on BBC TV. Seen together, one may place these men in a longer perspective, and say that they too have a place in the people's history, those people who began to find their historical voice only in the nineteenth century and for whom the mass circulation newspapers were an early platform of access to the forums

* R. G. Collingwood, *An Autobiography* (Oxford University Press, 1938), p. 155.

of history, however distorted the microphones. Somewhere in his biography of the newspaper tycoon, Alan Taylor identifies his close friend Max Beaverbrook and the popular press which he built up in competition with Northcliffe, as one of the major forces for democratization, the coming-of-age of the people, in the period. It is a wild but not wholly implausible idea.

When one looks at the Beaverbrook newspapers' record of empty rhetoric, braggartry, wishful fantasy and ridiculous misrepresentation, the temptation is first to laugh at the claim. When, again, one analyses the distribution of content within the popular press[†] – that consistent recipe of sex, crime and sport – then again the claims for the educative force of this pawnbroker's picture of social reality look derisory. The clear criticism is that these topics never grip upon that social reality, never deal with power, class conflict, wealth. These newspapers are manipulative to the extent that they peddle a view of society compounded about equally of gossip and impotence, a view in terms of style and range of interests which would have been immediately recognizable to the man-servant below stairs at whom Northcliffe was supposed to have aimed the earliest *Daily Mail*.

And yet all is surely not as lost as that. The English intellectual, with the strong justification I have advanced, has learned by heart how the mass circulation newspapers have betrayed and suborned the English people, especially its working class. Desmond Hackett in the *Daily Express* amply bears out the critique in a once notorious report:

> The World Cup quarter final was a riot. My jacket is ripped, my shirt torn, and I am minus a tie. And I have been thrown over a fence. So I do mean a riot . . . I tried to cross the field and ended up thrown over a fence by two policemen. Considering the riot going on around me I was grateful to be out of it.
>
> But I was able to help Mrs. Ellis, the wife of the Halifax referee, and her two young sons through a side entrance into her husband's dressing-room. (June 1954)

The hand is the hand of Hackett, but the voice is that of the post-war *Daily Express*, which has chosen to give the people that special sense of helpless participation in great events which typifies the world-picture of most of us, by creating a reporting style for all its contributors in which the 'personality' of the reporter and what happens to him provides the framework of selection. What he sees is a function of his view of himself as giving a *personal account*. To that extent he reflects the developments sketched out in the beginning of this chapter. The personalness of the personal account is validated by the (always secondary) personal presence of the given sportsmen. Thus, what counts in such reporting is the personal touch which lights up the otherwise vast, inaccessible, public event. Some such device is probably essential in order to give a reader imaginative

* A. J. P. Taylor, *Beaverbrook* (Hamish Hamilton, 1972; Penguin, 1974).

† I offer a theory about these content-analyses in my *Ideology and the Imagination* (Cambridge University Press, 1975).

purchase on a distant event, however strong he is on catching hold of abstractions. But the final intention of this method, embodied as the defining dogma of *Express* reporting, is to render all news palpable by making it an 'event',* and to define the event in terms of certain personalities. On this view, the *Express* has indeed helped to shape popular response to the times, has given people a *way* of understanding the times.

That way accepts certain absences. The central absence is of standards by which to judge the significance of what the different groups and classes of men and women do in society. Without any common standard of judgement, without much understanding of social worth, the only criterion people find they can hold on to is that of the likeableness of others, and its entertainment world correlate, 'personality'.

Let me explain. To speak of social worth – the *value* of a man's work – is not, in this discussion, to put a monthly cheque on his head. It is not to arrange a league table of value in which we decide whether a bus driver or an airline pilot, a surgeon or an MP, a welfare worker or a poet, come out ahead of one another. An adequate valuation – the value which would remain if, as one would like, we were all paid the same and lived by an ethic not of universal competition but of mutual help – could only make sense in an understood totality of social relations. That is, everybody would in a more or less muddled way know the social function of his or her work, wherever it fitted, what truly counted in its performance, but not as a matter of arbitrary prestige nor as a matter of productivity. To be a better car mechanic is not always to do with working faster or even harder. In both cases, function and value would move together as people recognized the spaces in the lives of others which their work helped to fill. The dimensions which their work kept open. Fulfilment would be possible on many more varied planes of being and understanding. The car-mechanic would have some sense not only of the relative importance of keeping cars on the road generally, but also of the particular community he worked in, its mechanical shortages and likely orders; he would know something of the pleasure to be found in the intricacies and variety of the job; he would know closely the men with whom he worked. He would be honourably paid.

It is not all that improbable a Utopia. People make the effort to value others on these terms already. But without a shared scheme of judgement, disgusted by the common recourse to the weekly wage or monthly salary as a measure of social function, they fall back on judging others simply as likeable or not. To be a good man is to be likeable and popular. And then with 'public figures' – the notion itself the product of a mass communications society – the substitute for 'likeability' at the level of people whom one will never know well enough to like or dislike, is 'personality'.

* A concept 'news-as-event' – which I take from *Demonstrations and Communications: a Case-Study* by J. D. Halloran, et al. (Penguin, 1971).

Personality is the strange configuration of qualities which makes a public figure what, in the popular imagination, he is. And what he is is not always what he supposes himself to be. Probably he can only become that again when he no longer is, in the subtle, vulgar sense, a personality. As we shall see, the personality is in a very powerful sense a product of his own image, and that image is in part what he has been made to be, at least in public. (This is partly the process which John Arlott looks at in *Fred*.)

These pressures bear differently upon different public roles. For the personality-makers are themselves personalities. The best-known journalists, the telecasters and interviewers, the former sportsmen–become–commentators – the Richie Benauds, Jimmy Hills, Jack Kramers and so on – are themselves the mediators of sporting experience, who create and interpret the events which people watch on their TV sets and read as reported in their newspapers. Their qualitative presence is not the same as that of the people they write about, but it is hardly less potent and is certainly more continuous.

In one interesting piece of research,* the researchers thought they had found that viewers of television *preferred* the important political events of the day to be interpreted for them by a fairly familiar intermediary from the television channel concerned. Most people, that is, would rather that Ludovic Kennedy and Robin Day at least began for them the difficult process of political absorption when they were faced by the great heap of the day's, the week's history. In the same way, one would guess, viewers daunted by the colossal range and variety of world sport, want a familiar, cheerful, friendly, and infallibly omniscient guide and organizer of the torrent of information relayed from the screen every weekend. Each sport has its mediator; each programme, as David Coleman showed, its master-mediator, critic, archivist, commentator and poet, most importantly, accessibly nice man, all improbably combined in one. Coleman found and developed with his peers a style admirably suited to the special role which is required of him. It is a role supremely the product of television. Marshall McLuhan advances a general hypothesis which, however wrought-up, tells us important truths about our perception of the world.

> In the electric age, when our central nervous system is technologically extended to involve us in the whole of mankind and to incorporate the whole of mankind in us, we necessarily participate in depth, in the consequences of our every action. The aspiration of our age for wholeness, empathy, and depth of awareness is a natural adjunct of electric technology ... The mark of our time is its revolution against imposed patterns. We are suddenly eager to have things and people declare their beings totally.†

The truth to get hold of here is that television indeed involves us in the whole of mankind; but we are not yet as wholehearted about the business

---

* J. Blumler and D. McQuail, *Television and Politics*, Longmans 1967.
† H. Marshall McLuhan, *Understanding Media* (Sphere Books, 1965), p. 64.

as McLuhan says we are. Bewildered, ignorant, or afraid before all that enormous pageant, we turn gratefully enough to those who offer to give its episodes some shape and meaning. This is the central importance of these demotic figures in and out of sport. The main thing to understand about any chat-show chairman is not that he is so mediocre an intelligence nor so banal a platitudinarian, but that it is precisely this that some weird, temporal necessity of history, opportunity and genetics have required him to be. There is a dismayingly close fit between, say, David Frost as public personality and as social function. In the case of David Coleman, the no less exact fit moves in the service of a less ruinously wide range of moral references and meanings. Coleman and the lesser figures doing the same job on BBC and commercial TV know better to whom they speak and what the proper speech would be. Consider Frost chairing a discussion on highly unpopular go-slow industrial action by electricity power workers:

> *David Frost:* Let me at this point, now there's a lady – there is someone here from 'Meals on Wheels' I think. Mrs Tinker is it? Yes. Let's have your point of view, because you were quoted somewhere this week.
> *Mrs Tinker:* Well, I can only say that – I am from Brent, as you probably know, and we in Brent serve 500 people a week with 'Meals on Wheels', and some of our ladies – as this gentleman said – do have to climb a lot of stairs, but they've even had to rub the old people's hands to make them warm enough to be able to get hold of their knives and forks and this is really true.
> *David Frost:* Wally, I think you should answer that point . . .
> *Medlicott:* At the moment you are holding this country to ransom.
> *Tom Diss:* I would like to say . . .
> (*Medlicott rises to his feet, shouting*)
> *Tom Diss:* Will you shut up.
> *David Frost:* No, no, I think you can sit down. I think you should sit down.
> *Medlicott:* Bloody Communist.
> (*Medlicott fiercely removes his jacket. Diss starts to take off his too, as the audience laughs. Medlicott then strikes Diss, who falls to the ground*)
> *David Frost:* No, sit down Mr Medlicott. Just sit down again will you. Just one second, one second. I think we should realize the Mohammad Ali fight was Tuesday, and this is a talk show.
> (*Audience applause*)
> Although this was almost as exciting. But the thing is, the gentleman there, what you were just saying; in answer to the charge, do any of you accept the charge that you're communists?
> *Voice from platform:* No, no, we don't.
> *Tom Diss:* I ask this gentleman. I respect you for what you did, because he's under the misapprehension that we go to work, and we do nothing. I'll ask this gentleman – I took your thumping just now . . .
> *Medlicott:* You're going slow.
> *Tom Diss:* We are not. I'll ask this gentleman . . .
> *David Frost:* Well, what are you doing . . .
> *Medlicott:* He's got no rights at all.
> *David Frost:* Give him a second.

John Wroughton: We've got as many rights as you.
David Frost: Give him a second, otherwise you'll do a Jerry Rubin and put
everyone on his side rather than yours.*

Coleman was never faced with such uncertainties; the context of his work
was much surer. The absolute domination he won on 'Grandstand', a
domination then institutionalized in 'Sportsnight with Coleman', marked
his emergence as the first sports commentator on television to become a
fullblown show business 'personality' who remained entirely within
television's sporting world.† His success was no doubt partly his own,
partly a structural consequence of the BBC's system of presentation which
requires this special group of mediators to gather and focus in a style
suitable to the subject, the world-wide variety of news and events, and to
give them shape, intelligibility, and safety. Coleman is as surely one of this
group as Frank Baugh is not. He represents television's insistent tendency
to push not only sport but any mass audience subject into the terms of
show business spectacle, and to substitute compères for chairmen. The
'professionalism' for which Robin Day is so admired and disliked is
identical in structure with Coleman's: the same astounding knowledge of
their subject, the same eye for newsy controversy and ear for shadow-
boxing questions, the same tendency to define their topic in terms not of
issues of history, but in terms of individual differences and personal
intrigue.

I suggest later why this is inherent in national television. Within its
frames of mind and reference, Coleman has been, in his irritating way, a
notable force for good in his work for sport. *His* problem was to prevent real
emotion becoming banal and sentimental. Not surprisingly, he often
failed. He was, after all, required to receive, screen, interpret and judge at
astonishingly high speed an enormous range of information. He had to
weigh the significance of transient events for a few million people in
seconds. The insistent faults were more of fake nationalism, worked-up and
bogus excitement, and a folksy sentimentality. When at the 1972 Olympic
Games, Black September guerillas from landless Palestinian forces held
hostage and then murdered a group of eight Israeli sportsmen, Coleman
was by turns strident, irrelevant, and then silent.

I wonder if this is to judge someone in such a position too harshly. One
would like to think not. In the face of always breaking pressures, he has
learned to speak in an idiom which permits about as wide a range of
reference for his audience as may be imagined. But the irruption of the
terrorists' gunfire into the Olympic Games suddenly shrank the high
heroics of victory in a harmless race into a tiny scale. Those high-pitched

* Transcribed from the show and reprinted in *Open Secret 6*, journal of the Free
Communications Group, London (1971).
† A point I take from Andrew Tudor in 'The Panels', *Football on Television* (BFI,
1975).

events became abruptly trivial beside another, hardly less arbitrary but much more imperious and cruel measure of human and racial aspiration. In such circumstances, and given the way we see the world, it would have taken a much more comprehensive soul than this best of sports commentators to do justice to the dreadful sequence of events. As it was, the BBC and ITV inevitably took off their sports experts and put their news and political mediator-kings on to the case. Divisions of labour on the media. Yet the case I have made here is that Coleman is master of an extremely rich and socially flexible idiom; he is able to speak to his audience of beauty, heroism, tragedy and triumph within a few sentences of each other. Is this a rare achievement, or is it simply the devaluation of a priceless currency? If tragedy is defeat by a few yards on a 1500 metres track, how shall a TV personality speak of the utterly unlooked-for murder of a group of harmless lads come several thousand miles to pick up enormous weights?

The valuable difference between Coleman and other 'personalities' of television is that, unlike Alan Whicker or the other forgettable presenters, Coleman is not the main point of his own programme. His subject is not himself, it is sport. Of course he commands wickedly high fees – but the morality of television payment is not at issue just now.* His strength is his capacity to present the sport and not himself, but also to remain unmistakably a presence on the screen, not just a rearrangement of the transmission lines like some of his successors and imitators.

Alan Whicker – with whom Coleman belongs on the same shelf in Madame Tussaud's, alongside David Frost, Cliff Michelmore, Michael Parkinson, Bruce Forsyth, Joan Bakewell (sic) and others – Whicker in the guise of the honest bourgeois TV man relentlessly transmits himself as the centre of the programme. The professionalism is, according to its severe limits, real enough; but it is according to its rigid standards that the subjects are chosen and the questions asked. Thus, in a famous interview with the then dictator of Haiti, Papa Doc Duvalier,† the emphasis of the programme was first of all on Whicker's audacity and initiative in ever having got there at all, and second on the exotic travelogue-rolling of the island, a dishy fantasy in which Whicker eyed the girls and drank the drinks, and ignored the starvation, the yaws, and the corruption. The effect was as of a self-aware Podsnap:

> 'We Englishmen are very proud of our Constitution, Sir', Mr Podsnap explained with an air of meritorious proprietorship: 'It was Bestowed Upon Us By Providence. No other country is so Favoured as This Country . . .'
> 'And *other* countries,' said the foreign gentleman, 'they do how?'

* His salary was reported as being 'in the region of' £40 000 per year (*Evening Standard* July 1973). It was not, as he genially says, for more money that he took up a year's work in the USA in 1973–4.
† 'Whicker Way Out West', 15 September, 1973.

'They do, Sir', returned Mr Podsnap, gravely shaking his head, 'they do – I am sorry to be obliged to say it – *as* they do.'*

By contrast, Coleman presented as a weekly *tour de force* the amazing variety of detail and statistics of which he is complete master, without the least ostentation. He is liable to sentimentality, for instance in his misty treatment of the 17-year-old Olga Korbut's first appearance at the 1972 Munich Olympics – 'little Olga'. He has his clichés, especially of intonation. But his gusto, amiability, and unfailing pleasure in all the varieties of sport, a vocabulary sufficiently varied without being inaccessible, tirelessness, and an easygoing, classless charm suit him excellently for his strange job. He interprets the sporting world to a vast audience. To do so, he has had to speak of aesthetics and politics, of beauty and rivalry and heroism, in innumerable circumstances. He is the window which shapes the frame of reference for the viewers. If we say, with McLuhan, that the medium is the message – meaning that the TV frame itself shapes how we see things – then a man such as Coleman is the dominant medium, a strong invisible frame along with the producer and the channel director and so forth. The strength of the man is that, both in reporting and interviewing, he lets the subject speak. The weakness – and it is the radical weakness of many so-called professional TV men, their clipboard at the ready with questions from the researchers – is that he never pushes his insights right home. I do not mean that he does not search out the men and women he interviews hard enough, though this is true. No. Rather, he does not expect his audience to be as intelligent as they are. He is content to sift the torrents of information off the telex machine in his own pleasantly casual style. He does not make his extraordinary store of knowledge work for him. He has theories only about events, never about processes. The contrast in sport is with Danny Blanchflower. Think what it would be for him to manage 'Grandstand'!

So there are real virtues here. But the conventional divisions of labour, and therefore of mind and conversation, prevent those virtues trying for anything but a 'professional' reach. 'Professional': that great contemporary honorific. It signifies on television that scrupulous regard for a certain control of the events broadcast such that they embody the values proper to the programme in question. For the sports programme, to be professional means that the pictures are unfalteringly precise and clear, the angles varied but unobtrusive – faithful to the event and not just to the producer – the technology commandingly deployed and impersonal. The commentator adjusts idiom, diction, and morality until it fits the value-judgements carried by the picture, and the adjustment becomes, as a matter of familiarity and long practice, so rapid and instinctive that nobody is aware of it, let alone that anyone could be thought of as imposing it. The process is, one presumes, much the same in any TV programme. It

* Charles Dickens, *Our Mutual Friend.*

is in something of the same way that newspapers conserve and transmit through their editors and journalists their 'house style'.

Now a mass society needs its mass communications. They are not simply the top-dressing of the technology. But where the specialisms of production force unprecedentedly deep divisions of labour, their system can sustain the conversation of a society. The system permits the society to have a whole view about itself, and to talk to and about itself. I said earlier that the 'personalized personality' which the *Express* (and in a comparable way the *Mirror*) took for many years as the style which embodied its view of its own social position and its social function, did provide a way of looking at the world. Desmond Hackett and Peter Wilson, for all their jaunty assurance, their pushy declarations that on behalf of their readers they would reveal all, are in fact the spokesmen of the helpless. Their way of writing shows this. They share with all newspapers and their men the notion of news-as-event.* What is selected for attention from a day's news is what most readily identifies itself as an *event*, as opposed to a process. If there is a process to be reported, then as far as possible the way to deal with it is to put frames around a portion of the process, and to create an episode *in* the process, which can then become an event.

This organization of the world experience which is received by the agency as news is the result of many causes and conditions. It may be held to be part of some modern malaise which requires daily sensationalism in order to stimulate its dull nerves. Well, perhaps. This organization of news seems more attributable to conventions of lay-out: to the banner headline and radio-transmitted news-photography. And these are in turn due to a complex series of causes, some of them the products of market forces – the assumption that the headline and the photograph which catch the eye sell more copies; some of them to do with assumptions made by editorial habit and custom that a supposed readership is too short-winded to read news stories longer than a given number of words; some of them to do with the technology and economics of typesetting in narrow columns and keeping available space open in order to make room for stories which come in late and alter the order of presentation and importance.

Such a hierarchy of forces operates within every organ of mass communication. To tease out the precise loadings of the forces within, say, each newspaper or the day's reporting and commentary on BBC Radio 4's 'World at One', 'P.M.', and 'World Tonight' would be another book. The point is this. That according to the style which these forces create for a given newspaper or broadcast programmes, so the contributors will select and present the day's experience. The surprise is then not the variety of forms and content, but that the social experience which every day is presented to us as news should be so uniform and predictable. Given world electronic cover, it is remarkable that newspapers and broadcasters so

* See J. D. Halloran, et al., pp. 90–198.

often all agree that what the earliest or quickest of them happen to have chosen as news should be reprocessed and re-presented by them all, throughout a day.

The interest for our purposes then lies in the nature of the reprocessing by particular sportswriters. Men like Alan Hoby, Frank McGhee, Wilson and Hackett turn process into news (according to the style of their paper) by their presence in the events chosen. Here is a minor example, from Peter Wilson. (The dateline: Barcelona, Thursday.)

> Stan Smith, one of the world's greatest lawn tennis players, gave a dazzling performance to reach the semi-finals of the Commercial Union Masters tournament here tonight, when in thirty-nine and a half minutes, he destroyed Jan Kodes of Czechoslovakia, 6–1, 6–0.
>
> Afterwards I asked Smith if he had ever played better in the twenty-six years come three weeks he has been on this earth. And it was typical of the man's honesty that he paused for a quarter of a minute before he replied: 'Perhaps I have . . . but I can't remember when!'
>
> Certainly I can't remember seeing the tall, powerful American play better.
>
> *Daily Mirror*, 1 December 1972

The distinguishing note of such reporting is not only that the reporter appears in his own news story, but that he has to keep reminding us in the details that he is still at our elbow. It is easy enough to criticize the fake accuracy of that 'thirty-nine and a half' – to say 'forty minutes' would be too unobtrusive; the claim to tiny, irrelevant accuracy is really a way of giving the reader a nudge and reminding him that Wilson is still at his elbow – but the whole nature of such reporting is that this corner of the world's experience is seen through the temperament of the personality resident in it. The concepts which make the style are then not directed towards the detached understanding of the total shape of the experience. They permit a different sort of access to the experience. They push on to the stage where the experience is taking place, and apprehend it entirely on their own terms. They obtain purchase and understanding by shaking hands with the event. Now this may be ruthless. But it makes for a certain sort of grip on the news. Wilson, like his colleagues in other sections of the *Mirror*, appoints himself the people's representative at every event. And the special blend of cheek, assertiveness, relentless familiarity ('Afterwards I asked Smith . . .') is all a way of asserting *presence*. A way not so much of conceit – it is not really important that it is Wilson who is there – but of speaking on behalf of all the people who in the past have been excluded from public events, or have only attended them in a spirit of deference, and on condition that they were hardly seen and never heard except to cheer their rulers. The pushing, bluff, rather too assertive presence of the main tradition of *Mirror* reporting (their motto, printed on every front page, is 'Forward with the people') is a function of the arrival of the paper's readers on the public stage. If that presence then comes over as larger than life – as it surely does in Peter Wilson's case – then this was perhaps once to do with a certain defensiveness about pushing in where no such spokesman had been before. This was perhaps the case when Wilson – who is undoubtedly about as informed as one can be about most sports and really expert (as a former practitioner) on tennis – first constructed his style with the *Sunday Pictorial* where he began in 1938. The problem, which is hardly peculiar to the forms of popular culture but seems to be unusually recurrent within them, is then to prevent a necessary social gesture becoming a rigid attitude. The style of the old school of popular sportswriters has not always kept up with the changes elsewhere in their newspapers. They sometimes sit uneasily beside the new typography. The house-styles have changed, the voices of the old guard have come on occasions to sound rather hoarse. It is worth looking closer at the company they keep.

II

	Daily Express	Mail	Telegraph	Mirror	Sun	Guardian	Times
Total pp. (av.)	14	32	26	27	28	20	28
Sport pp. (av.)	3.60	5.80	4.86	6.50	7.0	3.0	2

	Sunday Express	Sunday Telegraph	Sunday Mirror	Sunday People	Sunday Times	News of the World	Observer*
Total pp. (av.)	21	36	48	24	64	24	34
Sport pp. (av.)	4.25	4.5	8.68	5.55	4	5.2	2.75

 * excluding supplements

		BBC 1	BBC 2	BBC radio	ITV
Hours broadcast/	Saturday	15½/6½	11/1¼	61/5	15¼/5¼
Hours of sport	Sunday	15/1½	9/0(4½*)	62/0	14¼/1
	Monday	14/½	13/0	71½/1	13/6½
	Tuesday	14/0	7½/0	71/1	14½/1½
	Wednesday	14/1	5/0	71/2	14½/1½
	Thursday	14/1½	4¾/¾	71½/¾	14½/2½
	Friday	14/½	5½/¼	71/1	14½/½

 * In cricket season.

ITV hours averaged over four channels (HTV, Yorkshire and Tyne Tees, Granada, London Weekend). BBC covers all four radio channels but no local radio. Test match coverage increased radio hours by up to 18 hours per week. Wimbledon, World Cup and Olympic Games coverage in 1970 and 1972 reached peak figures of 72 hours on BBC TV and 67 on ITV. On

Audience estimates
*Audience estimates for some regular sports series in 1973**

Grandstand (BBC-1)
(52 broadcasts, 12.30–5.30 approx.
audiences measured each half hour)
Audience sizes (% *of population*)
(averaged over full transmission)
Lowest audience   3·3%
10% of audiences below   4·6%
25% of audiences below   5·3%

Median Audience   6·1%

25% of audiences above   7·1%
10% of audiences above   9·0%
Highest audience   15·5%

Match of the Day (BBC-1)
(42 broadcasts)
Audience sizes (% *of population*)
Lowest audience   8·6%
10% of audiences below   12·9%
25% of audiences below   14·7%

Median Audience   17·4%

25% of audiences above   19·5%
10% of audiences above   23·1%
Highest audience   24·1%

Rugby Special (BBC-2)
(35 broadcasts)
Audience sizes (% *of population*)
Lowest audience   0·2%
10% of audiences below   0·7%
25% of audiences below   0·9%

Median Audience   1·0%

25% of audiences above   1·3%
10% of audiences above   1·5%
Highest audience   1·9%

Sportsnight (BBC-1)
(28 broadcasts)
Audience sizes (% *of population*)
Lowest audience   5·2%
10% of audiences below   10·4%
25% of audiences below   11·4%

Median Audience   14·2%

25% of audiences above   16·4%
10% of audiences above   20·9%
Highest audience   24·2%

Pot Black (BBC-2)
(16 broadcasts)
Audience sizes (% *of population*)
Lowest audience   4·9%
25% of audiences below   6·2%

Median Audience   7·4%

25% of audiences above   8·2%
Highest audience   10·4%

---

*Appendix A, *Coverage of Sport on BBC Television*, BBC General Advisory Council, December 1974.

Bank Holidays all broadcasting channels extend their sports broadcasting
to normal Saturday hours. Throughout the cricket season BBC 2 covers
one of the Sunday League games in the afternoon, and shows an interview
with well-known cricketers, past and present, during the tea break. From
the beginning of May to the middle of September, therefore, BBC 2 on
Sundays would regularly include $4\frac{1}{2}$ hours more sport.

There are no figures available about the sports reading habits of
newspaper readers, but it is worth quoting audience estimates for some
regular sports series, particularly where – as with, say, snooker or rugby –
what we might normally think of as minority sports command really very
large audiences. (See table below.) But I have already spoken of the
confusions and grossnesses to which we are liable when we counterpose the
categories 'mass' and 'minority'. A 'minority' of 1 per cent of the
population generally watches 'Rugby Special': half a million people. Any
man lives in many minorities, some distinct, some overlapping. More
directly to the point, can we speak of these figures as generalizable not in
terms of the 'minorities' who watch the programmes, but in terms of the
form of the programmes themselves?

The percentages, of course, generalize the peculiar uses to which the
individual viewer puts his watching; but then the gross readership of a
given newspaper conceals as great a variety of purposes and intentions. For
all the fact that these programmes are broadcast as sport, do they share a
'house-style' in form and presentation, in the way in which newspapers do?

There are the structural similarities in the presenters which I have
looked at: the regular collaboration of compère and hired expert, and the
latter's gradual transformation into the former – as with Jimmy Hill, Tony
Lewis, Cliff Morgan. There then follows the placing of compère and expert
in a panel of discussing experts chosen less, it sometimes seems, for the
depth of their knowledge and experience, than for the readiness with which
they suit the styles of show business and chat show. Brian Clough is better
television than Don Revie. The inherent tendency of television to make
sport, and indeed all public affairs, into public spectacles, and thence into
television's very own spectacular, comes out most clearly on Cup Final
Day. Screening begins at eleven in the morning, and the homogenized
mixture of presenter, footballing expert, show star, and public figure as
forming a series of frames through which to enter the game itself, is nicely
parodied by the programme's including as it did in 1975 Mike Yarwood
imitating Brian Clough, the Prime Minister, and the tame pop singer, all of
whose prophecies for the match had just been solemnly canvassed. In that
mélange, we find the most distinctive and ostentatious of television house
styles in which personality is become niceness and geniality, news and
events are all become spectacle, rational discussion simply the assertion
and counter-assertion of opinion (caricatured as 'balance'), and public
celebrity replaces intelligible political power.

To speak of style like this concentrates attention on the people we see.

We may, with Marshall McLuhan,* also look at the total frame of presentation, and its life as a process. When we do, we find 'channel-style' to be no less unmistakable, but always adjusted to the timbre of the sport in question. 'Pot Black', on BBC 2, takes its tone in a discreet murmur by the commentator from the men in shirtsleeves, the heavy, hipped lightshades and the bright green baize and bright primary colours of the ivories, from the ritual stillness and containment of this intensely trigonometric and ballistic game. This game, too, is the 'dancing of an attitude', spurts of dynamic colour upon a still, green surface. Television faithfully reflects it. By contrast, the bursts of noisy, catchy music, the quick, flickering sequence of images at the start of 'Grandstand' serve to create the expectation of virtuosity, of instantaneousness, of geographic range, which comprise the pattern of the programme. The images themselves – a try, a football foul, an ace service, a steeplechaser hurtling to the ground, a swirling hammer thrower – express excitement, drama, physicality, conflict, success. The techniques are largely those of the advertisement; these are the glamorous images of publicity. The images and the music run down, of course, until the camera rests on the decent dullness of Frank Baugh, but all the same, all that the presenter hopes for in the preamble to the afternoon, all that commentators look for and ask the camera to emphasize in the sport or match they report, are the actions which emphasize the central meanings of publicity. Their most popular apotheosis is the sportsman of the year annual album, with its action replays, applause, and forced creation of personality in the rhetoric of celebrity.

Television inherently glamourizes all it touches. The album style of programme sets out to celebrate virtuosity; the programmes about a single sport are less flashy. In turn, the obvious mass publicity sports get more of the mass publicity treatment than do sailing or bowls. (But status changes: look at swimming.) By and large, the instantaneousness of television, the cultural importance of spectacle, the technology of colour and instant playing back, all serve the publicity values. They make televised sport colourful, vivid, utterly thrilling; they do little for quieter and slower qualities.

It is easy of course to spot the main differences of newspaper style as soon as you open the pages. There is not the brute size of the *Mirror*'s banner headlines – the most obvious detail of the house style – to be found in the much smaller typeface of *Guardian* or *Telegraph*. The *Mirror* displays all the jaunty assertiveness of the idiom. Take a single day, the day after Billy Bingham went back to Everton, the club he played for in the early sixties, as their new manager.† The *Mirror* ran a one-and-a-half inch back

* In *Understanding Media* (Sphere, 1964). I take him before the latter-day semiologists or students of signs, because he does look at substance and content, where semiology lacks any such grip on the real world.

† For £50 000 for a five-year contract (*Daily Express*, 29 May 1973).

page banner, BILLY 'YES' TO EVERTON; The *Express* a one-inch left-hand inside page headline reading BINGHAM'S BONANZA; the *Guardian* a middle-of-the-page lower-case half-inch headline, 'Bingham back at Goodison as manager'. In the same issues, secondary stories included: 'Illy's in charge again' and 'Ruth shows a touch of Lilian's class' (*Mirror*); 'Winnie and Peter roar back with easy wins', 'Ruth, 16, raps out warning', 'Kids seek hat-trick' (*Express*); 'Reluctant Ramsey may have left it too late', 'Lancashire are rewarded for enterprise' (*Guardian*). Leafing through the headlines, glancing at layout, appears to provide a simple set of contrasts for the purposes of classification and of discrimination.

Some comments on these contrasts may be so obvious that they may not even be true. The immediate contrast lends itself too easily to the old class distinction between 'quality' and 'popular' newspapers, terms whose general discriminations could hardly be more simple-minded if each came in wearing a monocle or a flat hat. On this division, quality signals itself by quiet good taste and calling sportsmen by their surnames; popular by using a much noisier manner and calling people by their first names. The contrasts between the breezy and the lofty, warm and cold, hearty and arty, body and mind: all the easy oppositions of a two-sided (especially where the sides are classes) view of the world. But who could confidently assign either of the following two passages to their parent newspaper?

> Siliciana showed herself a really bright hope for the Irish Sweeps Cambridgeshire when running away with yesterday's Virginia Stakes at Newcastle. Success entailed a 4 lb penalty for the big Newmarket handicap on Oct. 6 and her weight is now 8 st 5 lb.
>
> Ian Balding, Siliciana's trainer, is anxious to avoid any further penalty, so he may not run her again before Cambridgeshire day. Siliciana brought off a big win at Saint-Cloud last October and Balding considers the autumn to be her best time.
>
> Le Levandoll set a strong early pace in yesterday's trial. Bamburi lay a close second, with Siliciana in third place.
>
> Bamburi took a brief lead two furlongs from home but then Philip Waldron unleashed Siliciana. Mr David Back's filly swept into the lead and drew steadily clear to win by six lengths.
>
> Bamburi hung on to second place from La Linea, who had set a course record at Newcastle on Saturday. Regal Lady, ridden with much more restraint than in last week's Yorkshire Oaks, made steady late progress to be fourth.

> There seems little doubt that Peter Walwyn is on the way to turning out more winners than in any previous season, and his five-horse raid on the Epsom and Chepstow meetings today could yield a 100-per-cent dividend.
>
> The one who seems most likely to let him down is South Africa in the River Plate (4.45) at Chepstow.
>
> This filly who raced in France last year, made a promising start when third to Eastern Blue at Newbury.
>
> Not surprisingly, she was odds-on to win her next race at Salisbury, but could finish only fourth to Tiercel.

Even allowing for the fact that she was amiss that day, it was not an encouraging performance.

Now she may have a job to cope with Springo – my selection – and Vaunted. The rest of the Walwyn contingent seem likely winners.

Santa's Sister has only four rivals in the Rubbing House Stakes (2.30) at Epsom. With Great Somerford, the only serious danger, she is going to be odds-on to complete her hat-trick.

Stablemate Cesarea has not run since failing in the soft ground at Royal Ascot. She had previously put up a pleasing display to win over this course and distance.

It will surprise me if she cannot give the weight to Hyde Park and Sure Loser – her only rivals in the Archie Scott Trophy (3.5).

Both passages are close, technical, informative and, as such writing is likely to be when read by those who are not on the inside of a special language, dull. The reporter has in both cases a lot to include in as few column inches as possible. The straight news, in as unambiguous a meaning as possible, is what concerns them and makes the flat, transparent manner so appropriate and so welcome. In neither case is the 'house-style' obtrusive. The first passage is from the *Daily Telegraph*, the second the *Daily Mirror*, but they could be as well transposed. And it is also to the point to look at the proportion of the newspapers (and TV channels) that horse racing takes up.

Newspapers (Saturday)	*Express*	*Mail*	*Telegraph*	*Mirror*	*Sun*	*Guardian*	*Times*
Sports pp.	3.6	5.8	4.9	6.5	7	3	3
Racing	1.5	2.6	1.75	3	2.8	1	1

Television (Saturday)	*BBC 1*	*ITV*
Sporting hours	4.5	5
Racing	0.75	1.5

Of this mass of newsprint, a great deal is taken up by lists of runners and odds. The racing pages are in status and manner something akin to the investment pages, and in each case the style of the writing is clearly oriented towards expected cash interests. This is particularly obvious on television where commentating is largely a matter of consistently reading through the order of the runners as it changes during the race. Peter O'Sullivan's voice rises in a ritual crescendo, but he – good though he is – pays scant attention to the colour, beauty, and excitement of the race.

It is only gradually that racing reporting, and its special kind of austere figure-telling which is vivid only for insiders, takes its place in the paper's house-style. And even then, in composition and manner, in attitudes and expectations, it seems that the world of sporting journalism is very much more regularly patterned than those simple binary divisions, 'quality' and 'popular', could ever have allowed for. Each fragment of reporting is stitched in with the others to complete the texture which I have described as 'house-style'.

> It could be 13th time lucky for Squeak Fairhurst's Red Desire in the Curfew Handicap (2.30) at Ripon today.
> Squeak's grand old sprinter, now eight years old, had had 12 races this year and, although running his heart out, has yet to notch a win.
> But his sporting owner, Desmond Redhead, doesn't seem bothered. Every time you meet him after Red Desire has run, you would think he had won the race.
> Desmond says: 'It's great to see the old fellow still enjoying his racing and putting up such a good show'.
> After Red Desire had finished sixth behind Day Two in the Great St Wilfrid Handicap at Ripon last time out, Desmond said: 'Wasn't that marvellous'.
> For a moment I thought I had the wrong result.
> Then Desmond said: 'I know Old Red didn't win, but it's so nice that he turned in such a run against these good horses'.
> Perhaps Desmond's sporting outlook will be repaid this afternoon.

This engaging little anecdote also comes from the *Mirror*. Again, it could as well come from another newspaper, and is only worth remarking in its being rather more chatty and unbuttoned than the packed austerity of the earlier examples. Indeed, the whole atmosphere of racing is much less demonstrative than the other sports: the riders quiet spoken, modest, and rarely subject to jockey club discipline, the trainers self-effacing to a degree, the journalists undemonstrative and exceptionally well-informed. Racing (and who could mean anything by the word other than *horse*-racing) is perhaps with football the most intensely colourful of the mass spectator sports; it is also and obviously the richest. It remains a paradox that the men at its centre are reticent, dignified and withdrawn in these rather impressive ways. It is, however, part of the thesis of this chapter that the channels of public communications reflect pretty well what is there in sporting reality, that their distortions are the product not of some private conspiracy but of their technology, their modes of financing and production, and most of all, of the way we have all learned to see the world.

The differences, to say it again, are much less telling than the similarities. As here:

> No miracles. The rump of the English batting down to, but excluding No. 11 was disposed of in a couple of hours, or a little more. Underwood obstructed for an hour in all, and so enabled Fletcher to give the crowd rather better value for their money.
> This he did in yet another admirable Lord's innings. However it was a solitary effort against a side that bowled and fielded with a fire and purpose not to be denied.

There is a moral balance in these great sporting events that can be beyond rectifying, and before venturing any post mortems on English cricket (which has died many deaths and been as regularly revived) let me offer the warmest congratulations to Kanhai and his team on their first success in a rubber for seven years.

A respected West Indian journalist remarked with praiseworthy under-statement: 'We needed a little injection'. Now it's England for the needle!

Kanhai on giving reasons for the victory laid stress on the great improvement in the West Indian catching. This is true, and he must take credit for keeping his side so splendidly on their toes.

Fielding apart, I would ascribe the rejuvenation of the West Indies to three factors, the emergence of Julien, the sudden and unexpected elevation of Boyce to new, undreamt-of heights of achievement, and not least to the glorious Indian summer of Sobers.

Again though they were so incontestably the better side, things were clearly made easier for them by Kanhai's success three times running with the toss.

There has been a fair amount – indeed, I think, rather more than that – of short, fast bowling from the West Indians in this match, and in particular from Boyce.

After 40 minutes play H. D. Bird decided to invoke Law 46 and issue a warning on the grounds of intimidation to the bowler, informing the other umpire and the captain of his decision.

My view, for what it is worth from beyond the boundary, is that the umpire was right to apply the law. I wish it were done more often. But having spoken to Boyce, why did he need half a minute to issue a few formal words, accompanied by much gesturing, to Kanhai?

The latter, as could be seen through the glasses, accepted the decision, as indeed he was obliged to do, without demur. Umpire Bird is highly regarded by the players, and is likely to be umpiring in Tests for a long while. But I do hope that he sheds the histrionics. There's often too much of that on the field, without umpires joining in.

The best umpires, like the best judges, are generally the quietest.

E. W. Swanton in the *Daily Telegraph*, 28 August 1973

The margin – or chasm – between the two sides was an innings and 226 runs, annihilation so complete that England's Ray Illingworth was obliged to write the whole thing off with the saddest words of his cricketing career: 'We were out-batted, out-bowled and out-fielded. Finish'.

England's cricket indeed looked finished after the battering it suffered in a match lasting only three-and-a-half days.

In 491 Tests, England have only once experienced a heavier defeat – at Brisbane in 1946, where Australia won by an innings and 332. And that was on a 'sticky'!

This season's disaster springs from technical flaws and a fibreless attitude by cricketers allegedly at the top of their profession.

On the evidence of what has passed for Test-standard batting by England, only Fletcher, with 68 and 86 not out, has shown us pure cricket.

Yesterday, he stood straight and fearless against everything West Indies could hurl at him, never once failed to get his body behind his bat, and thus made nonsense of pre-summer doubts about his match temperament.

In stark contrast Brian Luckhurst timidly, Hayes unthinkably, and Tony Greig wildly, embarked on strokes that would not have been acceptable in the Sunday League.

Worse than that, Geoff Boycott, the alleged champion of champions, has approached this match like an optimistic schoolboy.

Twice he has thrown his wicket away in a manner his captain found unforgivable in a cricketer so quick to lecture others in the do's and dont's of his craft.

Finally, we are confronted by West Indies' incomparable skills and teamwork, which built a massive total of 652 for 8 declared, and hounded England right through to the bitter end.

On batting technique, Kanhai, Gary Sobers, Bernard Julien, Clive Lloyd, Roy Fredericks have been untouchable; Keith Boyce, with 8 for 99 (19 for 294 in the series) became undisputed man-of-the-match for seam bowling that never abated in its ferocity.

Sobers, the old master, also collected 6 catches in the match and thus shared a world record.

But, in the final reckoning, it is not flashy individualism but the joyous capacity of these West Indians to play their hearts out for each other over and again, that has beaten England to her knees.

Peter Laker in the *Daily Mirror*, 28 August 1973

One old myth goes out the door if we read the full report of this Test match in two newspapers, and that is that the *Mirror* only gives very very brief space to *words* in its reports, and that quality papers like the *Telegraph* cover a story in much greater detail. Whether or not this is true for front page news is another matter: in the leading sports news, as here, the two stories were within a few dozen words of one another. The greater amount of newsprint in the *Telegraph* is simply a consequence of covering more matches, which may be a virtue but does not affect the first point – that the two papers give the same space to the news story.

It is also held that popular newspapers require their man to intrude into the news after the manner we have seen at work in the reporting of Hackett, Wilson, George Whiting, and J. L. Manning. But in fact the *Mirror*'s report is interspersed with a longish verbatim interview with the English captain, Ray Illingworth, and it is E. W. Swanton whose presence in his piece is very much more obvious. 'My view, for what it is worth', 'I do hope that he sheds the histrionics' – come, come now, good taste in an umpire. Beyond these simple points, Swanton's manner is much the more portentous – 'There is a moral balance in these great sporting events that can be beyond rectifying . . .' What *can* he mean? In this comparison, Peter Laker's narrative is much crisper, his congratulations more generous – 'it is not flashy individualism but the joyous capacity . . .' – and his criticisms more tart and less self-regarding.

The *Mirror*'s prose is pointed and honest; the *Telegraph*'s more fleshy and large in assurance, at least in these hands. 'Quality/popular' are unusable categories here. And if we turn to the *Observer*, the following football report exhibits all the crassness, the over-written trendbending and familiarity which once was held to be the property of the *Mirror*.

> Bearing promises of good behaviour, bony, blue-jawed Leeds formed a chorus line in the centre circle and waved genially to the crowd. Everton, an odd assortment, but boasting a new manager and a beefily reconstituted Joe Royle, sneaked in a few ironically limp-wristed waves of their own. So much for the pre-season gestures.
>
> Leeds got straight down to business, with Gray and Jones, and then Clarke and Bremner, causing panic with low passes slid between the back-pedalling legs of the Everton defence. Jack Taylor's whistle was wet, indeed, when the Clarke–Bremner combination fiddled its way through somewhat luckily for a second time, Bremner ending the move amid disbelief with a walloped left-foot goal.
>
> Three minutes had passed. For a while the Leeds talents were generously displayed. Giles enjoyed a sizeable acreage in front of the defence, and Gray was given plentiful space down the left to shimmy the tassels on his numbered garters, not to mention the celebrated china ankles. Madeley, who had looked ponderous when required to think in attacking terms, suddenly decided to go through on his own, but the gliding Clarke just failed to collect his cross. Lorimer blasted in a low free kick, which momentarily escaped Lawson's clutch, allowing Bremner to risk controversy yet again by rushing and and colliding ambiguously with the grounded goalkeeper.
>
> The flying boot of Hunter, unpenalised, flicked a bouncing ball away from Harper's ear. Nothing had changed at Elland Road.*

This sort of writing is the worst result of the intellectualizing of football, and of other sports in the *Sunday Times* and *Observer* as well as on television. The prose is more dressy than George Whiting's (and all the worse for it, too, as we shall see) and the colours are those of Carnaby rather than Coronation Street. The 'human angle', as the pre-war editors used to call it, is contemptuously included in the first paragraph. The footballing details are picked out to give the piece a spurious vitality. 'To shimmy the tassels on his numbered garters', the fake-violent verbs – 'walloped', 'blasted' – do not give anyone a sense of the reality of the writing so much as of its shiny surface. The details are like those of a really well taken and touched-up advertisement for the beautiful people; they glamourize reality, they make it all appearance. Style for style's sake.

Just compare with that piece of mandarinese this brief, decent example of strong-lining from George Whiting. The old reporter will out in the first paragraph, but the admiration in an unsensational but memorable fight is all for the fighters, and none for himself. This is undoubtedly the old-stager's style, the writing of a man confident of himself, his craft and his audience. Clean, clear, immediate reporting under his famous name. The Beaverbrook Press at its best.

* Russell Davis, *Observer*, 26 August 1973.

Then came those two perfect gentlemen, Cooke and McCaffrey, to biff and to bang and to blast without respite or retreat – hammering each other to an absolute standstill after fifteen rounds that had every man in the hall stamping and clapping and cheering and tossing money in the ring like millionaires at a Mardi Gras.

Brave stuff, brimming over with dignity. Never one doubtful dodge, never one sneaky liberty. They just stood there and slammed joyously – Cooke, thirty-two, with his right eye cut and his homely face resembling a much-abused gargoyle; McCaffrey, twenty-eight, pitching his dark aquiline features into punishment that would have put lesser men in an ambulance.

Winner Cooke (73¾ pts), ten years in the trade, reckons to be fighting again when his hurts have healed. Loser McCaffrey (73½ pts) ponders the question of retirement – as he did last year.

Textbook science? We forgot about such trifles as the pair pummelled each other – Cooke hooking, McCaffrey countering and the crowd committing such uproar that on at least two occasions neither warrior could hear the bell and carried on clouting.

Cooke won because he had a fighting brain in that battered head of his. He rolled with the punches, busied himself 'inside', made legitimate use of the ropes, and was nearly always first to the punch.

I doubt if either Cooke or McCaffrey will ever rate raves in the international ring at this stage of their careers. But they have contributed their measure of history to the British welterweight championship. They fought like men.*

Yet the main differences between all the newspapers is still the merely visible one of layout and typeface. We are so used to associating a certain size of photograph and of headline, a certain texture of presentation with a whole set of attitudes in this or that particular newspaper that we no longer look and see. If we do, then I suggest that the main structures of presentation, style, and feeling hold fairly solidly in all forms of sporting communication. There is no doubt a world of difference in style and ethic between E. W. Swanton and Frank McGhee or the late J. L. Manning, but they are the same in function in that they are each their newspaper's resident luminary, its man for revealing all and taking off the lid. These reporters are the main repositories of the house-style in the way the extracts quoted suggest, and their presence, it is true, looms over the sports page in an inescapable way. It is also worth noting, however, that individual manner adjusts itself to the sport: football takes a much more energetic language to itself, but also a language much more liable to tricksiness as well as to cliché. Of course the one is generally the other, and most football writing is stuffed with tricksy cliché, 'part melodrama, part slop', as Arthur Hopcraft puts it:

But it must be admitted that the student of the language has plenty to clout when he looks at football writing. Our sports pages are weighted with brawny scoring aces, they trip over our breakfast on the heels of impish little baggy-pants

* George Whiting, *Evening Standard*, 13 February 1967. Reprinted in *Great Fights of the Sixties* (Frewin, 1967).

geniuses, they glower with veteran centre-halves who silence elfin forwards like severe schoolmasters, and they drip with the blood of mud-caked battles *almost* reminiscent of the Somme. Every other teenage newcomer to a team's forward line either gives the opposing defence a lesson or gets one from it. Chelsea's forward, Peter Osgood, was Sogood; Manchester United's opponents were lucky not to suffer six of the Best. Red-haired players are fiery, little ones big-hearted, big ones gentle giants. Managers never *say* anything, but snap, declare, deny or challenge.*

The alleged vigour in these clichés is partly the product of hasty reporting from a phone box after the game, and partly the odd way in which conventions in any part of social life harden until they are simply part of the interpretative framework of ordinary life, only to be noticed when someone breaks the rules deliberately. No one would *talk* like a football report (though a football reporter probably would talk in much the same manner as the racing journalist writes), nor would they really notice, critically *attend to* the way the report is written. They simply accept the message as it is encoded, and the changes in sporting style which undoubtedly occur do so, as I have suggested in connexion with John Arlott and Neville Cardus, as men more or less consciously receive and reorganize the language they have for understanding the world. The deeper, the more novel and responsive their understanding, the more they will have to change the language in order to register their change in the way of seeing the world. If you see things differently, you will have to say things differently.

Now whereas the bright lights of a newspaper will speak in a manner distinctively the product of themselves-as-the-voice-of-their-newspaper, they are surrounded by assorted reporters who have often been prac-titioners of the sport in question, whose writing and talking is a great deal less sprightly and self-conscious than those of the leading figures. ('leading' here is a question of layout; it denotes whose name is generally in the biggest type). Thus Crawford White is flanked by Keith Miller in the *Sunday Express*, Swanton by Tony Lewis and a troop of other internationals in the *Telegraph*, Langley by Fred Trueman in *The People*, George Whiting by Henry Cooper in the *Evening Standard*, and there are a dozen other pairings in dailies and Sundays alike. A list of former internationals who are at least part-time in journalism and television would include Richie Benaud, Keith Miller, Trueman, E. R. Dexter, Jim Laker, Denis Compton in cricket; Clem Thomas, Cliff Morgan, G. W. Wynne-Jones, Nigel Starmer-Smith in rugby; Brasher, Hill and Disley in athletics; and of course a huge list of footballers, from Tom Finney in the *News of the World*, via Blanchflower, Crerand, St John, Jack Charlton and dozens of others, to Jimmy Hill as being since 1973 the doyen of 'Match of the Day'.

* *The Football Man* (Collins, 1968; Penguin, 1971), p. 212.

There is, then, a certain dynamo of presentation, on and off television, of which the familiar 'Grandstand' and 'World of Sport' sequences can serve as type.

First, and top of the presentation layout come the resident commentators – the Colemans, Dan Maskells, Desmond Hacketts, and Raymond Baxters. These men generally, but not always, specialize in one or two sports. (Coleman is the most notable exception, but as I have indicated he is a special television polymath like CBS's Walter Cronkite in the USA, or like Richard Dimbleby was in the UK.

Second, there are the practitioners past and present, some of whom I have listed, who stand largely in relation to the resident commentator as expert to interpreter or mediator. In the newspapers, they may be sending in a straightforward report when the main man is reviewing the national panorama; on TV, they will be around a table for interrogation and summing up by the polymath-chairman.

Third, there are contributions from the people who actually made the historical event. In the papers, these will take the form of longish statements or, more rarely nowadays, interviews. On television, the people from the event will appear in three ways: directly broadcast while the event is taking place; repeated in a series of recordings, both in immediate action replay and later on; in person, hot from the performance and asked to describe their own part in the events which are immediately run through for them and us on the TV monitors.

Fourth, there are the great columns of newsprint from the minority sports which, as we see in Chapter 9, take up the time of the millions of unsung and, on the whole, unwatched sportsmen. This journalism is much more technical and to the point (more like racing journalism). The facts of swimming, hockey, cycling, netball, canoeing and squash, are barely and briefly recorded. It is true that many of these sports are pushing strongly upwards in the amount of time and space they receive on television. It is also true that many less spectacular sports like fishing have always commanded considerable prestige and space in local papers, not surprisingly in a country issuing 2.75 million angling licences every year. This language, too, has its private conventions:

> Turning from a hard fighting species to one that is notoriously lacking in fighting ability we find that no really huge bream were landed in 1973, for not a single one of the seven double figure fish reported made the 11 pound mark. Billericay angler Kenith Rickesburg bagged one weighing 10 lb 2 oz from the Aquatels fishery at Basildon (Essex) on worm bait in July, and this same water produced three other double figure bream. An unknown angler got one of 10 lb 4 oz in July, and the same month saw the best fish of the year weighing 10 lb 8 oz taken on maggot by M. Pankhurst. In August Harry Stevenson got one of 10 lb 2 oz on a flake and maggot cocktail bait.
>
> The other three double figure fish all fell in October. One was a very welcome capture for famous angling writer Peter Stone who took the fish on legered

maggot from a water in the Oxford area. The other two fish provided the biggest surprise of all however; they took fly fisher's lures on famous trout water Grafham water in Huntingdonshire. Both fish weighed 10 lb 2 oz and one fell to Northampton angler Arnold Haddon; the other was taken by his companion Peter Dobbs of Wellingborough. On the same day they caught a 31 lb chub and several big trout!*

Worth noting in this sort of report, is that the main news is the statistics of the fish, a universal sporting obsession which I have mentioned but not accounted for.

For our immediate purposes, however, it is the third item in this ideal-type of sporting news presentation which counts; the process of event-analysis. This process is the produce of the intensely *recoverable* nature of events on video tape-recording. It helps to make reporting at all levels a peculiarly circular sequence of event-manufacture. Any process is ransacked for what can be removed and studied in short close-up. The close-up is then commented on by a quartet of experts, chosen in the interests of inexplicit but highly organized ideas of fair composition or 'balance'. Finally their views are sieved and sorted for us by the chairman-layman, the panel is dismissed, and the chairman summarizes their conclusions in affable accents.

This manufacture is common to all portions of the newsmaking industry, and sport exemplifies it neither more nor less than politics. Such a manufacturing process grows from the dynamic of a centralized communications industry and its vast bureaucracies. That is to say, to run such an industry according to cost-efficient principles you need regular and recognizable structures of production. These structures are of time and space, knowledge and evaluation. You need men who will integrate them and make them comprehensible and interesting to millions. Cameramen, producer and linksmen-chairmen must mesh with complete smoothness, clarity, regularity, facility; these are the criteria of that professionalism by which journalism and broadcasting set so much store. Nothing chippy. No disconcerting unfamiliarity which shakes you outside the preferred frame of reference.

There is no plot about all this. The system of presentation is the regular outcome of centralized communications and the limited access this creates. 'Stars', 'personalities', and 'experts' are to be expected as part of such a system. And while these men and women are no doubt gifted and remarkable in their way, they are also the raw materials of the industry. Understanding sport must be as much as anything a matter of understanding that industry. One road to understanding is to consider how it makes men into heroes.

III

Honour where honour is due. But the creation of the personality as a public

* *Derbyshire Times*, 22 February 1974.

hero has its own politics. It is the ghoulish politics of the image. An image not just in the sense of a picture – a sort of snapshot in the memory – but an image as keeping some of the associations of religious (graven) image. A rich set of associations such that if you speak of an image of behaviour, you imply a strong, more-than-usual idea of how a man should comport himself in many different situations, against which you may check this or that individual piece of behaviour in front of you. Image used like this incorporates values. Now when we speak, as we very often do, of a man's public image, something of this meaning remains. We intend by this a series of associations, part pictures (snapshots), part judgements and standards which are called into play by the mention of the man's name. And when we speak of this personality or that public figure as trying to change his public image, we are not talking about radical changes in the self; we are talking about some projection of the self as it is perceived by a mass public which does not and cannot know the man concerned, and whose version of him is monstrously refracted through the many lenses of the mass media.

The process may be imagined as the magnification by many times of a normal social sequence whenever people are reported on and gossiped about within a social group. They then measure a particular person's actions against their sense of what he ought to be like according to his social role, his age and appearance, and the special needs of their community. They report the results of their measurement, and that person's identity is then in some very important way the product of other people's social view of him. You cannot simply be the product of your own, existential decision. Who you are is partly the inevitable result of who the others think you are.

The distance, however, between your self and the self you are reported as being depends on your relation to the reporters and in what sense their reports count for you. The disparity can be tolerably wide as the commenting group recedes with the social distance, as it has less and less sharp, precise, social reality. But there is a difficult problem when the reporters are literally that: the newsmen of the media system whose version of your public behaviour to a large degree determines how the public will see you. No doubt it is then possible to live with a pretty large disparity between your private and your public – and publicly constructed – self. And it is also possible to go your own unregarding way and let the media go hang. What a public figure cannot do is prevent the mass media constructing a version of him. Like their own cartoonists, they will select an exceedingly simplified and distorted set of characteristics which are there to see in a person and measure that against a shortish list of stereotypes, adjusted according to absences at the time or changes of values, or strategies, or taste, or the complicated process we have to gloss as fashion. Think of some examples. The most consistent and successful example of aloofness among sportsmen is Alf Ramsey. He gives few, bare interviews; he does not make fortunes out of his own successes. His austerity, however, in no way rescues him from the manufacture of images of him: he is presented in a large parody of the self which he may actually be in a small group, as distant, obscure, incommunicable, dedicated, and so forth. These are the qualities which take on in the man's public image curiously solid reality – curious because they are really no more than names for the journalists' and broadcasters' puzzlement. But in the processes of the mass media, the response is detached from the responder and assigned to the image. The image is then incorporated and modified – everybody is robustly sceptical of what the papers say – and given different weight and value in the popular imagination.

Perhaps the process can be put like this. The impressions we take from the newspapers, radio and television of famous public figures (as the phrase goes) are bound to be fleeting. But the figures recur. Each time they appear fleetingly, and each time they carry with them certain associations. They recur, at least in sport they recur, because we want them to. Sporting heroes on a mass scale become heroes in response to that weird mixture of manipulation by a few people and expression by many people which is the energy of television and newspapers. So we want, partly, the heroes we get. But what we get, we get at a distance. The heroes remain on a screen or a newspaper photograph. And so the characteristics which we come to attribute to the heroes are partly those suggested by the reporters, and partly a variable set of characteristics imposed upon the hero by the inarticulate wants, needs and desires of a mass public – a mass defined only by a common interest in football or racing or whatever it is. The set of characteristics we project upon a hero must in some sense 'fit' the real person: Fred Trueman could not have been seen as a quiet man; nor Eusebio as a flashy one. Yet those characteristics are very crude and unspecific, as though the extraordinary magnification of normal encounters which television in particular makes possible – instead of face to a small group of faces, we have one man facing several million invisible faces – makes a satisfactory view of a person impossible.

We have not thought about these processes hard enough, or imaginatively enough. It seems to me first of all that people do not *want* to make the effort to understand the celebrities of sport whom they watch on the media. They are fascinated by just this non-reality: the impossibility of thinking of the celebrity as a solid human being. The throngs of autograph-hunters or sightseers, the interested surprise with which we gape after a celebrity doing something ordinary such as getting on a bus, are not so much recognitions of the heroes' presence as commonplace human beings, as verification that the picture on the screen does have physical reality. Just that: the moving set of dots on 625 lines does correspond to a living body. Secondly, they find the characteristics which can be so organized as to fit a simple set of stereotypes. The hero can then be used as a very broad outline upon which his admirers (and his detractors) can project and explore their own fantasies and preoccupations. Or they can use the hero to confirm their own values: think of Bobby Charlton's status as the embodiment of endurance, courage, modesty, and resignation. No less, the celebrity may be a necessary object of vilification. Danny Blanchflower, one of the most intelligent men ever to have played professional sport for a full career, often and bitterly mentions the promoters' *and* the sportsmen's preference for 'the white man's hope – the black with a good punch who knows his place outside the ring',* the footballers who are simply the honest work-force of the directors. So Cassius Clay (as he was then) broke all the rules when he burst on the sporting scene with his inordinate boastfulness in 1963, and everyone looked to see him beaten by the dogged fighter Sonny Liston.

Fifteen years afterwards, we can understand how much more plausible it is to see Muhammad Ali's whole colossal performance as a daring subversion of his own social position. He created by sheer outrageousness a different set of expectations in his fans. Slowly, and in a puzzled way, they came round to him. But only because he was an astonishingly fast and beautiful boxer. For a while, as Blanchflower puts it, Ali was 'so good that we could leave the pack and all its pedestrian little ways behind'. He was able to break open the prohibitions and the conventions which define the narrow possibilities of the sportsman's life – even the life of a very rich and successful heavyweight champion of the world. So even after defeat came in 1971 he had forced the giant crowds which came to see him, to see him – and other black sportsmen with him, as the 1972 Olympics made clear – as a very different sort of hero, and they followed him back to the great winner of 1975. At this distance, fifteen years after his remarkable campaign of self-advertisement began, it is easier to see his enterprise as quite conscious, intelligent, and disdainfully detached from what his crowds wanted to make of him.

Mostly, however, the vast unconscious processes of image construction have things their own way. In much the same way as they live by racial stereotypes – about Frenchmen, West Indians, Pakistanis and so on – mass-media audiences carry around caricatures of their sporting celebrities. These caricatures are not like the pop images of teenage girls; the girls' devotion is precisely hysterical because it has almost no content at all. They could not, that is, describe the human characteristics of their idols. The idols exist as a large blank into which the girls can pour all the pent-up passions, aspirations, and appetite for which their lives provide so little satisfaction. To speak so generally of mass-media audiences is not to fall into the old fallacy first of meaning by 'mass' the mass of the working class, and second, of supposing that the mass audience moves and is moved as a single organism. Because nine million people watch 'Match of the Day', we cannot take for granted that they are all football enthusiasts, nor even that 'Match of the Day' is what nine million people most want to appear on

* 'Muhammed Ali', *Listener*, 11 March 1971. Blanchflower is speaking, of course, of Joe Frazier. See also his review of Hunter Davies' book, *The Glory Game* (Weidenfeld & Nicolson, 1972) in the *Listener*, 15 November 1972.

their sets on a Saturday night. None the less, I think it is possible to say something generally about people's perception of events seen on television.

Televised events are seen and recollected as at a distance. The degree of reality attributed to them is also a condition of their geographic distance. This is notorious. People are much more affected by a severe accident involving two or three children in a motorway crash than they are by the deaths of several dozen people in, say, a Spanish air crash, or by the deaths of hundreds in a South American earthquake. There is a natural, if disagreeable tendency to feel greater shock at a letter bomb in London than millions of tons of bombs in South East Asia. Television, then, does not make people insensitive to reality, as the cliché view goes, though it might emphasize tendencies already there. But quite apart from the question of geographic distance, it seems that people perceive television itself as picturing something not-quite-real or believable. It is not at all clear what we are all doing imaginatively with the pictures in which we appear so absorbed, but there seems to be some sort of glass wall in our consciousness which we interpose between ourselves and the world-as-televised. The world-as-televised then stands as it were somewhere over the shoulder of the world-we-live-in. This means that we view it in rather ambiguous ways. And 'view' is the word. Because it is a part of seeing the world-of-the-media (that is, on TV and in the newspapers) as being on the other side of a glass, that we see it as spectacle, not as a situation in which we act.

I don't mean quite by this the old chestnut about 'TV making us all into passive receivers'; because while we watch, the distance at which, sensibly, we keep ourselves, makes it perfectly possible for us to keep sceptical, to judge, comment, criticize, think of other possibilities, and so on. To a very marked extent – and how marked it is can be seen by the way in which anybody who is not alone with a TV set (and some who are) talks back to it – viewers of TV are not at all passive. But they *are* detached. At one level viewers want to make it clear to themselves that they are sceptical and independent of what they watch. Much the same is true of newspaper readers. And so people seem to weigh up the events and celebrities of the mass media in distancing ways. First they are seen as from an enormous distance, as though through the wrong end of a telescope. (Unlike the radio, on which disc jockeys for example can chatter ruminatively on while you go about the kitchen getting the supper ready; the point being that you do not have to watch.) Secondly, they are seen as objects, not subjects for thought; that is, you can do what you like with them. You can call the Prime Minister names; you can switch him out. You can gaze adoringly at Ilie Nastase or Tony Jacklin; you can forbid Eddie Waring the house. But this response, however healthily bloody-minded it may be, is at once the product of politics as we have learned them over the past few decades and the product of the technology which has produced our special versions of mass communications.

What does this mean? It means that we expect the events of national news to be available as information of a completely unusable sort. They become knowledge which cannot be translated into action. Hence the idea of a 'celebrity': a person who is famous simply because he or she is famous. Their status as celebrity does not depend much upon their ability to debate intelligently and lucidly and in public the special interests which mark them out; they are often arbitrarily appointed to signify the master images of their society:* this TV star as sex-kitten, that announcer as homely virtue; these footballers as gladiator-gentlemen, as buccaneers, as playboy-geniuses; the distance runner as dogged hero; the negro boxer as Uncle Tom, pugilist. In each case, the very roughest outline of the person's immediate self is used to contain these gross cartoons. As this chapter has tried to show, the mass media act both to manipulate and to express the popular forms of these cartoons. Without clear and responsible debate on the huge variety of social life, deprived of rational and reliable sources of information and standards of judgement, most people fall back upon a heavily and helplessly 'personalized' view of society and its leaders. The celebrities of politics, the men who wield power, are largely immune to influences from mass communications, at least as they work now. The celebrities of entertainment, however, can appear to be the creation of their own public. The sportsmen of the mass spectator sports (and more and more sports take on that designation, as Chapter 6 shows) of football, rugby league, cricket, tennis, motor-racing, boxing, swimming, athletics – these men are the public gladiators. They must absorb the huge projections of their audience into themselves and live out its intense aspirations, if they are to keep its favour.

It is a tricky business in which to keep your balance. Some personalities are praised 'for getting on with the game', and praised generally by the same sports reporters who also complain about the lack of 'rich personalities in the modern game'. Whatever the game is, the quiet, modest men and women – the Arnold Palmers, Colin Cowdreys, Rod Lavers and Mary Peterses – are contrasted (to the latter's severe disadvantage) with their stormy, 'temperamental', 'colourful' or 'wayward' opposites like Virginia Wade, Martin Chivers, John Snow, Gordon Pirie, Terry Downes, David Bedford. Only a few tough people like Trueman, Muhammed Ali, Jimmy Hill, or Henry Cotton and Fred Perry before the 1939 to 1945 war, have had the strength and staying-power to push back the conventional limits of the sporting hero which are marked out in the folklore of the mass media. Much of this change had to do with the new, vigorously independent way in which these men saw themselves. It is the change implicitly set out in John Arlott's book on Fred Trueman. In the case of such strong men as Henry Cotton and Fred Perry, the change was

* c.f. C. Wright Mills, 'The Celebrities', in *The Power Elite* (Oxford University Press, 1956).

principally to do with their determination to make a great deal of money out of their sporting talents, and in so doing to change their position in the social structure. In the teeth of the most bitter snobbery, Cotton won a much sneered-at fortune for himself* and a social status which the later golfing heroes now take utterly for granted. The same went for Fred Perry. These two men were among the first to see the entrepreneurial possibilities of vastly increased leisure and the wider spread of social opportunity and of cash. For these men stood and stand for an unusual resiliance before the off-the-peg categories of the reporters. If we look at a now famous case, that of George Best, we can see at once, and quite briefly, how attitudes towards media celebrities in general and sporting heroes in particular can – at the very least – damage and distort one of the chosen figures.

IV

There is a very good short story by Brian Glanville about the part that a football crowd – which, as anyone knows who has played in front of a big crowd, possesses or rather *is* a powerful mixture of frightening identities – the part it took in driving a young player away from the team he had joined and was doing well for. The crowd have it in for the lad because he has edged their ageing hero out of the first team:

> They never left me alone for a minute, not even when I got a kick on the knee and Jackie Morris, the trainer, had to come on; even *then* I could hear them shouting, 'Get up, Prentice, there's nothing wrong with you!' and I felt I never wanted to get up again in my life; I was so choked I could have cried. I said to Jackie Morris, 'Listen to them, Jack,' and he said, 'Those buggers? You don't want to take no notice of *them*.'
>
> Even the centre-half on the other side, he said to me, 'They don't seem to like you down here, do they?' †

And after several Saturdays of this, he asks for a transfer and the manager says 'Look ... this'll pass. This is a crowd that *needs* someone to get its knife into, it's always been the same.' For a while the hero (who is only 19) played only in away games, and then the manager tries to appeal to the crowd's generosity.

> The trick he'd got was he broadcast to the crowd before the match, he made this appeal to them. All I could hear from the dressing-room was somebody's voice coming over the loudspeaker, and then what sounded like the crowd all giving whoever it was the bird. Then Jackie came in and said, 'That was the Boss, he was asking the spectators to lay off Ray,' and one of the other lads said, 'Told *him* where to get off and all, didn't they?'

* See his autobiography, *This Game of Golf*, for details of his success and those who did the sneering. It is a dignified, good-tempered book.
† 'A Section of the Crowd', in *The King of Hackney Marshes* (Secker & Warburg, 1965) pp. 131–8.

I was finished before I'd even kicked a ball. Once, in the second half, I just couldn't take any more of it. I turned round to the crowd behind the goal and I shouted, 'Call yourselves supporters? You're worth a bloody goal to the other side!' But that made them worse than before, it was what they'd wanted, really, I'd shown them they'd got under my skin.

In the end, the hero scores a magnificently reckless goal and, even more disgusted by the crowd's immediate adulation, leaves the club the following week.

The truth which Glanville brings out in such a convincing way is that very large groups of people like football crowds may well 'need someone to get their knife into', and may certainly act in strange and grisly unison, week after week, when the knife is out. Any such action is no less certainly the result of believing in some crude stereotype about an individual player or about a whole team. 'So-and-so "is yellow" ', 'X and Y aren't speaking to each other', 'that young man has got a very swollen head', can all be said with equal portentousness and equal ignorance by one man in a pub or thousands on a terrace. What is frightening is both the vindictiveness – we have all seen or heard of this – with which a section of the crowd can pillory its victim, and the utter fickleness with which their demon can be transfigured into their favourite.

The strange case of George Best provides us with a very full study of this sort of behaviour. In his case we can also see how the newspapermen and broadcasters act as spokesmen for the primitive and malicious impulses of the mass audience. Everything that is worst about the public faces of the media comes out here. For Best's footballing brilliance and precociousness have meant that he made an extremely large amount of money very young. He seemed an attractive and vivid enough man, though not remarkably so, and his ostentatiously rich style of life off the field fell easily into the clichés of pop music, show business, fast cars and unforgettable girls. He wore the decorations of his success flashily. He had none of the discretion and quiet fastidiousness of Bobby Charlton, his one time team-mate, or the assurance and calm of the English captain, Bobby Moore. Both Moore and Charlton were reported during their playing life as being paid from all sources well over £10 000 a year. Best has owned a £50 000 house and three boutiques, though he has obviously spent his fortune very freely indeed. But the point at issue is the way in which he is presented in the newspapers and on TV, and what the possible consequences may be for the shape of his life.

Now Best brought back into the first-class game at a wonderfully developed level the technique of dribbling at a time when the whole pattern of football, with its long, quick, sweeping passes and the movement of blocks of players about the field, was planned to exclude the technique. Best made it work again, and in doing so recaptured the special spotlight which plays upon the man who holds the ball, baffles opponents, and transforms matches on his own. He was countered, during the rise of such play, by shattering fouls: cut down from the side and behind under a sequence of very heavy kicking at his feet and shins, and just as heavy tripping and barging. He retaliated by losing his temper, often and demonstratively.

Best is another example of what happens when someone who combines amazing talents at one of the big sports with his vibrant, flashy but oddly fragile and tender sensibility, becomes a popular hero. 'As for living, our heroes will do that for us.' He took to the dazzling girls, the pop star world, the long white cars, because he liked them, and he liked them because they are the recognized symbols – no, not symbols, but *realities* – of success, fame, recognition. This is not to sound prissy and censorious. As though I should say, 'he oughtn't to like these things; he ought to play a courtly, gentleman's game of football and then go back to his motherly landlady and sit waiting for training the next morning.' What I am saying is that the glitter and the fresh, conceited brilliance of Best's footballing style is also the style of his life. And that style, given the money, expressed itself naturally in the opulent colours of advertising images.

But of course you can't ignore such style, on or off the football field. And the television's and newspapers' honest enough attempt to see people as people and not simply in their specialist roles means that they follow a Best from football field to Miss World's apartment and back. Someone like Best, it is a truism to say, found success too soon. It might be better put to say that he could not ward off success for long enough at a time; could not keep the camera-lights from lighting up the intimate corners of that self which any man would keep private. Conventional 'no thoroughfare' signs will not do in such circumstances, and the 'seamless, private thoughtfulness with which the decently mannered young excuse themselves from contact'* which Arthur Hopcraft gently describes will not do to keep at bay the grosser intrusions of the nation's cameras.

It is important to emphasize that the cameras are there as agents and the interviewers as representatives of an entire society. The sporting hero has to carry in hugely magnified terms the weight and glare of many other peoples' complex and contradictory aspirations. Unless he can devise presentations of himself† which face the glare but do not melt under it, he is likely to break or quit the job.

In Barry John's direct, honest autobiography, he speaks of this exposure and of his defensive responses to it. Finally, when the prominence had destroyed, through no fault of his own, the pleasure he took in his rugby, he left the game.

It began to worry me that the adulation was alienating me from the human race. In a crowd at the National Eisteddfod I was talking to people when I heard

* *Football Man*, revised edition (Penguin, 1971), p. 13.
† See Erving Goffman's book, *The Presentation of Self in Everyday Life* (Penguin, 1969), especially the chapters 'Performances' and 'Teams'.

a mother tell her small son to touch my hand. Well, I suppose that is a compliment, but I am not a god or a prince or a healer, but a man. Once, in Swansea, I was visiting a hospital and, to my embarrassment, a woman curtsied to me. In Rhyl a girl approached and, as I was saying beneath my breath, 'Don't do it, don't embarrass me,' she, too, curtsied. The people around me thought that was a great gesture and they laughed with pleasure, but it was to me another indication of the way I was being drawn away from people and reality.

Living in a kind of goldfish bowl is not living at all. I went to see George Best a few times and I quickly grew to understand his outlook and to have tremendous sympathy for him. People were pulling up outside his house to point at it and to photograph it; many times I have heard cars stop outside my house, wait a minute or two with the engine running and then drive slowly away . . .

I felt I could not tolerate this kind of existence much longer. Occasionally I had the curious sensation of not being in my own body, of looking at it as if it were some kind of robot. I was Barry John the rugby star and machine; the real Barry John had stepped outside for a while. In the year up to my retirement from the game I saw my doctor more times than in all the other years of my life put together. And I got into the habit of having a few drinks late at night as a drug to get me off to sleep.

The demands were unbearable. Leaving rugby had nothing to do with the game itself – the very thought of playing a match made by blood race just as it did when I was a schoolboy. But family life had become impossible and, as an amateur player, I could not have continued leading this kind of life for many more months. I would have been doing no justice to myself, to my family, my firm, the Welsh team, or the devoted followers of Welsh rugby. In the end I would have let everyone down.

By the time of the Wales v. France match my resolve had hardened. I had decided that rugby should not be a total obsession, burning me out emotionally. It was a fulfilling and marvellous and large *part* of my life. But only a part. Yet to give it up was the hardest decision of all. Many times I wrestled with that insistent voice in the back of my mind which said: 'You were born to play rugby. Don't quit now.' It was the devil of a job to keep that voice quiet. I still hear it today from time to time.*

Barry John, who wasn't paid to play rugby for Wales, was able to leave the game pretty blithely. Best, with very different contractual obligations, had to try and live through the bright lights and develop a protective skin. This is difficult enough in itself. The relationship of sports page to gossip or news pages varies with the house-style and the public image of the person concerned. Best, obviously, features on that front page in a way in which Bobby Moore, even when charged with theft in Bogota during the 1970 World Cup, never would. Moore's cool self-possession made it possible for him to hold off public attention from those areas of himself he was resolved it should not touch. The forms of news production and layout, both in broadcasting and newspapers, create a rigid structure for the presentation of the public image – the media self, we may say. It is hard to force these

* *The Barry John Story* (Collins, 1973), pp. 32–34.

wide, crude categories to register the tiny, rich variations which make everyone their own individual.

The sportman is in a rather harder case than longer-lasting celebrities, so far as the presentation of himself goes. As Christopher Chataway remarked during an interview:*

> 'politicians are around for longer; journalists have to respect them as sources far more than they need sportsmen, who last no time at all.'

For sportsmen, like great artists, are seen in popular culture as interesting not for what they can do but for what they are. And, as I have said, what they are is in important part a product of the extent to which the sportsman in question allows the TV and press to make him into what they – and we, the readers and viewers – want him to be.

The admonitory prissiness, the satisfied and full-mouthed malice with which the newspapers reported the fall of George Best, across the winter of 1972 and autumn of 1973, is a case in point. After Best had missed training and broken for the severalth time the close nunnery rules which are usual for footballers paid anything between £25 and £1000 in a week, his club dropped him, fined him, and put him on the transfer list. On a Friday with only quiet news, he moved from the sports to the front pages, and came respectively third in the BBC 1 9.00 p.m. news, and in the first half of ITV 'News at Ten' (all sporting matters generally coming after the 10.15 break).

The *Sun* produced full banner (1½ inch) headlines: 'GEORGE BEST UP FOR OFFERS', with a 3½ × 6 inch photograph of Best's very pretty girlfriend:

SACK FOR UNITED'S WAYWARD SUPERSTAR
George Best, soccer's Number One truant, is up for sale. His club, Manchester United, finally lost patience with the runaway last night and put him on its transfer list.

Grim-faced manager Frank O'Farrell announced that 26-year-old Best would also be suspended for 14 days.

The bombshell decision was taken at a two-hour crisis meeting of United's board.

They said they had 'no alternative' after the superstar failed yet again to turn up for training on Monday.

The player also disappeared from his lodgings in Chorlton cum Hardy, Manchester.

On Monday night he was reported to be in London's trendy Tramps discotheque with actress girl-friend Annette Andre until 3 a.m. He drove off, alone, in a taxi.

Annette, aged 29, one-time girlfriend of matador El Cordobes and star of several TV series, refused to talk about her meeting with him.†

---

* With the author in January 1974.
† *The Sun*, 6 December 1972.

The *Daily Mirror*, above banners announcing Princess Anne on a foxhunting truancy, placed a large box advertisement ($5\frac{1}{2} \times 4\frac{1}{2}$ inches) on the front page, but covered the story at the back. The box read:

> For sale! George Best, footballer, age 26. Price £300,000 or near offer. Interested parties should apply to . . . etc.

The back page report, however, was given over to long, quoted statements by Derby County's chairman (this club was said to be interested in bidding) and by Best's manager. The statements were careful and dignified. The Manchester manager, Frank O'Farrell said:

> Best has delighted millions of fans all over the world. Yet he has never been able, while I have been here, to realise the responsibility he has to himself, the manager, his colleagues and the club's young players.
> The problem existed with the two previous managers – Sir Matt Busby and Wilf McGuinness – before I took over at Old Trafford. Who knows Best's mind? Certainly no one seems able to get through to him, and the board simply had no alternative but to place him on the transfer list.
> We are losing a great footballer, but the decision is final.
> This has come about through breaches of club discipline, not over months, but over a period of years.
> We have got to think about the morale and the general discipline of the rest of the players here and, most of all, of the players of the future. *

The *Express*, though 'Best for Sale' was the topline (but secondary) banner with a full-length photograph on the front page, kept most of the story on the sports page. There, however, the house-style reasserted itself (personalized, as they say, by the sports editor John Morgan – 'he told me in his Marbella hideaway that . . .'):

FADING GLORY
> And before you judge him, remember this: Best was never a problem when Manchester United were winning trophies here and in Europe. His discontent grew as the glory of United faded.
> He felt last May – as I'm sure he feels now – that Manchester United cannot provide him with the platform he needs to express his talents.
> It is easy to say that he should stay and play his part in making the club a powerful force in Europe again. It is easy to say, and perhaps it is right.
> But it is also true that Best is a showman, supreme, one of the greatest footballers the world has known.
> He isn't playing the game for money any longer. He wants to show off. †

The only explanations the sportswriter can fall back on are the tired clichés of the fagged-out and still censorious schoolteacher: 'Best was never a problem when Manchester United were winning. Best is a showman . . . he wants to show off.'

* *Daily Mirror*, 6 December 1972.
† *Daily Express*, 6 December 1972.

On such a view, the footballer-hero must remain a gentle genius on the field, and a quiet, orderly, tax-paying, fireside lad-of-the-lodgings the rest of the time. It is worth noting that when Best returned briefly to the front pages in 1973 for a short-lived comeback, the *Sun* picked his landlady to comment, beneath banner headlines, 'Best is Back', and a shaggy, wry close-up 5½ × 5½ inch photograph:

> George's No. 1 fan, his landlady Mrs Mary Fullaway, said: 'I'm thrilled and delighted. I always wanted George to go back to football.' Mrs Fullaway, George's 'mum' since he joined United at 15, added: 'He's easy to look after, though I might have to ration his cream cakes, now he's back in training.*

And beneath a small girlie photograph, the *Sun* followed this with:

> 'I knew', says girl friend.
> Blonde Joan de Kuyper was one of the few people who shared George Best's big secret.
> Joan, a 25-year-old secretary, met him on a beach in Majorca.
> They have been spending a lot of time together and George told her that he hoped to play for Manchester United again.
> Joan said at her flat in Mill Hill, North London, last night: 'I know he's had lots of girlfriends, but so have other men.'

In spite of its careful and lengthy reporting the *Mirror* turned to one of its bluff, no-nonsense folk heroes, Frank McGhee, to send from 'The Voice of Sport' this:

MESSAGE TO GEORGE BEST:
> Georgie, you have committed the one unforgivable [sic] crime in the world of entertainment. You have become a bore.
>   END MESSAGE

And again, at his attempted comeback, the *Guardian* launched a rather more deliberate character analysis:

> Not even Best's sternest critics – and I am one of them – would deny that at the peak of his form, and before he became involved in the whirlpool of commerce and hectic living, Best was a genius. He may still be one.
> Nevertheless, Best faces a tremendous task, and it must be the final challenge to the better side of his character. He knows better than most that he let down the public no less than he let down United and himself. He knows as well as anyone that many people hoped that they had heard the last of him. He knows better than anyone that he must mend his ways off the field as well as on it, where.he has an ominous record of indiscipline. Above all, he must spare no effort to show that he is sincere in his determination to win back his place in the team and in the estimation of the public. Frankly, I consider that he is a very lucky man indeed even to be allowed inside Old Trafford again, let alone given the chance of getting back into the side. If he justifies United's faith, then good luck to him; but as I have said before, I will believe it when I see it.

* *Sun*, 7 September 1973.

But if ever he transgresses again, please let there be no more attempts at salvage.*

Throughout the conversations of the newspapers about Best, there comes through the clear sense that the footballer is a perfectly proper object for severe and condescendingly personal criticism and advice. The stereotype of Best's kind of pop and sporting hero is divided into various parts, and reported on accordingly.

There is, as the relentless cliché insists, the *Dolce Vita* component – the marvellous girls, the cars, the discos and the late flight to Ibiza. There is the artist-as-wayward-adolescent, for whom art is the precisely tempestuous expression of his personality. There is the homely working-class lad who has made good, but whose proper place is at home with his mother or his landlady (same person, really). The newspaper welcome given to the tough and formidable Mrs Charlton emphasizes the continuing strength of this component in the stereotypes with which public communications on present terms interpret our sporting life to us.

Best is an object for news because he is rich: he is one of the very few men who have made fortunes out of football, whose feet have transformed their life. He lives in that high style which remains a complicated symbol for the whole society because it is both enviable, while remaining at best trivial, and at worst, greedy, wasteful, cruel, and corrupt. With a similar double focus he is seen as showman and sportsman. And it is impossible to be both, at least without very severe wear and tear. For the showman is expected to play up in the histrionics of the sport – to be, that is, genuinely brilliant at his arts, but to play them off against the mediocrity of his opponents for the various gratifications of his audience, for their contempt, hilarity, admiration, and warring, bloodthirsty sense of the transience of human achievement. The sportsman, on the other hand, is expected to be in all things gentlemanly and assured. In a novel about a political painter whose life's work was to paint a masterpiece of the 1948 Olympic Games, the hero writes:

> In sport . . . liberation is collective. I have seen games of football in which I have glimpsed all I believe the productive relations among men might be.†

The tradition of the showman-footballer desires this liberation in the interests of the exhibition; the tradition of the sportsman-footballer desires it in the interests of aesthetics – beauty before freedom. Sport, I think, is always struggling for its purer nature against these ways of seeing. Yet sport still makes it possible to those who play, and occasionally for those who watch, to become purely heroic, not just pop-heroic. The Sportsman as Hero.

Heroism consists of understanding that the achievement can be greater

* *Guardian*, 7 September 1973.
† John Berger, *A Painter of Our Time* (Secker, 1958; Penguin, 1965), p. 122.

than the individual achiever. That is a way of saying that a destiny is more important than a set of interests.

These speculations seem to move a long way away from the particular case of one contradictory, recalcitrant footballer. But the case of George Best, his wealth, his recurrent appearances in the publicity columns and the courts, the ambivalent nature of his gifts and his identity, make him a suitable subject for exploring the way we make our popular heroes out of the images of public communications. As the *Daily Mail* put it: 'Whatever Best is, he has been created by Soccer's star system.'* Well, that – as I have tried to show throughout this chapter – is not quite true. But there is a close, alternating relationship between a man's private self and what he is said to be in terms of, in the general phrase, public images. And 'public image' is right. It is the image created of a person out of the materials that person chooses either to make available or else involuntarily betrays to that public and its publicly accredited image-makers. When, as in Best's case, the materials available are so colourful, dashing, so petulantly self-conscious and ardent, then the ambivalences of projecting such a personality on to a television screen are likely to force him out of work. As, with Best, they did for two years.

The really bad mistake in trying to understand all this would be, in a vulgarly common-sensible way, to blame the image-makers. Mass media are as they are because of the whole texture of society, and to criticize them at all intelligently is to criticize the human priorities and encounters of that society. That is why, in the passage I quoted, the painter was right to say '*glimpsed*' when he spoke of the liberation and productiveness which sport makes possible. These fine things are there: they are the grounds of this book. But they are there often in spite of and a long way beneath the disfigurements.

Sport in all its forms has to contain and express a vast jumble of fantasies, hopes, embitterments, and regrets. So, no doubt, do any forms of art. But sporting forms at the present time have to bear more than most, and more than ever before. In this industrial society, they try to give shape and sense to what is dammed up in other places in people's lives. As I have said before in these pages, their sport is for people their expression of beauty, passion, tragedy, delight, and history; of meditation and serenity; of creative imagining and energy. A lack of these experiences and ideas thwarts and distorts a people. At the moment, the stridency and confusion of so much mass media coverage of sport simply reflect back to us the same din in our nation. It is a wonder so much sports writing is as good as it is.

V

When it is good, it is careful, spirited writing in the plain style. One of the best bits of sporting journalism I ever read was a piece Danny Blanchflower

* 6 December 1972.

wrote for the *Observer* after visiting the Cambridge University rugby team
of 1959 in training. With his keen eye for such detail he at once picked the
amateurishness of the undergraduates as their distinguishing characteristic, but his charm and tact in writing were able to place this quality as at
once attractive as well as merely boyish. He wrote of 'the uneconomical
line of their kit' as 'matching the reckless, hair-raising enthusiasm with
which they threw themselves into the dangerous rigours of their training',
and this in turn as being of a piece with 'the shattering obscenity of the
songs they sang in the communal baths at the end.' What Blanchflower was
immediately shrewd enough to measure was the vast gap in ability, in
expectations, in attitude, which separates university and professional
football. And from this insight he is able to touch the cultural meaning of a
whole heap of details in the mixture of nervous, natural grace and heavy,
undisciplined effort which is a first-class rugby tream in training.

Such writing is exceedingly rare. Blanchflower, writing weekly in the
Sunday Express, rarely reaches that far inside himself these days. In the plain
style of honest reporting, you would go a long way to improve on Michael
Davie's report of Christopher Brasher's gold medal run in the 1956 Olympic
Games. (For the virtuosity of stamina, single-minded and -handed
covering, thoroughness, and lively accuracy, Brasher's own reporting in
the *Observer* of the 1974 Commonwealth games would take some beating.)

Melbourne, 1 Dec., 1956.
Brasher has so far received about 150 telegrams congratulating him on
winning his Gold Medal in the 3,000 metres Olympic steeplechase. He is moving
about between the Olympic village, the stadium and restaurants in the town in a
state of dazed satisfaction rather than open jubilation, uncertain whether he has
achieved something worthwhile or not. He is very polite to strangers who ask if
they may shake his hand. He thinks he has degenerated from physical fitness to
unfitness faster than anyone in the history of athletics. His face is a tired, muddy
yellow, and he looks as if he could do with a long holiday . . . At lunch the day
before the race he was already a little distracted. He had a filet mignon steak and
two large glasses of lemon squash, went through the list of runners for the next
day, and reckoned the winner must come from one of five people. He
complained he had something wrong with his back, but agreed it might be
psychosomatic. He said it was funny how the body worked (like other class
athletes, he thinks that doctors still know practically nothing about the human
body) because the metatarsal arch in his foot had a brain of its own and had
started to ache in acknowledgement of the fact that it would shortly be required
to hit the ground hard landing from hurdles.

Chataway that afternoon was running in the 5,000 metres, but Brasher said he
wasn't going to watch in case it dragged too much nervous energy out of him . . .
He decided to go to the pictures to see 'The Vanishing American' at the
Lyceum, saying half seriously that Wild West heroics would put him in the mood
for laying down his life before 100,000 people in the stadium next day . . .

Brasher went back to the Village after the pictures, had a meal, took a knock-
out pill and went to bed. He woke at four in the morning in a panic, thinking he

had wrecked everything and wouldn't be able to go to sleep again. He did go to sleep again, however, and was woken up by the women coming in to clean. He had had 10 hours.

Before the race began, he experienced no nerves at all. His legs felt very strong. Just as the gun was about to go off Disley, Britain's first string steeplechaser (Brasher was only the third string), said to him: 'Well, Chris, if I don't win I hope you do.' Brasher knew when there were two laps to go that he could be in the first three. The disputed hurdle, four from the end, when he jumped it between Rozynoi, the Hungarian, and Larsen, the Norwegian, seemed to have no special significance. As he came up the final straight ahead of the field Brasher's brain was saying 'I've done it, I've done it, I've done it.'

Up in the stands the incredulous *Evening News* man was on his feet yelling 'No, no, no, not Brasher! No, no!' In the adjoining stand as the race ended Chataway's face was suffused: his eyelashes were very white and his eyes as bloodshot as they were when he beat Kuts at the White City, 'How does he do it? How does he do it?' he kept saying. 'Those last two laps . . .' Bannister, sitting next to him, said Brasher's legs had looked terrible, but then they never did look good.

Twenty-four hours later, in a Cypriot restaurant in Melbourne called Florentinos, there was a discussion about how Brasher had in fact done it. Chataway, who knows Brasher as well as most people, said the secret lay somewhere in Brasher's behaviour during the last month. Since they had arrived in Melbourne, said Chataway, Brasher had become testy, moody and dogmatic.

Brasher demurred, but it is certainly true that since he reached Melbourne he has somehow seemed to feel the ground firm under his feet . . .

Asked why he, a sensible fellow with plenty of interests, had gone on running in the first place after having had a comparatively undistinguished athletics career at Cambridge, Brasher said that everyone else seemed to be packing it in and he thought he would go on and see what happened. Then, after he became involved in personal and athletic relationships with Bannister and Chataway, and especially after the four-minute mile, he became really committed. He began to resent his role as the third man, at being introduced as the person who helped Bannister with the four-minute mile or as the friend of the celebrated Chataway. He became aware, too, that the ability to run faster over a certain distance than anyone else on earth might be due less to natural athletic ability than to the kind of will the runner possessed.

Brasher said he found the most interesting thing about human beings to be the degree of control they can develop over themselves. How does a man like Hermann Buhl find the resources to climb Nanga Parbat? How do you react when you are lost on a mountain-side, alone and in fog? The first thing, if you are going in for this kind of investigation of the limits of human capacity, is to discipline the conscious part of your mind. That accomplished, you can hope that your unconscious mind, too, will begin to learn discipline . . .

Brasher added that if a year ago he had had an ache in his metatarsal arch such as he had had before the Olympic race he would have assumed he had really injured himself. This week he knew the arch was merely expressing a point of view.

It is perhaps because he thinks like this and is this sort of person that Brasher has been capable of producing his best on the right day, whereas other English athletes, who in a formal sense are very much better runners than he is, have been unable to do so.*

This is not great writing – nothing like Arlott at his best. It does, however, represent a sound piece of instant historicizing. It is also notable that the reporter – in his vivid mixture of local detail (the glasses of lemon squash), of English understatement, especially by very close friends ('his face is a tired, muddy yellow', 'Bannister . . . said'), and of rather interesting psychological biography – shows us very fairly the hero-athlete and his event. The article is not maudlin about Brasher, and it does not sink the man in the event; it keeps runner and race in a nice balance. It is further worth remarking, as part of the style and its morality which penetrate our sport, that the reporter concentrates entirely on the virtues of endurance, resolution, introspection, and *will*, in some rather narrow sense of which 'iron' is more than the cliché description. Where Leni Riefenstahl, in her famous film of the 1936 Berlin Olympiad stressed above all the grace and poetry of the human body in motion, the British movie *Tokyo 1964* stressed the strenuousness, the pain and lonely effort of that body. This report does the same, and that is the nature of its limitations. It reminds us of the judgement to which I came early in this chapter: that to talk of sport as John Arlott does, and as on their day Danny Blanchflower, Chris Brasher, Jack Charlton, and Tony Lewis in their smaller voices do, is to speak in a rare and admirable and human voice.† It would be good, in those channels, to hear it more often.

* *Observer*, December 1956.
† Contrast this fake aestheticizing – sport for art's sake – and over-intellectual stuff, from *The New Yorker*'s baseball critic:

The pitcher, immobile on the mound, holds the inert white ball, his little lump of physics. Now, with abrupt gestures, he gives it enormous speed and direction, converting it suddenly into a line, a moving line. The batter, wielding a plane, attempts to intercept the line and acutely alter it, but he fails; the ball, a line again, is redrawn to the pitcher, in the center of this square, the diamond. Again the pitcher studies his task – the projection of his next line through the smallest possible segment of an invisible seven-sided solid (the strike zone has depth as well as height and width) sixty feet and six inches away; again the batter considers his even more difficult proposition, which is to reverse this imminent white speck, to redirect its energy not in a soft parabola or a series of diminishing squiggles but into a beautiful and dangerous new force, of perfect straightness and immense distance. In time, these and other lines are drawn on the field; the batter and the fielders are also transformed into fluidity, moving and converging, and we see now that all movement in baseball is a convergence toward fixed points. Roger Angell, *The Summer Game* (Viking, New York, 1972), p. 302.

6 Gesture as language—sport and its stories

SUPPOSE THAT YOU ASKED for something a lot sharper than those good voices give? After all, talking about the sport is nothing like the same as actually doing it. (Which is not to say that talking about it is just a second-hand business. Talking about your sport is as much what gives it continuity as playing it.) But if the games at least partly match up to what I have been saying about them – if, that is, they are a people's art – then somehow talk about them should at times take your breath away with the suddenness of diving, flat and heavily, into a very cold swimming bath.

Is that the way to put it? Is it possible for a whole game – a full athletic match, say, or a swimming gala – to be as unselfconsciously *happy*, and as full and sweet as a Mozart symphony? (A quartet would be something different.) Or as a really big, busy, crowded Raphael mural?

Well, why ever not? The happiness of such a symphony or such a painting is not the product of innocence or naivety. People make an artist into an innocent in order to claim that he cannot really manage living in the ordinary toughness of the world. (They forget millionaire Picasso on this argument; and they forget the engineer Gabo, exiled from USSR, or Michelangelo, flat on his back on his plank high below the ceiling of the Sistine Chapel for four years.) Artists, on such a showing, do not *think*; even less can they *do*. They are. But the Mozart symphony and the Raphael painting are only unselfconscious as a consequence of an extraordinary effort of learning. And then what they see becomes their way of changing their history; they make statements about a different kind of seeing. The unselfconsciousness is then nothing to do with naivety – it is not a feeling or even a quality, it is a way of describing the certainty that they are telling the truth.

Bobby Charlton in the photograph in the first chapter, or Joe Brown, tell the same truth in the unassuming line of their bodies. We mean, when we say 'unassuming' that we approve of a becoming modesty. Indeed, both men in those pictures are modest in that what is important to them is what they are doing, but of course both of them are also supremely confident – the expression on their faces tells us that. Such confidence is anything but 'unassuming' in the usual sense; it assumes a range of technique and a certainty of capability which permits them their complete and unselfconscious freedom to create what they can. And, then, as Tolstoy put it, they create 'to improve the world, to establish brotherly union among men'. That is faith, and faith (being of the flesh) lives for the time being in sport.

All these remarks are preface for saying that the players or the artists writing and talking about their games (their work) will not necessarily unlock any very profound meanings. Like most people, including officially systematic talkers like politicians or intellectuals, they have learned no method in talking. I have written of the big media and of public communications as telling us not so much what these circumstances are, as how we talk and think about them. The small universal screens enormously magnify, and therefore make easily available for discussion, not the way we live now but the way we talk about the way we live now. To get hold of the actual living is much harder. A few television programmes come near, no doubt – but never capture the endless process, the undammable flow itself. A few books – John Arlott's, for example. A few people talking – Christopher Brasher. David Storey's novel *This Sporting Life** is one framework within which to place the other accounts I shall turn to in this chapter. It is an amazing book, though in places weak and irritating because it is so over-assertive, and it is doubly hard to go back to it because it is now so well-known, filmed, and in 1971 rewritten by the author (its best parts, at any rate) as the play *The Changing Room.*†

As most people know, the novel tells the story of a steelworker in a medium-sized Northern town of the late 'fifties who gets out of the grinding bleakness and meanness of his job and its surroundings by becoming one of the best players in the local, big-time Rugby League team. He is taken up by the club's chairman, a weak, wealthy businessman who is distinctly one of the town's leaders, and he comes to hope for a richer fulfilment than his car and local prestige can provide by pressing, with insensitive, bullying gentleness, his landlady Mrs Hammond to marry him. She, in her turn, has drawn back from the dead routines of her poor life by settling into a dull, dumb immobility of spirit. It is the settlements of this sort, either the beaten Mrs Hammond's, or those of Arthur Machin's friends as they boil themselves a hard, flashy outside with which to contain their own vulnerable, manly softnesses and their unexpressed longings – these settlements rouse Machin to violent anger and a proper hatred of what is hateful.

The truthfulness and ardour of the novel are a harsh antidote to the optimism and gladness with which I have so often written about sport in this book. Its bold, clear lines give us a number of structures with which to understand sport in society. There is, first, the structure of power which sets Weaver and Slomer at the centre of the town. Weaver's factory dominates the bottom of the valley overlooked by his house at the top. Slomer's cash

* Longmans, 1960; Penguin, 1962.
† Cape, 1972.

loan is to set up the footballers in business when they retire from the game. Machin is doubtful about the proposal; he feels that he sold himself to the Slomers of this world when he took the £500 cheque and went professional. The other players – strongly attracted as they are by the idea of not sinking into the anonymity of the mines or the steelworks again, or indeed the equal blankness of a job at the side of the pitch – are put off by the risks of going into business together, put off simply by the prospect of the lack of all the strong, good things which hold them together in football, and most of all put off by their own deep sense that there is not much they can do to change their world for the better, and that the wages won from football are just a temporary respite from the inevitable beatenness of life.

In the event, Slomer dies before the loan is made.

> The funeral was a procession. It seemed the town stood back when Slomer died, and nobody was quite sure what it meant or what should be done. The result was that hardly anything was not done, and all the big businesses sent representatives, and all the taxi firms sent all their cars. The hearse was a solid mass of flowers, from which seemed to protrude only the four wheels below and the driver's head on top. The haphazard and instinctive spectacle brought out large crowds, and the whole thing went off in an atmosphere of awesome bewilderment.
>
> George, Frank, and I shared a taxi with a couple of other men who'd known Slomer slightly, in a business way. One of them, impressed by the number of people who ducked down as we passed to peer in the window, was saying, 'It's the end of a way, you know'.
>
> George lifted his shaggy eyebrows, and looked lost without the dog. 'How do you mean?' he said patiently.
>
> 'With Slomer gone', the man told him, 'You'll find all the big combines finding it easier to move into town. You mark my words. There'll be no king-pin any more. We'll become like all the other big towns – socialist, impersonal, anonymous. The only thing we'll be known by' – he waved his gloved hand at me – 'will be the standard of our football team'. (p. 228).

He is succeeded by the club's former chief trainer, and when Weaver quits football and the town in a rush of petulant dissatisfaction with the ill-concealed, sneering subordination which he has purchased from the players, Wade is left in charge, and his buttoned-up and stifling banality is marvellously conveyed by the ubiquity of his repellent little dog, his conspiratorial and trivial whispering, his frightened, over-assertive watching of the time, as in the familiar image of work-disciplined capitalism, he portions out the minutes for the benefit of his men and on behalf of his superiors.

That is one main structure of the book, as it is of sport, and as it is of our society: the relations of employers to one another and to their men. Weaver wants to be liked; in an arbitrary, fickle way courts affection where there could only be either sponging or defiance in response. Slomer keeps his authoritarian and disillusioned manipulation of people according to his

Catholicism. Wade then runs things by the clock and the short change of a frame of mind utterly without imagination or aspiration. He is hopeless because he cannot understand what he might hope for.

The slow death of hope is a main subject of the book. Machin is a man who hopes for a great deal, hopes for it passionately and with determination. He hates and is made angry by hopelessness, such as he finds in his landlady Mrs Hammond, and in the creature Johnson who first gets him access to the club.* The anger is not, however, self-interested. It is the generous feeling of a man who wants to shake others out of failure and into both independence and fineness. But of course he only rarely can find the terms in which to do this, or in which to express the fineness he knows he wants.

The fineness comes through in the best moments of what the footballers make together. There on the page David Storey brings to life the sense I have that in football as in other sports we may glimpse all we believe the productive relations among men might be. And yet all the time the stains and smell of the defeats enforced by the desolation and horror of so much of people's lives today are there to poison the brief comradeliness and gladness of the footballers' lives. Frank Mills, the giant, ageing miner who captains the team, draws these threads of perception together, but Frank himself is living through to an end which waits for all the players.

> And I knew what occupied Frank most – the fear of letting go of football, of the popularity, the money, and the friendship maybe, and subsiding into the obscurity of his fellow miners, a has-been. This abrupt diminishing of life, just at the point when according to the rules it should be getting larger, was a fear he'd come to recognize too late. (p. 245).

In the remarkable and beautiful conclusion to the book, Machin takes an elegiac farewell of the game. In the closing pages, this second structure of feeling in the novel is finely rendered – a structure, so to speak, built from the strong webs of particular human values as they intersect with one another, values in this case such as familiarity, friendship, warmth and intimacy, all living in the detail and the cadences of the language. But by this stage of the book, these values are crossed by Machin's deep, mature sense of loss, failure, pain, exhaustion, resentment.

This generalizing vocabulary reduces to a crude diagram what the novelist really gives our imagination. The day is bitterly cold, and raining. A new boy is playing, Arnie:

> He had a lot of talk had Arnie – he talked all the time he rubbed the grease in, his abnormally developed muscles quilted with a restrained confidence. Unmarked, they impressed on me a sense of my own maturity . . . I watched, fascinated, the flesh of the kid's heavy shoulders, the lithe muscles sliding across

---

* In these remarks I am turning to a fine review of David Storey by John Newton in *Cambridge Quarterly* (Summer 1966).

his back. It seemed a greater flexibility than anyone else's, fluid, without hesitation. Had I been like that? (p. 245).

And at one point, when Arnie looks at the hero 'with unmistakable challenge and ambition', Machin turns away, with ten years football behind him, thinking 'Why be burnt up about it? Wait a few years and see how you feel then'. Young Arnie is contrasted with Machin's friend and one-time rival, Maurice Braithwaite:

> Maurice was naked. He jumped up and down with his customary pre-match excitement, amongst the coated, impatient players. His body, heavily and indifferently scarred, was some consolation. I watched him as if I'd never really noticed him before. His muscles were hard and knotted, fierce little physical intensities. His bowed and prodigiously thickened thighs tucked in to the tight knot of his knees, red and scabbed and about to be bandaged by the masseur. (p. 243).

What fills this, the last match of the book, is Machin's sense of the pointlessness which has gone to mark and misshape Maurice's body. By the end what is most emphasized is the tiredness and pain of this futile labour. Machin acknowledges 'I was ashamed of being no longer young', and finally he misses the sort of tackle which he once would have accomplished 'running fast yet feeling poised at the same time, and taking most wingers in my stride I'd throw them neatly over the touchline and against the concrete balustrade'. But in the last game of the book, 'I could only stare unbelievingly at my legs which had betrayed me'.

He has come to the end of a road which had always only offered ambiguous promises. The closing paragraphs, dense with implication as they are, move us outwards into the third, encompassing structure of the book.

> Arnie took the ball and with his boy's shout of triumph threw himself into the confusion of mud and men, his body searching, like a tentacle, for an opening. He ran ten yards to a scream from the crowd, then fell into the sea of limbs.
>
> I was still kneeling, absorbed in an odd resigned feeling. My back teeth chattered as I pulled myself up, my hands shook with cold, and I despised myself for not feeling hate for the man who'd torn my nostril. I was used to everything now. Ten years of this, ten years of the crowd – I could make one mistake, one slight mistake only, and the whole tragedy of living, of being alive, would come into the crowd's throat and roar its pain like a maimed animal. The cry, the rage of the crowd echoed over and filled the valley. (p. 252).

Once more, David Storey reminds us of the central tension in his novel between the players and those whom they play for, between entertainers and entertained. This tension is in the end what has broken Machin and exhausted Frank Miles; it is what fires Maurice Braithwaite's narrow egotism and the young boy Arnie's ambition. I shall go back to it. For the moment, though, it is worth quoting from the last paragraphs of the book, those which immediately follow the tackle which causes the defeat.

The water rose to my shoulders. It pressed on my chest and I fought for breath, coughing in the steam. Its heat brought my bruises to life. Over to my left Maurice chatted, just his head and a lighted cig above the water. Frank, drawing relief from his fag, turned his bull's back to me, I rubbed the soap over his familiar stained skin. I knew it better than my own.

He submerged and left half the soap on the surface. When he brought his face up again he said, 'Somebody's pissing i' the bath again'. And after looking round with a vacant grin added, 'It'll be Arnie, thy can bet'.

'Who me?' The kid looked hurt and pointed to himself.

Frank lunged through the crowded bath at him. Maurice and me joined him, the others shot out. He screamed for help. We got hold of the wild animal and shoved his obscene head under the cold water tap. Maurice tickled his ribs. Water cascaded into the dressing-room. Everybody joined the shrieking. Arnie was tortured with his own laughter.

Then Dai cleared us out with the hose. We stood in front of the coke fire and were rubbed down. Maurice lay on the table, another cig in his mouth, having his knees dressed. The masseur bent over him, staining his body with orange liniment.

Frank, his belly relaxed and protruding, rubbed his head slowly with the towel, his biceps bunched like rocks. I had my ankles strapped, got dressed, and put my teeth in. (p. 255)

In spite of the weary mixture of relief and resignation which the tone and cadence of these sentences so vividly express, no man who has ever played football of any sort can fail to be pierced by his own changing-room memories at this point. As much as anywhere it is the atmosphere of the changing room after a match which best embodies the comradeliness of team sports: the unforgettable, pungent smell of embrocation, very heavy sweat, shampoo, and cigarette smoke; the thick steam from the vast communal bath, the easy, unembarrassed nakedness and the sheer variety of physiques; the shared jokes, the reminiscence, the long anatomizing of the just-finished game as small events are isolated, laughed or raged over, and gradually become part of the folklore of the club. The friendships settled in such surroundings go very deep among its garrulous but inarticulate membership. Men who would never speak of their affection and loyalty not only towards one another, but also towards their club and its continuity (what old player but looks up the result for his club in the Sunday papers), keep that love thriving in the way they insult one another or punch one another on the pack of muscle at the shoulder. And then, long after, these friendships are maintained by the shared recollections of particular games, of how a certain player disliked tackling and what another one did to be sent off. It is to this feeling that David Storey gives brief but glowing significance.

Even at its best, however, these relations – which are not so much of work, nor of play, but of *possibility* (I would have written *productiveness* if the word were not so narrowly economic in its usage) – are part of the larger structures of power and manipulation in Primstone. There is an excellent scene which describes Machin's standing out for a £500 signing-on fee during which time the committee try, as a *principle* of manipulation, to force him down. He digs in, gets his money, and is then vigorously chaffed for his stubbornness.

> For a minute I hated the stinking money. It burnt a hole in my pocket. Then I remembered it was mine, and I was smiling.

The cheque links Machin to Weaver; it also ties him to the town, and places him in the weird social position of the professional footballer, part hero, part hired entertainer and buffoon. Remember the treatment of George Best? That is an example of the way the public communications magnify the ordinary transactions of the street which Machin bitterly describes here.

> Quite a few people recognized me. They nudged and pointed. They were always doing that. I didn't like Middleton talking about footballers strutting about town as if they owned it. It was the way they were treated that made them like that. The way people looked at me, spoke to me, handled my affairs generally whenever I wanted to buy a suit, a stick of chewing-gum, a gallon of petrol. They *made* me feel I owned the place. Course I strutted about. They expected it. I couldn't help it. I walked in front of these people now, and I felt a hero. They wanted me to be a hero – and I wanted to be a hero. (p. 162).

But the footballer, as the newspaper reports have shown us, is only a hero on other people's conditions. He has to look at himself the whole time, because he is their property (as opposed to being their representative). In 'normal' life he would be one of them.

There is something permanently unreal about being a well-known sportsman. The unreality is the feeling we describe as self-consciousness, but it is more complicated than that. It is, certainly, the consciousness of being looked at; it is also the sense of not quite living inside their own bodies. A public sportsman or entertainer must constantly be joining the rest of the crowd in order to watch from a distance his own actions. (I am guessing at this feeling, of course.) Only in the rare moments of absorption in the game can he become completely unified. In those circumstances he fills the content of other people's lives with his own. At such a moment the sportsman is indeed the representative of the people.

Perhaps what I say applies only to the sports which are, regularly, public dramas. There will of course be differences of degree and occasion: the first ascent of Everest in 1953 became public drama after the event; so did Bonington's victorious climb in 1975. Normally, climbing is immensely remote. On the other hand, some men are more than usually able to hold secure this relation of their public, watched self to their other, watching, and judicious self: I have already suggested that Fred Trueman is one such man. None the less, what David Storey makes his hero say, and my earlier interpretation of newspaper and TV treatment of their heroes supports this analysis, is that the gladiator paid for by the town's public benefactors is the town's own property. He is the prompt to the crowd's savage and unpredictable expressions of itself; if he fails, they will hate him, because then they fail also.

> I could make one mistake, one slight mistake only, and the whole tragedy of living, of being alive, would come into the crowd's throat, and roar its pain like a maimed animal (p. 252).

If he fools about, he wins the crowd, because they can make him their own fool. If he is dazzling, it is to dazzle them. The difficulty is to do these things, and remain his own man. What Machin wanted was money, power, success, not for themselves but for his own freedom from the dead life which he started from.

> Thou hast shook hands with reputation
> And made him invisible.   (*The Duchess of Malfi*, III, ii.)

But he finds that when, for instance, he goes home to the narrow, proud, and dogged decencies of his parents, they can only judge his money as heavily tainted by the hypocrisies and the old corruption of its source. And when Machin lets himself fall through the gap between his home street and the flat the club has given him, he drops into the mind-stopping squalor and brutality of the dosshouse underworld. The similarities and con-nexions between the beastly, comic drunkenness of a wandering Lith-uanian bus-conductor vomiting in the bedroom and the appalling party at Weaver's are left to speak for themselves.

Storey's novel, then, gives us these three structures (or sets of relations) with which to interpret public and spectator sport: the first, that which defines and contains the *rentiers* and their employees, the power élite and their hired men; the second, the relations strictly internal to the game and the players; the third, the relation of town or 'crowd' – literally, this time, 'the masses' – to its hero-entertainers.

It is worth taking time over Storey's novel because it is so exceptionally good. By and large, novels about sport are pretty poor: they turn on the conventionalities not only of the tritest ideas of the sport in question, but also of the tritest novels around at the time. In so far as such novels are much read, or such films are watched, then we can learn quite a lot about the actual consciousness of the time. The strength of Storey's novel is that he goes well beyond what people actually think to what they could possibly think. To put it simply, he shows what might be thought if only people noticed the limits of their imagination, the tightness of their 'frame of mind' as the familiar but very accurate phrase has it.

It is worth pointing out that there are few films about sport. *This Sporting Life* was a famous version of the novel produced by Lindsay Anderson but in my view crass and uncomprehending of the real fineness of the novel – 'actual consciousness' indeed. *The Final Test* (1951) with screenplay by Terence Rattigan is the only box-office fictional movie about sport in Britain. It told, in Rattigan's special brand of controlled sentimentality, the story of an ageing Test match hero who gets a duck in his last test (commentary by John Arlott) and just snatches his favourite barmaid from the arms of the caddish new star who made a century that afternoon. There is a goodish American version of the famous (I think overrated) Budd Schulberg novel, *The Harder They Fall*, and there was Chaplin in the boxing ring. Unforgettably, there was the Marx brothers' *Day at the Races*. Apart from these you have to go to the documentaries like *Olympiad 1936* by Riefenstahl, which is a classic, *Goal!* the dullish 1966 World Cup film, and the fair-to-middling *Tokyo 1964*. Films like the last two are not very different from run-of-the-mill TV sporting scrapbooks. Odd that there still have not been any successful TV sports serials.

The obviousness of ordinary or actual novels is readily documented.* There is, supremely, the middlebrow cricket novel deep in the great illusion of the changeless English village, and pasted lovingly into the pages of as mixed a bunch of patriots as Ian Hay, R. F. Delderfield, L. P. Hartley and the early P. G. Wodehouse. The most famous of all these georgics is itself the gentlest and most loving of parodies, loving as all successful parody must be. It is the cricket match in A. G. Macdonell's *England, Their England*.† It is worth mentioning that the eleven literary worthies in that novel who come to play the village side were closely modelled upon the similar team run by the benignly inept poet, J. C. Squire, who authorized and edited genteel poetry in fashionable London in the 'twenties. The cricket in *England, Their England* is not so precise and informed as in *Pip* or in Aubrey de Selincourt, or indeed as in the excellently close descriptions in P. G. Wodehouse's serials from *Mike* for *The Captain* in 1912 to 1914. But Macdonell is writing parody, and is very funny. Almost all his literary-gentlemanly Londoners are drunk on village beer from the start, sixes abound, blacksmiths are demon bowlers, and (of course) the match ends in a tie. He gives us the fraily exquisite (but saucy) novelist who hits the tax-collector's most crafty deliveries out of sight (the leg-break, the fast yorker, and the slow, swinging off-break out of the laurel bushes), the ferocious Major whose fast bowling is anaesthetized by local beer sneaked from the back door of the pub, the mammoth oarsman 'in all the majestic trappings of a Cambridge Blue', and the innocent American abroad, supposing himself to be playing a hilarious version of baseball which only a Scot who knew nothing of baseball could ever imagine, full of college whoops and pelting the running batsmen between the shoulder blades. It is all done with terrific zest.

* See for a start this very mixed bag from the 'twenties and 'thirties: Ian Hay, *Pip*; A. de Selincourt, *The Cricket Match*; John Moore, *Brensham Village*; L. P. Hartley, *The Go-Between*; R. F. Delderfield, *A Horseman Riding By*: Siegfried Sassoon, *Memoirs of a Fox-Hunting Man*.

† Macmillan, 1933, pp. 98 ff.

The scores were level and there were two wickets to fall. Silence fell. The gaffers, victims simultaneously of excitement and senility, could hardly raise their pint pots – for it was past 6 o'clock, and the front door of the Three Horseshoes was now as wide open officially as the back door had been unofficially all afternoon.

The Major, his red face redder than ever and his chin sticking out almost as far as the Napoleonic Mr Ogilvy's, bowled a fast half-volley on the leg-stump. The sexton, a man of iron muscle from much digging, hit it fair and square in the middle of the bat, and it flashed like a thunderbolt, waist-high, straight at the youth in the blue jumper. With a shrill scream the youth sprang backwards out of its way and fell over on his back. Immediately behind him, so close were the fieldsmen clustered, stood the mighty Boone. There was no chance of escape for him. Even if he had possessed the figure and the agility to perform back-somersaults, he would have lacked the time. He had been unsighted by the youth in the jumper. The thunderbolt struck him in the midriff like a red-hot cannon-ball upon a Spanish galleon, and with the sound of a drumstick upon an insufficiently stretched drum. With a fearful oath, Boone clapped his hands to his outraged stomach and found that the ball was in the way. He looked at it for a moment in astonishment and then threw it down angrily and started to massage the injured spot while the field rang with applause at the brilliance of the catch.

Donald walked up and shyly added his congratulations. Boone scowled at him.

'I didn't want to catch the bloody thing,' he said sourly, massaging away like mad.

'But it may save the side,' ventured Donald.

'Blast the bloody side,' said Boone.

Donald went back to his place.

The scores were level and there was one wicket to fall. The last man in was the blacksmith, leaning heavily upon the shoulder of the baker, who was going to run for him, and limping as if in great pain. He took guard and looked round savagely. He was clearly still in a great rage.

But the point of such fantasy is not to make fun of the long-lived mythology (why should it be?) which we find in Ian Hay, and in some Ian Carmichael movies (remember also the early (1939) Hitchcock, *The Lady Vanishes?*). *England, Their England* confirms and strengthens that saturating nostalgia which is so important a part of the English popular imagination. Not, of course, that nostalgia need be a swear-word, although it almost always is used disapprovingly. It conveys a uniform tone of pitying disparagement. At once more generally (because without disparagement) and more precisely, we could say that nostalgia is an outcome of an incomplete membership of any social group.* When it is so universally felt and referred to as it is in England, we could go on to wonder whether at the moment it is possible to find a form of social membership in which fulfilment is such as to make nostalgia less a substitute for action and more a small refreshment. At any rate, it is worth noting that cricket is very often a symbol of nostalgia even when the main course of the game itself has gone

* Denys Harding's definition in *Experience with Words* (Chatto, 1963).

in drastically different directions. It is a case where the gap between social myth and actuality is often very wide – a point I shall come back to. The continued popularity of Macdonell's book – a film version of the cricket match was broadcast on BBC 1 in July 1974 – is a measure of that gap, of the need for an image of the timeless, changeless English landscape, for village cricket is the living expression of an unmoving social structure free from the industrialization which brought class war and big sport with it.

I am putting these things into words which cricketing nostalgists would hardly accept – 'class war' 'social structure', and so forth. But that is my argument. Macdonell does not make it possible to think these things; he depends on a view of an unhistorical, impossible past which can then be used to show up the awfulness of the present. Nostalgia is a weapon of defence against an unsatisfactory present. The same is true of Bernard Malamud's novel, *The Natural*, hardly less famous in the USA than Macdonell's novel in this country. *The Natural* is in the tradition of the Wild West's tall tales: the fabulous unknown baseball hitter with a no less fabulous appetite who pulls the joke side up to the top of the league. In the end, he is bought up by the no-good bookie, the no-good lawyer and the no-good pin-up. For all the relentless high writing and wild, cinematic force of the novel, at its heart is the old American cliché: the innocent genius from the backwoods corrupted by the city dudes. There is no team brought to life, nor coach nor journalist. The only structure is made from the crooks who buy and sell games, the good woman wronged, the hypnotizing statistics, and the magic baseball bat – the tired bits and pieces of locker-room analysis.

Put together in this reach-me-down way, a book or a painting or a television programme or, indeed, a conversation, makes everyday life more manageable. Such simplification can do so by fogging up a superimposed perception of the present – as in *England Their England* and its progenitors – or, in what is really the same process, by telling a useful set of lies about the present.

This is what another range of myths do for our imaginations even when they purport to be 'realistic', 'harsh', 'a scorching look at . . .', 'an icy acceptance of a world which too patently exists' and the rest of the blurbwriter's jargon. The 'harshly realistic' novel or film says to us, in effect, 'Life is brutal, crooked, sexy, noisy, amoral. There is nothing you can do about it, but you can find a good deal of fascinated satisfaction in really relishing the brutality, sexiness, etc.' And big sporting events lend themselves to this tasty treatment, as in Hugh Atkinson's, *The Games*,* which mixes up power politics, criminal, greedy administrators, Olympic crowds and killing races all in one savoury 500-page mess. It is the sort of writing which fills the run-of-the-mill Harold Robbins novel; what animates the dead cliché of most of the writing is the thrill of inflicting pain.

* Cassell 1967; Corgi 1968, p. 491. Filmed with Robert Shaw in 1972.

At these points, it moves along the line of the nerve with a crude power.

> When the track bent and the tape waited on the straight opposite the official
> stand, Scott Reynolds straightened and drove for speed. He did not hear the
> great gasp of apprehension. Blind, lost in the effort, running from the agony that
> seared him, Scott Reynolds crashed, face first, into the concrete wall. Above him
> they heard distinctly the breaking of bones, like the snapping of kindling wood.
> He was sprawled on his back in the cinders, one knee slowly flexing to draw the
> quivering leg up to his stomach. Under the fair curled hair the face was a pulped
> mask of jetting blood.

However gripping such a story often is, the book does nothing really to
understand what is going on. The nasty self-immolation with which it ends
is a suitable image of its terms of reference.

Such books can tell local truths, no doubt, and tell them plainly. Brian
Glanville's *The Olympian** is a useful, sensible objection to time-crazy
athletes and their monomaniac coaches. Glanville catches the joylessness
of such competitive running neatly enough. The hero is pitted against 'the
usual African police sergeant with eighteen or nineteen children' who will

> come out on to that track in Tokyo – I can already see it – cool as can be, the way
> these Africans are, quite expressionless, closed in an envelope of calm, and when
> the gun goes, he'll be off like a gazelle. He may not win, but that's how he will be.
> While Ike will be sick and tense, his muscles knotted, full of thoughts of pain
> barriers and sacrifice, lap times whirring in his head like wasps, conscious of
> What's Expected of Him, conscious that he's Running for His Country, beneath
> the Eyes of the World – and all the thousand shabby clichés.
> He *might* still win. I don't believe he will.

The point is well taken. But Glanville cannot break out of the pre-
dictabilities of a broken marriage, charismatic coach, casual liaisons, and
the final crack-up in the big race. A very intelligent reporter, he cannot
imagine and shape the significant structures nor the consciousness possible
to someone who takes sport to have the meanings David Storey finds in it.

These strictures seem to me largely true of the whole pile of sporting
books and films. Dick Francis writes goodish thrillers about horseracing.
Bonecrack† is typical enough and, as they go, holds you well for a train
journey. The ingredients are those of *The Games*, much crisper and more
intelligently and modestly written. But the casserole of crooked organizers,
death on the course, the busy, rowdy, colourful details of the race-
meetings, is familiar enough. The tip to the atmosphere is given in the title:
the grisly and audible vividness of 'Bonecrack' as a word is what makes
Francis's writing alive. He likes and is excited by the buzz and colour of
race-meetings; but his prose only moves with its own energy when people
or horses are badly hurt.

* Secker & Warburg, 1967; Pan, 1968, p. 224.
† Michael Joseph, 1971.

What I am looking for are the images which, within one novel, or across several, blend into a single structure. A scheme, that is, of values carried in the words and phrases, in their cadence also. You might get them on television – the old start to BBC 1's 'Sportsnight', that brilliant sequence of glittering moments from half-a-dozen sports which they used to use, for instance – but the ones in the novels stand still to be looked at. There are two or three images I want to take from two novels, to add to what Storey offers and to use as measures of what sportsmen themselves have actually had to say about their sports.

The first comes from Jim Hunter's novel, *The Flame*.* It is a story specially preoccupied with the simultaneity of events, the sense of the simultaneous movement of a society as time and the globe turn. He puts a horse race at the centre of this teeming movement, the momentary focus of many people upon a single event.

> It's a large crowd, for April and poor weather; the race is a three-thousand pounder, three miles two furlongs, nine good ones to go.

The jockey, Stafford, and the owner, Lord Cort, walk slowly towards the horse, Cort 'with an arm spread around the small shoulders . . .'

> She stands still, ears pricked, forelegs cleanly bandaged, the smooth dark coat silvered with moisture. Stafford listens to the rich man, not grinning now, head stooped slightly, glancing up at moments and nodding; his whip taps the calf of his boot in a fidgeting habit. As other jockeys get mounted, he nods more frequently, edges nearer the horses. At last Pawson gives him a leg-up – Keep with 'em, Mike, you'll be all right – and he tugs his cap down over the crash helmet, flexes his gloves in the reigns, fingers the girths automatically as his mount is led out. Past scanning faces, Stafford eyes them without interest, and on to the course, he nudges the mare into a canter. Under the glistening grass the ground bangs up, through her joints and his own. Ah well, it's money we're bein' paid.

And Hunter moves on to the central agent of the vast connectedness which he presents: the television cameras.

> On the roof of the stand a damp cameraman tilts to chase the horses in his viewfinder. – Ready, two . . . take, two. Tilt up a bit; hold that . . .
> – . . . most of the runners already out on the course, so for a description of the race . . .
> The husbands are called in from the garden.
> – Dad! It's nearly started.
> The spade stuck into the hard soil. Nice to straighten your back.
> – You're not coming in here with those boots on. Come on, you've time to take them off.
> The kids are watching already, cross-legged three feet from the television set, rocking back and forth. That's Mummy's one, and that's mine. Their

---

* Faber, 1966.

grandfather leans forward, his elbows on his knees, rubbing his thin hands together.

In Glasgow wet snow blizzards down the yellow afternoon, the betting shops are crowded and fuggy, the floors wet with dripping coats and umbrellas. The screen flickers indistinctly, thwarted by fluorescent lighting; all the chairs are taken, many stand, clutching pencilled newspapers. Men gabble down telephones, the palm of the other hand pressed flat against the ear to shut out the hubbub. In the big bookmakers, in Glasgow, Aberdeen, Edinburgh, Manchester, Leeds, Birmingham, London, batteries of clerks sit in shirt-sleeves, holding their telephones like violins between jawbone and collarbone, scribbling thousands of figures. One of Britain's biggest industries, and this is peak hour. This afternoon there are three race-meetings, and seven divisions of Pools football, plus F.A. Cup Semi-Finals . . .

. . . The wire stretched across the course is lowered; the starter, in bowler and jodhpurs, moves to the rail, and the men and horses walk watchfully up, to choose their places.

– Won't be in your way, Mike?

– You bloody try it.

The wire rips up, the horses are kicked almost casually into action . . .

. . . On the far side of the course the race goes on privately shut in by mist. Three plain fences and an open ditch. Two men hired to repair the fences watch from a temporary hut; otherwise nobody. A jockey shouts across to the man riding alongside. In the grandstand and enclosures people wait impatiently for the first colours to emerge.

The betting-shops are quieter. The television camera just picks out galloping wraiths. Grey against lighter grey. They all rise at a fence and drop fluidly again. The commentator is silent.

– There they are.

Lord Cort lifts his race-glasses, drops them again almost at once. This is only the first time round.

Stafford's mare almost kneels on landing, tips him forward, his mouth is full of horsehair but he keeps the stirrups, wriggles back, boots her up to catch the leaders again.

The first minutes of hundreds of professional football matches. At some grounds the floodlights are on early, a white ball; and the fourfold brightness pouring down from a giant height on to the mist makes almost a mystery of the swift movements . . . like a ceremony, with indistinct ranged masses of ardent watchers, on every side. They roar, rumble, chatter, roar again. In the streets outside people look at each other, and work out the events.

Going into the last Lord Cort's horse is upsides with the leader. A faint hesitation in the mare's stride, a hint of refusal, draws a grisly yell from Stafford,

– Geeeeerrrup!

and she rises just in time, brushes the clipped birch, and lands full of running. In five strides the other horse is past and beaten, and Stafford tucks the whip away under the ball of his thumb and rides her home with his hands. (pp. 66–9).

The writer's attention, and ours with him, moves easily from the race, to the camera eye and the huge electronic web which it concentrates, and then out, out into the millions of people with their varying interest, now intense, now casual, caught for a few minutes by the trivial event, the horses, fleet and silent in the dim rain. Flowing down the lines of busy communication with the electrons, less physically there but energizing that intricate technology, goes the cash.

It is a stirring image, one made possible no doubt by television, or at least by modern communication systems. Men give their lives to this complicated mutual interdependence, and yet so many of the images of our lives which we cherish deny the links, or see them as chipping away at our precious selves and freedoms. Hunter has spotted that sport on Saturdays, wet, murky, late winter Saturdays, is a better occasion than most for registering this strong surge of life of the times, pushing unrepentantly on. He notes the details as they come along, without having to moralize about them: the racehorse peer, the bookies, the families in front of the telly, the great crowds and the wet streets, as well as the race and the football matches themselves. And in the end they come together quite without dewy writing or throbs in the voice, to make a single, solid image of lives, for that time, worth living.

It is another version of the relations David Storey gets clear in *This Sporting Life* between the sport and the people, and between the sport and power. In what is a much more famous novel, though still a remarkably quiet and modest one, Ernest Hemingway catches and, in his turn and accents, celebrates the individual side of things. He gives us a lovely image of a depth of affection expressed in the manly joking of two friends out fishing, and he gives us just as powerfully a picture of the professional sportsman at just the moment at which he becomes an artist. The novel is Hemingway's *The Sun Also Rises*,* and about halfway through, Jake Barnes, the hero, and his friend Bill Gorton go on a fishing holiday in the Spanish Basque mountains above Burghete.

> I got my rod that was leaning against the tree, took the bait-can and landing-net, and walked out on to the dam. It was built to provide a head of water for driving logs. The gate was up, and I sat on one of the squared timbers and watched the smooth apron of water before the river tumbled into the falls. In the white water at the foot of the dam it was deep. As I baited up, a trout shot up out of the white water into the falls and was carried down. Before I could finish baiting, another trout jumped at the falls, making the same lovely arc and disappearing into the water that was thundering down. I put on a good-sized

---

* First published in 1927 by Cape. It is also published under the title *Fiesta* but under the first title, Hemingway sets this epigraph from *Ecclesiastes*:
> One generation passeth away, and another generation cometh; but the earth abideth forever . . . The sun also ariseth, and the sun goeth down, and hasteth to the place where he arose . . . The wind goeth toward the south, and turneth about unto the north; it whirleth about continually, and the wind returneth again according to his circuits . . . All the rivers run into the sea; yet the sea is not full; unto the place from whence the rivers come, thither they return again.

sinker and dropped into the white water close to the edge of the timbers of the dam.

I did not feel the first trout strike. When I started to pull up I felt that I had one and brought him, fighting and bending the rod almost double, out of the boiling water at the foot of the falls, and swung him up and on to the dam. He was a good trout, and I banged his head against the timber so that he quivered out straight, and then slipped him into my bag.

While I had him on, several trout had jumped at the falls. As soon as I baited up and dropped in again I hooked another and brought him in the same way. In a little while I had six. They were all about the same size. I laid them out, side by side, all their heads pointing the same way, and looked at them. They were beautifully coloured and firm and hard from the cold water. It was a hot day, so I slit them all and shucked out the insides, gills and all, and tossed them over across the river. I took the trout ashore, washed them in the cold smoothly heavy water above the dam, and then picked some ferns and packed them all in the bag, three trout on a layer of ferns, then another layer of ferns, then three more trout, and then covered them with ferns.

They looked nice in the ferns, and now the bag was bulky, and I put it in the shade of the tree.

It is a lovely piece of writing, but of course it is not something you could simply lift out and lay in an anthology. The lightness and delicacy of such writing, Hemingway's famously hard-won style, is of a piece with the whole book, and Barnes's open level candour – so much the moral stance which Hemingway aspired to – while it responds with special gladness to the fishing holiday, is consistent right through the book. Hemingway's intention, sometimes mannered and overwrought, was always to give plain, solid, conversational words their due weight and currency; here it comes off perfectly. He *sees* the beauty of the sport – the arc of the fish, their colours – but the pleasure is the product of very much more than a series of beautiful pictures or of keen, sensuous moments: the cold water, the hot sun. The pleasure, as in all sports, is produced by the perfect coming together of all the components of the game. Hemingway's beauty of organization is present in the readiness to use phrases taken straight from a rather trite letter home, 'They looked nice in the ferns', 'He was a good trout', and to make them tell, to lean on them until they mean what they mean in everyday life. He also is able to make the same simplicity of phrasing vivid and exact in the presentation of physical detail. Finally, he completes the pleasure of the whole experience with the wine, the picnic, and the knockabout conversation in which two men friends typically express deep affection for each other, happiness, and pleasure in what they are doing. (It is odd that the deep happiness of male friendships – and women's too, for all I know – is so rare an occasion for explicit rejoicing. Is it really harder now to have and keep close friends?) It is perhaps worth pointing out* that pleasure in this rich, real sense is not sufficiently

* In the company of Alasdair MacIntyre, 'Pleasure as a reason for action' in *Against the Self-images of the Age* (Duckworth, 1971).

emphasized as a reason for doing something, especially in sport, and that indeed to say you play a game because it gives you pleasure can sometimes be frowned on. Glanville's Olympic runner gets no pleasure from running. Of course, there are times when although it would be quite easy to do something pleasurable – we have the money, say, and plenty of leisure – we still do something else. Well, there are many values and pleasure is only one of them, and in any case the word 'pleasure' may be used in very different ways. You may fish because it will give you pleasure; or you may fish for a living, but find your job pleasurable; and you may sometimes enjoy fishing (as the men do in Hemingway's novel) and, because you feel ill or are worried, you sometimes may not. But sport for people who do not practise it for a living is largely a distinct object of pursuit for the sake of the pleasure it provides, even though all kinds of other values must come into it (a question which returns sharply when I come on to mountaineering).

What is so impressive about this whole chapter in Hemingway's novel is the easy, unpushing way in which the pleasure in all these strong and good ways is allowed to come through. The delight in talking nonsense is both expression and cause of pleasure. It is part of the way the whole experience comes together.

'How big are they really?'
'They're all about the size of your smallest.'
'You're not holding out on me?'
'I wish I were.'
'Get them all on worms?'
'Yes.'
'You lazy bum!'
Bill put the trout in the bag and started for the river, swinging the open bag. He was wet from waist down and I knew he must have been wading in the stream.

I walked up the road and got out the two bottles of wine. They were cold. Moisture beaded on the bottles as I walked back to the trees. I spread the lunch on a newspaper, and uncorked one of the bottles and leaned the other against a tree. Bill came up drying his hands, his bag plump with ferns.

'Let's see that bottle,' he said. He pulled the cork and tipped up the bottle and drank. 'Whew! That makes my eyes ache.'
'Let's try it.'
The wine was icy cold and tasted faintly rusty.
'That's not such filthy wine,' Bill said.
'The cold helps it,' I said.
We unwrapped the little parcels of lunch.
'Chicken.'
'There's hard-boiled eggs.'
'Find any salt?'
'First the egg,' said Bill. 'Then the chicken. Even Bryan could see that.'
'He's dead. I read it in the paper yesterday.'
'No. Not really?'
'Yes. Bryan's dead.'

Bill laid down the egg he was peeling.

'Gentlemen,' he said, and unwrapped a drumstick from a piece of newspaper. 'I reverse the order. For Bryan's sake. As a tribute to the Great Commoner. First the chicken; then the egg.'

'Wonder what day God created the chicken?'

'Oh,' said Bill, sucking the drumstick, 'How should we know? We should not question. Our stay on earth is not for long. Let us rejoice and believe and give thanks.'

'Eat an egg.'

Bill gestured with the drumstick in one hand and the bottle of wine in the other.

It's a bit heavy footed to take to pieces the satisfaction which is so richly there in these pages. Perhaps it is enough in the way of justification to say that we do not always recognize the pleasures we *can* have, and this fishing holiday of Hemingway's is, in its way, an image of possibility. If we can't imitate that, what *can* we expect?

The other possibility which Hemingway offers is the bull-fight,* and here he is much more liable to tell lies by mystification, and by a good deal of nudging and winking and I-know-what's-what in the margins of what he actually says. But then bull-fighting is a mystifying business: really dangerous, and in its ritual, its anachronisms and courtesies, its brocaded early baroque dress, more profoundly linked to Spanish Catholicism than it is linked to other sports. What there is to say about it is difficult, although no harder than what there is to say, for example, about ballet to someone outside the group of people who understand it.

The leading *matador* in the novel is Pedro Romero, a beautiful boy of nineteen, idealized slightly by Hemingway in order to make him a perfect gentleman-athlete (but a professional, to be sure). He is natural, dignified, has beautiful manners, and is very, very good. After a fist fight between Romero and the man in the story who is jealous of his irresistible success with the beautiful philandering heroine, Romero puts on his most ravishing show. Or, better, he fights at his beautiful best. Hemingway contrasts Romero with an old, once great but now cautious, damaged fighter for whom, 'when he felt the greatness again coming, just a little of it through the pain that was always with him, it had been discounted and sold in advance, and it did not give him the good feeling. It was the greatness, but it did not make bull-fighting wonderful to him any more.' Hemingway's own ethic comes callously near one of the main brutalities and facts of sport. When you are too old, you are no longer any good.

The usurper, as usurpers will, captures the lady, the crowd, and the glory. After Belmonte's yellow face, 'wolf jawed smile and contemptuous eyes', the calm and beauty of the young genius.

* Hemingway has written a famous study of bull-fighting called *Death in the Afternoon* (Cape, 1932) in which he takes further much of the analysis in *The Sun Also Rises*.

Pedro Romero had the greatness. He loved bull-fighting, and I think he loved the bulls, and I think he loved Brett. Everything of which he could control the locality he did in front of her all that afternoon. Never once did he look up. He made it stronger that way, and did it for himself, too, as well as for her. Because he did not look up to ask if it pleased he did it all for himself inside, and it strengthened him, and yet he did it for her, too. But he did not do it for her at any loss to himself. He gained by it all through the afternoon . . .

When he had finished his work with the muleta and was ready to kill, the crowd made him go on. They did not want the bull killed yet, they did not want it to be over. Romero went on. It was like a course in bull-fighting. All the passes he linked up, all completed, all slow, templed and smooth. There were no tricks and no mystifications. There was no brusqueness. And each pass as it reached the summit gave you a sudden ache inside. The crowd did not want it ever to be finished.

The bull was squared on all four feet to be killed, and Romero killed directly below us. He killed not as he had been forced to by the last bull, but as he wanted to. He profiled directly in front of the bull, drew the sword out of the folds of the muleta and sighted along the blade. The bull watched him, Romero spoke to the bull and tapped one of his feet. The bull charged and Romero waited for the charge, the muleta held low, sighting along the blade, his feet firm. Then without taking a step forward, he became one with the bull, the sword was in high between the shoulders, the bull had followed the low-swung flannel, that disappeared as Romero lurched clear to the left, and it was over. The bull tried to go forward, its legs commenced to settle, he swung from side to side, hesitated, then went down on his knees, as Romero's older brother leaned forward behind him and drove a short knife into the bull's neck at the base of the horns. The first time he missed. He drove the knife in again, and the bull went over, twitching and rigid. Romero's brother, holding the bull's horn in one hand, the knife in the other, looked up at the President's box. Handkerchiefs were waving all over the bull-ring. The President looked down from the box and waved his handkerchief. The brother cut the notched black ear from the dead bull and trotted over with it to Romero. The bull lay heavy and black on the sand, his tongue out. Boys were running toward him from all points of the arena, making a little circle around him. They were starting to dance around the bull.

It is, again, beautiful writing, but then Hemingway could be immensely good on such subjects, and I have quoted at such length because the finesse and graceful rhythms of the writing do for the occasion all we could ask. The writing is both leisurely and very intense; it presents us with the beauty of the sport, and the beauty, the accomplishment is such that we do not need to ask what the 'point' of bull-fighting is any more than we need ask the point of a tennis match. The sport is 'good-for-nothing' so to speak, because it is itself, utter, absorbing, ceremonious. To make another important distinction, it is not useful, it is creative. The possibilities it creates are a produce of the specific conditions of the sport and the society. *Corrida de tores* which, as Hemingway points out, does not translate as bull-fighting, is sunk deep in a tragic view of life which is the produce of Spanish history. I do not know a lot about Spanish culture, but I would guess that the abandon of the fiesta balances the normal social life of a people who are contained, proud, undemonstrative and suspicious, especially in their masculine relations.* Similarly, English football, one of the most powerful invisible exports we have ever made, is rooted in the concrete, historical conditions of the late nineteenth century and its industrial cities. It began in the English private schools and moved, for complicated reasons – among them the presumption that football would keep the masses quieter and break up the mobs who ripped out Hyde Park railings one wet weekend – deep, deep into the culture of the working class. Bull-fighting and football are both products of and responses to the history and technology of their time. They are shaped by social conditions; they in turn shape them.

* Compare with what Clifford Geertz says above about the Balinese cockfight, pp. 71–2.

7   Gentlemen, players and stars

THOSE SOCIAL and political bearings are worth emphasizing in a chapter which takes the voices of individual sportsmen and places them in their social totality. My comments simply link what they say.

Social life and culture are not after all (as Marxists would say) the inevitable reflection (or superstructure) of economic relations; but nor are they (as we most of us have learned to think in the traditions of this country) the spontaneous expression of the ideas of individuals, millions of them, who added all together make up a society. That is the old liberal's answer. People count. So all you need count are people. But the idea of totality is a critical weapon against either view of social life and culture. And then the effort to think in terms of totality is an effort to change the frame of your mind: to see analysis in terms of structures and not individual insights. There are always discoverable and regular ways of thinking: the ways we call 'commonsense'. (Get outside them and they may look decidedly uncommon, and distinctly partial to very many fewer people than the commonalty). Then there are the other, always possible, potential and *irregular* ways of thinking, which recognize and brace themselves *against* the underlying and formative modes of 'commonsense'.

This is the pulse of the creative tension. Never, of course, a tension between fixed points like the poles of an electric current, but a tension between mobile points, between (as I put it earlier) culture and being; or, to begin again, between form and content, actuality and possibility, rules and interpretations, chaos and identity, between radical and conservative.

> And I shall say: 'games' form a family . . . Here the term 'language-*game*' is meant to bring into prominence the fact that the *speaking* of language is part of an activity, or of a form of life . . . Instead of producing something common to all that we call language, I am saying that these phenomena have no one thing in common which makes us use the same word for all – but that they are *related* to one another in many different ways. And it is because of this relationship, or these relationships, that we call them all 'Language'.*

* From L. L. Wittgenstein, *Philosophical Investigations*, I, trans. G. E. M. Anscombe (Blackwell, 1953), paras 23, 65, 67. Compare with what I quoted, on page 68.

There could hardly be provided, as I said in Chapter 3, anything so general as a theory of games. What it should be possible to provide is precisely what this book intends: the description of the processes of learning, imagination, creation, performance, within individuals and within sports. Thence we can see the infinitely varied transformations which the individuals can create out of the forms and their contents which are to hand. And for all that the individuals each do their own creating, they do it within a given history, a particular and concrete social context which is evident in the arc of their gestures, their dress, their tones of voice, their minds and their carriage.

This is the relevance of my digression about language and its forms of life. You could say that in language you have the *type* of all creative experience. The many forms of language are related to one another. They are not simply and anatomically one thing. Having insisted that language-games and ordinary games have many purposes, we can say that they are alike in their creations. Games, like languages, have rules; their grammar holds certain meanings continually. In this sense, they are conservative because they conserve meaning. They also permit continuous and radical innovation and transformation within the permission of those meanings. Languages and games constantly and spontaneously create novelty.

Sport, in a noble phrase, expresses 'the inevitable creativeness of ordinary everyday life'. At its greatest moments, like a linguistic creation, a stage of a game dramatizes the constituting elements of real social life and beliefs* in such a way as both to present them and to change them – to experience them differently, to make people understand them differently. Thus, Hemingway's bull-fighter or David Storey's rugby footballer *in the way they play* make us see the world differently. In real life, so too do the great games and players. Brigadier Gerard's last race, Brazil's 1–0 victory over England in the 1970 World Cup, the Barbarians' victory tries over the All Blacks at Twickenham in 1973, Ann Packer's gold medal in 1964, Gwen Moffat climbing, Virginia Wade almost anytime: we each of us have our own rollcall of the games and the players which signify the transformation I am trying to catch and fix. Because this is a book and not a series of films, the transformations must be found in what sportspeople say and how they speak of what they have done, rather than in the doing itself.

I do not want to take my main examples of the process from football, which is the readiest instance but which can come to dominate rather too much the view of what sport is and does. I shall spend more time on mountaineering. But just because of its omnipresence football provides a useful, brief introduction, and cricket an even briefer support.

Football, after all, very visibly embodies *and* makes possible a response to 'the constituting elements of real social life and beliefs', as I put it earlier. It

---

* I am drawing here on Raymond Williams in 'Literature and sociology', *New Left Review* 67 (1971).

presents them and experiences them differently. Derek Dougan, now chairman of the Professional Footballers' Association and an intellectual of the game, puts it like this:

> Satisfaction for me in the game is intuitive, the thrill of the sport combined with show business. It's an art and a craft, combining commercial exploitation. I believe it should wear its sales tag proudly. We have a product to sell and should go out and sell it the best way we can.*

There you have the mixture I am talking about, and you have it in Dougan's position in the game and the PFA as well as in what he says. I suggested in Chapters 3 and 4 that popular culture is marked by its contrary pulls in two directions: towards the manipulation and towards the expression, of real feelings and ideas. One imagines that this contradiction is what Dougan means when he says that football is 'an art and a craft combining commercial exploitation'. In a commercial culture in which, for instance, the natural, self-explanatory focus of political discussion is economics, he can say with this rather flat defiance, that 'it should wear its sales tag proudly', because these are the terms in which men expect to justify what they do. Yet professional football is notoriously *not* a purchasable commodity – the clubs pay no dividend and the game, in an economic sense, is strictly non-productive. So we have in what Dougan says that combination of expression and response which typifies creative activity. In football itself, the patterns and relations of players on the field similarly move from creative expression to that exploitative, narrowly calculating deception of the spectator in the interests of publicity which is manipulation and which poisons so much of our social life. It is what Hemingway speaks of when he disdains bull-fighters who 'twisted themselves like corkscrews, their elbows raised, and leaned against the flanks of the bull after his horns had passed, to give a faked look of danger. Afterward, all that was faked turned bad and gave an unpleasant feeling . . . ' This fakery is as well developed in football as in many forms of culture: it is the hallmark of the publicity image.

Such images provide much of the intellectual and imaginative life of very many people. They are always there at the corner of your eye and at the corner of a moment – a moment on TV or a moment in the street. The publicity image promises glamour; the typical figure of such an image, whether in an advertisement or on a football field, is glamorous and therefore to be viewed with envy ('I wish that was me') or admiration ('I could never be like that'). Publicity is the manufacture of glamour, and the entertainment industry is a main factory for the product. When sports, as they often do, give way to its pull, they are no longer playing, as we say, 'for the sake of the game'. The effects are aimed at for the sake of glamour, that

---

* Letter to the author, October 1973.

is, for the sake of appearing enviable: masterful, handsome, tanned, flourishing. (Which may partly explain why so many football teams play in all-white strip.) The gestures of publicity draw on and enhance the ordinary gestures of emotion as well as the movements which are not gestures at all, but are practical. But in the same way as television tends to make sport into a ballet (noiseless, bloodless, *controllable*), publicity makes natural sporting action into a fake. And since sporting heroes have become unusually self-conscious under the cameras of the public media, they are understandably liable to court envy and admiration by playing for glamour rather than just playing.

This pull is there in all the big spectator sports. It is not, as so much else in this book insists, all there is. Nor am I saying that histrionics is in itself a fake.* The public nature of spectator sport means that all gesture is heightened to an abnormally demonstrative extent. Joy, anger, anguish, all express themselves intensely and vividly when these emotions are shared on your behalf by thousands of watchers. But I do not want to fall into the different narrowness of mind which says that any sense of the beliefs and facts of a society which transpire in sport poisons the true nature of the sport. Sport is social – is political, if you like, of its nature. When Dougan speaks in his autobiography of what football has done for him, who was brought up in the working-class streets of Belfast, he is rightly proud (not, shall we say, 'grateful'):

> Since the end of the war many different nationalities have come into Britain and people with roots in many far-off places have become British subjects. As a result of all this the Irish have been up-graded. They are as a group no longer at the bottom of the immigrant pile. But I don't think that they are all that far away from the lowest rung of the ladder. They say truthfully that the Irish have long memories. I wouldn't be all that certain that the English are as good as they think they are at forgetting old prejudices.
>
> It is odd. Since I have established myself in the sporting world I am allowed some privileges.
>
> I have been very lucky in being a professional footballer. It has been a sort of passport for me, and through playing football fairly well I have come to be accepted in many places which otherwise might not have been so welcoming. Football opens many doors for me and takes me across many frontiers. Sometimes I think of all the Irish who don't have this kind of opportunity. I am immensely grateful of course, but I reflect with some irony on the situation. I am removed from the class distinction argument. I also have the impression that I am no longer regarded as a real Irishman. I am the footballer, the one who brought out that book, the one who is always on television, the Chairman of the Professional Footballers' Association. As a sportsman I – like others – am given

* cf Danny Blanchflower's remark that 'The great fallacy is that the game is first and last about winning. It's nothing of the kind. The game is about glory. It's about doing things in style, with a flourish, about going out and beating the other lot, not waiting for them to die of boredom.'

special priority and, as I say, am apart from the class business. I don't think this is very fair to the great majority of people. *

It isn't hard to link this voice to David Storey's hero in *This Sporting Life*, and that confidence and determination are there to see in the shape and line of the game played by men who have earned, earned hard and personally, that tone of voice. Dougan knows better than most – an Ulsterman who is not an Orangeman, nor a Catholic – the relation of football, his football, to the whole society and its structures of power. He knows also just how expensive this discovery is; he pays the cost of living.

> Football is a wonderful activity for allowing freedom of expression. When that is not possible, the game becomes meaningless. It is a great pleasure to 'play it off the cuff'. But one needs a new kind of discipline here . . .
> You don't have this when you are fifteen, whatever else you may have. Nor at twenty-five. You are lucky to find the right blend of qualities when you are thirty. For me it is a matter of sadness that, while I have got as far as I can get in joining together the qualities that make for fulfilment, I am past thirty. Time for me has almost run out. When a player has got to this point – if he has stayed the course that long – he faces a dilemma. A sportsman whose livelihood is sport has this great frustration. Although life has perhaps been good to him (maybe for five years) it has to come to an end. The crux of the matter for him is that life begins at thirty.

Dougan's testimony is important in particular as it throws light on the position of sporting heroes and their membership of the 'star élite'. I have constantly spoken of the creative potentiality of sport, and of the occasions it gives for the imagining of what is unprecedented within the frame of what is conventional. It permits speculation about the impossible. But this process tends to work in a specific way. †

We live, after all in a stable society whose positions are clearly marked out. People's work and functions in that society are strongly inter-dependent – we all count on one another to perform our tasks well as plumber, doctor, fitter, policewoman, housewife, footballer – and we keep just as clear our sense of differentiation between these roles and their duties. As a result, the way each one may prompt us to think about our lives is specific to what he or she does for us. We do not, that is, generalize the influence of what a person says to us, except within the limits of his power and our expectations about that power. We treat on different terms what a car-salesman and what a director of British Leyland might say to us (this because of their relative power, at least until we know them personally). And this would be true whether they were telling us about cars or about

* Derek Dougan, *The Sash He Never Wore* (Allison & Busby, 1972), p. 25.
† In the explanation which follows, I am drawing on and modifying a paper by Francesco Alberoni, 'L'élite irresponsable', reprinted from *Ikon* (1962) in D. McQuail ed., *The Sociology of Mass Communications* (Penguin, 1972).

politics, although – conscious of people's specialized knowledge – we would quite rightly be more believing when they talked about brakedrums than about inflation.

Everybody carries round with him a picture of how all these social functions interrelate. Mostly, we would be on the losing side in this conversation.

> What is he?
> – A man, of course.
> Yes, but what does he do?
> – He lives and is a man.
> Oh quite! but he must work. He must have a job of some sort.
> – Why?
> Because obviously he's not one of the leisured classes.
> – I don't know. He has lots of leisure. And he makes quite beautiful chairs. –
> There you are then! He's a cabinet maker.
> – No no!
> Anyhow a carpenter and joiner.
> – Not at all.
> But you said so.
> – What did I say?
> That he made chairs, and was a joiner and carpenter.
> – I said he made chairs, but I did not say he was a carpenter.
> All right then, he's just an amateur.
> – Perhaps! Would you say a thrush was a professional flautist, or just an amateur? –
> I'd say it was just a bird.
> – And I say he is just a man.
> All right! You always did quibble.*

People are, we think, what they do, unless we know them well. There are, however, two groups who are judged on other scales; they are the holders of political power, and the stars of sport and entertainment. The politicians are judged for how they directly affect main public and private institutions; the stars are judged in a wider, looser context, not as changing the world but as individual models for living. They are not so much a group, as they are – one at a time – symbols of success, of approved *or* disapproved ways of living, of possibility. As we live day-by-day the process described in Chapter 5, we respond to the presentation of the stars through public communication systems and their public performance as subjects of comparison and aspiration whose way of life and morality exert wide and deep influence. If they are people of force and complexity, then their *presence*, the strong charge of themselves which is released in any encounter, can push out and affect areas of social life which are not special to their faculties and skills. One may think of examples of this process in men such as the mountaineer-explorer Lord John Hunt, the footballer Pele in Brazil,

* D. H. Lawrence, 'What Is He?', *Collected Poems*, Vol. II (Heinemann, 1965).

Keino and Jipko in Africa, as well as Zatopek and Muhammed Ali who have already been mentioned in this connexion. Obviously the lead such stars may take – the 'generalization of their charisma' as one might put it technically – will be larger in countries where social roles are less specific and thoroughly rooted than in Europe or the USA. What happens in Britain is that the generalizing process by which people use the stars as models for living is opposed at the same time by people's sense of what an individual star is good at. The star's more public expression then moves into socially permitted areas such as charity work or alternatively is significant in a general form only for young people.

This account of how people refer to and judge their sporting heroes may help put in context some of the things that men like Dougan or Jack Charlton say. They are both intelligent and forceful men. They both understand clearly many of the hopes and promises of life which they make actual for their admirers, Dougan for the Ulster back streets, Charlton for the less bloody but no less depressed streets of Durham county. Charlton says,*

> I like to think I've transcended class. I can talk to Harold Wilson and I can talk to a man who pushes coal tubs for a living. I vote Labour of course. My family always did, but that's not the reason either, but because I think they'll do the right thing for the people who need it. My people. And there's too much class in England. I don't mean we think about it too much, I mean class, what class you're in, means too bloody much. If you're rich, you get power. So there's a lot of snobbery in football, some clubs there's players' wives and directors' wives, nothing to do with each other. We get over that here. I get three tickets for doctors, and three tickets for working lads and they sit in directors' boxes with me.

Jack Charlton, as all the world knows, is a very big, lanky man and he speaks with the energy and force of a man whose intelligence takes the edge off his jovial aggressiveness and makes it into a strenuous self-confidence instead. The north-of-Wearside accent with the long, lilted 'a', is strong but perfectly clear, and he speaks straight at you, with a bold, candid stare and the long curve of his grin.

> Me family were all footballers. You played for your street, your area, your school. And they're all mining towns, so there was no question of where you went on a Saturday. Always St. James's Park, the odd time Roker Park when Newcastle were away.'

Pulling away from that close, preoccupied life, Charlton knows what place he now occupies.

> You become a sort of international hero. They keep coming to have a look at you if you go out for a meal. Peek round the corner, you never get any peace. People think they have a right to ask you to do things, to come over to their table.

* In a long conversation with the author, January 1974.

You can't resent it, lad, because I've tried! Then you'll have caused more trouble than it's worth. You have to work very hard anyway to be liked, and I like to be liked. Everybody does, but when you play for a team like Leeds or when you're a manager like I am at Middlesbrough and doing as well as we are, well it's important, being liked. You *are* important. There's a lot of pride in an area like this – I *know* the North-East, me, why, I know it. There's a lot of pride in the football club, it belongs to *you*. There's all the influence of its success, the joy it brings, and what it does for the economics of the town can't be measured. ICI and BSC don't have half the trouble now we're at the top. Same in Sunderland last year when we were winning the cup. The drop in absenteeisms on Mondays, everyone's noticed it.

Charlton and Dougan – men of this stature can place their sporting lives solidly in the real world. They know as the grain of their experience the contrary pulls of real football and publicity football. They know that they play both, that it is of the nature of the work they do and of the place of entertainment in society. Charlton said, 'I remember against Southampton once we turned on all the tricks, backheels, flip-ups, the lot, but only when the result was dead sure. What I really admire, now, is players doing the game they've always wanted to do. A man like Geoff Boycott, now there it is. Or our kid [brother Bobby Charlton]. I was good, but he's a genius.' Tony Lewis, captain of the English Test team in India and Pakistan in 1973 said the same sort of thing.*

When I was a kid well, like you, I was caught up in all the postwar excitement about cricket. Miller and Lindwall and the great Australians in 1948, and Len Hutton and Denis Compton as our great heroes. Then of course Glamorgan won the championship in 1948 as well [Lewis was Glamorgan's captain for several years]. I remember when I was nearly 18, I was asked at the same time to play the fiddle in the Welsh National Youth Orchestra and to play for Glamorgan. It wasn't easy. I chose Glamorgan, as you know.

But then I was coming into county cricket in the early sixties and the grounds were empty. You felt you were going into a dying game, and that it didn't matter whether you made runs or not. What a transformation though! Now you get 30,000 spectators at a match and the small boys asking for autographs, and it all looks like my own childhood memories of 1948, rosy spectacles and all!

But you see there have been losses. We've had to package cricket up all shiny. It's changed enormously. Now it really is part of the entertainment industry. One-day cricket, well, it's a piece of showbusiness (I'm not saying I don't enjoy it). Three-day cricket is like a symphony. It has slow movements, it swells. You have the time, say, as a bowler to make very gradual adjustments in your bowling, and just move the umpteenth delivery out a bit further, and get your catch in the slips. One-day cricket isn't remotely like that. You can't *build* the match. But it's certainly brought back the crowds. You're much more visible as a player, they tell you that they've seen you mutter under your breath while at the wicket . . ., and it's certainly brought me my future career, television, broadcasting, journalism . . .

* Conversations with the author, 1973–74.

Maybe the game is work now. I want to make runs and I don't worry too much about how I make them, so long as they come. Aesthetics isn't so important as grafting away at a good innings. When I hear the 50 go up, that's what matters to me . . .

This, again, is what it is like to live where the pulls are strongest: the tension between player and entertainer. Lewis, again, knows what he owes to sport, and what success it has made possible. He knows, too, pretty well what the status of celebrity is worth, and how its influence spreads easily into the media which in part created it; but not much further.

Such, then, are some of the ways in which a few men experience their own sporting lives in the larger totality of social relations. These are, very roughly, the contours of consciousness and of commonsense for celebrated public sportsmen. What happens, however, if you remove that awareness of the outer structure of society (it is still there, of course), and attend only to the sportsmen in action? You still find that their actions express their social lives and beliefs and feelings, but you may also find that in what they *do*, their frame of reference is larger, rounder, more rich and exhilarating than in the more glamorous but duller world of publicity and entertainment.

Take mountaineering. As a sport, it connects much less visibly with the society round it. It appears to be much more individualist than most spectator sports (though in reality it rests precisely upon very developed teamwork and collaboration). It is more obviously lonely. No one makes a fortune by climbing mountains. What is more, it is a sport (rather than a game) the pleasure of doing which is tangled with values central to human life in much more pressing ways than with other sports. You must collaborate with your climbing partners in the right ways, or you'll all fall and kill yourselves. Or *you* might not, but someone else (it is not necessarily a matter of self-interest, that is). The activity embodies values such as courage, endurance, self-sacrifice, co-operation, generosity, collectedness. No doubt, one could make a similar list for many sports, but quite without the urgency of these values when you are well up the side of Cloggwyn d'ur Arddu. More tellingly, one could object that for 'endurance' you could read 'masochism', or for 'courage', 'pride'. Well, the low view of human nature is always visible from the top of the mountain. George Mallory, the great Alpine climber whose death somewhere on or near the summit of Everest in 1924 is one of the great national as well as sporting legends. acknowledged from the honesty that made him a good and beautiful man, this other view:

The desire to climb mountains is commonly held among laymen to be an incomprehensible psychological freak. One explanation, nevertheless, is commonly given – that we climb to win admiration. No mountaineer will accept that. And yet, when he remembers that this explanation is freely offered, he may forget that the admiration is not completely withheld. Or, in mere indignation at its inadequacy, he may neglect the suggestion altogether. It is incomplete, of course; but it is probably true to say of most mountaineers, as one among several reasons, that they climb to win admiration . . .

The feeling which we recognize in friends, as well as enemies, however modestly they disguise it, seems to be so deeply seated in the human breast that we can neither pass it by nor condemn it. There can be very few men capable of performing heroic deeds without some desire of being proclaimed a hero.*

Mallory himself provides a good case-study of the mountaineer and his meaning, both to himself and to other people. He wrote of climbing as a dance, 'for the climber responds to the mountains as a dancer responds to music'. He praised the few arts which express themselves in the play of the body, 'the poise of a man's head, the manner in which the legs support his weight, and the notion of an uplifted arm or of a hand stretched out'.

Turn to the photograph of Joe Brown, and the perfect poise, the unforgettable combination of grace, precision, and wiry strength is there to see and admire. Only it is not just a matter of admiring, but of living and doing. As Mallory's biographer puts it, 'If you were George Mallory, you went on climbing . . . you saw again the beauty of the hills, and felt again the joy of moving skilfully and gracefully in high places as one of a party all splendidly fit and climbing in perfect harmony.'

The climbing is not just an occasion for having beautiful feelings, any more than playing a Mozart string quartet is. Climbing and playing the quartet delicately articulate judgement and movement and intuition. Thought and action attain their rhythm and their completion. The mountaineer gets to the top, and to do so, in so far as the climb is difficult and he is a good climber, he takes the risks which move him clear out of the realm of what is commonly thought, the limits of ordinary consciousness and activity, of commonsense. A climber like Mallory takes risks in order to do what has never been done before (or what *he* has never done before). That is the most straightforward and understandable reason for climbing either Everest, or simply a new, impossible route up Stanedge Rock above the picnickers from Sheffield.

Climbers themselves are relentlessly down-to-earth in their contemporary styles – as witness the nickname 'Cloggy' for Joe Brown's rockface. They deny that they ever do take risks, and insist that their sport is far safer than motorway driving, provided you know what you are doing. These protests combine modesty, showmanship, sedative and superstition. As I say, the point of climbing, as of so much sport, is to go beyond what you did before; either to do something better or faster or first. Roger Bannister says the same, in his first-rate autobiography, of the first four-minute mile: †

---

* Unpublished fragment, quoted in David Robertson, *George Mallory* (Faber, 1969).
† R. Bannister, *First Four Minutes* (Putnam, 1958), p. 121.

The stop watches held the answer. The announcement came – 'Result of one mile . . . time, 3 minutes' – the rest lost in the roar of excitement. I grabbed Brasher and Chataway, and together we scampered round the track in a burst of spontaneous joy. We had done it – the three of us!

We shared a place where no man had yet ventured – secure for all time, however fast men might run miles in future. We had done it where we wanted, when we wanted, how we wanted, in our first attempt of the year. In the wonderful joy my pain was forgotten and I wanted to prolong those precious moments of realisation.

I felt suddenly and gloriously free of the burden of athletic ambition that I had been carrying for years. No words could be invented for such supreme happiness, eclipsing all other feelings. I thought at that moment I could never again reach such a climax of singlemindedness. I felt bewildered and overpowered. I knew it would be some time before I caught up with myself.

Mallory, in a tradition nearer to Bannister's than to Joe Brown's and today's climbers, was very brisk with the feeble justification (still being made) that man might climb Everest for information about the limits of human beings at 29 000 feet, or in order to have a look at the geology.

Were I asked to sacrifice anything of real importance merely to break a record – well, I should not repeat the question to myself. In the whole scale of values, clearly, I think, records of this sort can't weigh in the balance against the serious work of everyday life.

No. I suppose we go to Mount Everest, granted the opportunity, because – in a word – we can't help it. Or, to state the matter rather differently, because we are mountaineers.

Our case is not unlike that of one who has, for instance, a gift for music. There may be inconvenience, and even damage, to be sustained in devoting time to music; but the greatest danger is in not devoting enough, for music is this man's adventure . . . To refuse the adventure is to run the risk of drying up like a pea in its shell. Mountaineers, then, take opportunities to climb mountains because they offer adventure necessary to them.

Mallory gives voice to the reason many people have for pursuing their sport. Even when he is Being Sensible in the manner of climbers reassuring their mothers, the thrill of recklessness comes through.

There have been great climbers who have grown so confident that they have run the gauntlet of natural perils and paid for it at a great price, there have been some who, not satisfied merely with difficulties of the ordinary kind upon snow or ice or rock, have undertaken for their pleasure the climbing of places which no human being could climb with safety, and added so a fresh element of risk by pushing our sport beyond its natural limits. Condemn them if you like, but not us who don't do these things and don't get killed . . .

In his last expedition he did, and knew he was doing, just these things. In such ways, the 'natural limits' are pushed outwards.

Mallory's last expedition is an amazing tale in itself, and I cannot tell it here. In a recent BBC television film,* two of Mallory's companions, Noel

* Repeat showing on the fiftieth anniversary of the 1924 attempt: 8 June 1974.

Odell and Philip Somervell, now both pretty elderly, told their stories in slow and moving understatement, mentioning (Somervell) that for warmth he wore 'three pullovers and his waterproof windcheater' and that when their ordinary picnic thermos leaked, the groundsheet of their ordinary bivouac 'froze like a sheet of cardboard – very uncomfortable'. Listening to their account of the elementary equipment and the exposure they were all liable to too, it's incredible at this distance that Mallory should have declared himself breathily 'rejoicing in the undimmed splendour . . . the unconquered supremacy of Mt Everest' before 'the army of steel cylinders, the warlike sets of apparatus', etc. etc. The tale, told in various places, advances with the absolute and terrible certainty of accomplished fact. It is no surprise that now it reads so like an account of Scott's last expedition to the Antarctic in 1912, which ended even more tragically, and the famous last words of which nobody can well read without tears.

Mallory, so far as one can tell, probably made many of the same assumptions about life as Scott. The same bluff, utter openness, of both love and judgement about his situation.

> The physique of the whole party has gone down sadly. The only chance now is to get fit and go for a simpler, quicker plan. The only plumb fit man is Geoffrey Bruce. N. has made me responsible for choosing the parties of attack, himself first choosing me into the first party if I like. But I'm quite doubtful if I shall be fit enough . . .
> The candle is burning out, and I must stop.
> Darling, I wish you the best I can – that your anxiety will be at an end before you get this, with the best news, which will also be the quickest. It is fifty to one against us, but we'll have a whack yet and do ourselves proud. Great love to you.*

He *knows* how bad things are, and hopes to his mother at 'just a bare outside chance of success and a good many chances of a very bad time indeed.' They climbed tremendous distances at such altitudes without oxygen. Odell at one stage in search of news about Mallory, climbed alone and without oxygen from Camp IV to V, slept alone, and went on to Camp VI very early on 4 June.

> The early morning was clear and not unduly cold; later, clouds began to form, and sleet and light snow fell intermittently. Odell has never wavered in his belief that, from about 26 000 feet, he caught the last glimpse of Mallory and Irvine, hours behind schedule, but 'going strong for the top' (p. 246).

Then Robertson goes on in Odell's words:

> At 12:50, just after I had emerged in a state of jubilation at finding the first definite fossils on Everest, there was a sudden clearing of the atmosphere, and the entire summit ridge and final peak of Everest were unveiled. My eyes became

* Mallory, to his wife; Robertson p. 243.

fixed on one tiny black spot silhouetted on a small snow crest beneath a rock step in the ridge, and the black spot moved. Another black spot became apparent and moved up the snow to join the other on the crest. The first then approached the great rock step and shortly emerged at the top; the second did likewise. Then the whole fascinating vision vanished . . . (p. 249).

All the letters written in praise of Mallory after his death are too fine and noble to be read as the usual efforts at *In Memoriam*. One letter from his wife must do to indicate the beauty of feeling, the valiance and truthfulness with which such a woman and her friends spoke of a tragic death whose meaning they understood and took the measure of. The touch of resentment at his death, the burst of lament, are burned out by her sense that such a life is lived supremely well, and in part just because it ended as it did.

> I know George did not mean to be killed; he meant not to be so hard that I did not a bit think he would be . . . I don't think I do feel that his death makes me the least more proud of him. It is his life that I loved and love. I know so absolutely that he could not have failed in courage or self-sacrifice. Whether he got to the top of the mountain or did not, whether he lived or died, makes no difference to my admiration for him. I think I have got the pain separate. There is so much of it, and it will go on so long, that I must do that . . .
>
> Oh Geoffrey, if only it hadn't happened! It so easily might not have.
>
> It is not difficult for me to believe that George's spirit was ready for another life, and his way of going to it was very beautiful . . . I don't think all this pain matters at all. I have had far more than my share of joy and always shall have had.
>
> Isn't it queer how all the time what matters most is to get hold of the rightness of things? Then some sort of peace comes.*

In Mallory's life, in his climbing, and in such obsequies as his wife's letter, there is to be felt the very best of his class and its history. He was the type of scholar-gentleman and athlete; the language he spoke and his climbing perfectly fitted a set of values which were not, in spite of everything, killed off in the trenches. Heroism, self-sacrifice, beauty, set in these graceful, unselfconscious accents mark the way of life he and his fellows stood for, and such all-conquering attractiveness is none the less boyish for being party to such manly resolution. Mallory was so strong as a man, and his legend remains so strong also, because he filled to its limits one sort of ideal man for his class, and those ideals remain active enough to be still widely appealed to.

Mountaineering gives the chance of expression to such ideals. Being as it is an incomparably rich sport, it changes along with the lives of those who practise it. By the time Joe Brown was in a position to write his own biography, the whole style and meaning of climbing had altered out of recognition. It is too easy simply to say that Mallory was the fine flower of

---

* Ruth Mallory to G. W. Young, 30 June 1924, quoted in Robertson, p. 254.

the English *haute bourgeoisie*, and that Joe Brown is a working-class lad from the North. Mallory's ideals, though quite without vainglory and well able to *work* for a climber and for a man, inhabit a rather high, dry atmosphere. Brown's matter-of-factness, his quick and dogged style of climbing turn out finally to be more brilliant and breathtaking because less solemn, less conscious of Everest's 'undiminished glory' and more of the next jughold. The deliberate and laconic trenchancy, the jokey truculence, is itself a decided style, and the unorthodox and creative techniques changed a whole way of climbing and, therefore, of thinking about climbing. Technique changes, and so (therefore) does expression; the frame of consciousness of climbing was changed by Brown, and it takes a man of genius to do that.*

The title of his autobiography – which was spoken into a tape-recorder – is itself almost self-parody: *The Hard Years.*† Brief and terse and flat, like Brown's own speech. Brown's most famous innovation of many, both in techniques and the devising of new routes, was to jam his hand into quite small fissures in a rock face and then to lock the hold by wedging the palm over and across his thumb. This gave him purchase in hitherto impossible positions. In fact he says little of his creations, but simply describes, plainly and with absolute vividness, a sequence of dazzling (but understated) climbs.

I would like to quote several at length, especially the record climb he and Don Whillans made of the West Face of the Dru in the Alps. Both he and Whillans, as if deliberately subverting the mistily poetic view of mountains, treat the climb with nonchalant familiarity. Whillans, jauntily disdainful of the French climbers who have made such a fuss of a particular pitch is 'full of beans . . . calling out scornfully, 'big holds here, large holds there, jug holds above, piece of cake and so on'. The rhythm of Brown's storytelling is that of his climbing – fluent, attentive, precise and extremely technical. There are some very funny pages – pages of the sort of knockabout humour which would not have featured in old style Alpineering – when he and a close climbing companion are climbing at once with and against a Russian team, whose devastating pace up mountains finally exasperates the equable two British climbers:

> On their return Mac gave his usual greeting to Vladimir: 'Well done, Bloodymir! You mad, impetuous Russian dare-devil!'
> Moving stores up the glacier, the Russians invariably charged past us when we had flogged ourselves to a standstill. They flung a greeting without stopping and Mac replied by cocking a snook and shouting back, 'up your hooter'. As they receded at rocket pace into the distance Mac stood and roared at the top of his voice, 'balls to you'. This happened so many times that the Russians stopped and inquired if we could translate.

* Compare T. S. Eliot's formulation of this idea in 'Eighteenth Century Poetry' in *Selected Essays* (Faber, 1953).
† Gollancz, 1967.

What marks Brown's climbing is the ability to 'crack' unclimbable pitches by a combination of courage manifested as cheek (it is all so completely without flourish, and he unfailingly gives most of the credit to his friends and partners) and extreme technical ingenuity, as in the first climb across the girdle of Dinas Cromlech in Snowdonia:

> Don made several attempts to lodge himself on the right wall. He came back saying that he was not happy about it. He refrained from taking tension on the top rope. We agreed that enough had been done for one day. We would come back on the next and try again to cross the right wall. Don went down to the bottom. When he got there, on an impulse I asked him to hold the rope tight so that I could have a shot at getting on to the right wall before going down myself. In tension from the pulley rope on the chockstone I leaned across the first blank section and succeeded in reaching the line of holds leading to Cemetery Gates. I had cracked it. I put in a peg to save our strength on the morrow and retraced my steps.
>
> Such was the nature of the elaborate preparations and precautions we made for the girdle of Dinas Cromlech. Each stage was closely scrutinized beforehand and a technique appropriate to the problem was methodically applied. It took more nerve than sheer climbing ability to make the techniques work. Leaving the equipment in place we returned next morning and crossed the right wall without a lot of bother. This wall was impressively steep and the climbing very difficult, but our psychology and confidence in the techniques employed mastered the situation. The rest of the girdle was an anticlimax.
>
> Had we relied too heavily on modern techniques, such as rope tension moves, and moral support from ropes arranged above and behind us, for crossing the Corner? One of the old guard thought so. He had watched us traverse the right wall and I overheard him in the pub that evening saying what he thought of the performance. 'By Jove,' he spluttered to someone else, 'you should have seen it. Any of the old-timers could have done it with the gear that those young fellows were using.'*

There is a lot of Joe Brown in that passage – the modesty, the understating, the brief laconic way, the accuracy. There is also the new, important question: has technology caught up too far, and taken away the risks and difficulties which lies at the centre of climbing? (Just as with steroids: are you really the same person if you artificially acquire another 40 lb in weight across your neck and chest? Are you really sailing if you are using a burnished steel hull?)

All these are qualities which have made Brown leader of the new mountaineering. He notes himself that during the late 'fifties:

> ... more and more young men and women, from all walks of life, were visiting the hills regularly and several strong groups of climbers emerged. It was no longer possible to go to Wales and know everyone who was there and what climbs they had done or were planning to do ... Cloggy was still the yardstick by which advances in British rock climbing were measured ... It became quite common – as it is commonplace today – to go to Cloggy and see several teams all climbing on the hard routes and even trying new ones.

* Brown, p. 180.

Brown was both signal and accelerator to widespread changes in mountaineering and, indeed, in sport generally. He mobilized his own genius and the new climbing technology to make certain aspects of the sport brilliantly more simple. He (and Whillans, Gwen Moffat and others) opened up a far richer variety of climbs on domestic rockfaces than had ever been thought possible, and he transformed climbing into a weekend sport. He provided both a language and a style in which those who followed him felt at home, and his unflagging energy and inventiveness made him a model for almost everyone else who took up the sport. I shall quote once more to bring home the remarkable nature and achievements of a man who recounts what he does in such a crisp, plain way; it is a climb on the south western pillar of the Dru, near Chamonix.

... The wall was so foreshortened that I was deceived into thinking that I might get up it in two pitches. I ran out of rope and had to take a stance in stirrups. The next 50 feet was climbing on rotten wooden wedges in a crack. The position was superb but any one of the wedges was liable to pop out without warning. Then the pegs just ended in a blank wall. For a minute I thought I had gone up a blind alley. Looking round a corner to the right I saw a piece of rope hanging there. I made a tension move to this point, went up a little then moved in the same manner again to the right, and found myself above the wall. There were some fairly easy slabs above but in the mist it was hard to make out the route. All I could see were these slabs steepening into walls then overhangs about 150 feet above.

I set off towards the overhangs, hoping to find some sign of the route. Fortunately I moved in the right direction, over to the left, where the climbing was magnificent. After a corner I entered a superb layback crack with a wedge in it. I still had the diagram from the dissected route description, and checking this I was surprised to find how far up the climb we had come. Up to this point we had climbed with our sacks on, whereas we normally hauled them up on ropes ...

Next morning we scrambled to the summit where we found a rucksack with gear strewn round it. We thought it must have some connection with the rescue operation in progress. On the descent I moved slightly away from the correct line for about 300 feet, returning to the proper route on the shoulder. We heard later that the owner of the rucksack lying on the summit had fallen down the ordinary route and that 'he was sort of spread out all over it' – in the 300 feet section which I had unconsciously avoided.

Traversing towards the Flammes de Pierre we looked down the approach couloir of the normal route and saw a body lying in the bed with a rope beside it. This corpse was a guide who had been roping down the face on a bad sling which broke. All told there were three bodies from separate accidents on the Dru at this time. We were feeling a bit sick. 'I want to get off this mountain,' Des said glumly. We rushed down the couloir to the glacier and made another route-finding error. We finished having to rope down over a 120 feet overhang on to the glacier. Pulling the rope down after us it jammed. I couldn't see any way of climbing back up and we were in a filthy temper. 'What a bloody stupid thing to do right at the end,' I fumed. We stretched the rope out far to one side and the springy tension set up in it freed it from the rock. (pp. 236–7).

To be quite so laconic at such a time is almost macabre. But not quite. The tale is told with beautiful plainness. He speaks the facts and lets them make their own order. Climbing mountains is dangerous,which is why the detail of his own climbing is every bit as important as the fact of the bodies – not because *he* is more important, but because good climbing is. It is no slight man who can speak of his sport in this way, making no grand claims, doing no half-baked sociology on the way, and finally telling truths about himself and the lives of his friends and admirers which are much greater than the mere sum of events described on his tape.

Mountaineering stands here as the type of private or weekenders' sport over against the mass spectator and professional sports. Like many sports, it has been vastly extended since the Second World War; before 1939 it was, substantially, a rich man's and a restricted pastime. By now, Brown himself has been televised live several times by the BBC, once in a spectacular team-and-camera climb on the Old Man of Hoy.

The new interest in the sport has not just been a matter of democratization. Mountaineering is convenient: there are good rockfaces within a couple of hours of every big city. It is pretty cheap; you can build up your kit a bit at a time. It permits the closeness and intimacy of friendship and dependence, but puts that closeness on a reassuringly technical basis. It offers the satisfaction of temporary but acute physical discomfort. More important than any of these appeals, the activity concentrates people's minds in decent privacy on central human values. It answers in those private lives a call for adventure and danger; perhaps, as Mallory said, for admiration. And why not? There are few enough ways in which a young man or woman may satisfy a wish to prove himself or herself physically courageous. Joe Brown and his men have made that challenge explicit, but in such a way as to drain off any surplus heroics. Mallory, no doubt, was free of them, and he was a great and gallant man. A sportsman indeed. But Brown, following and enormously developing that great tradition, has done more. He has, so to speak, thought the unthinkable right through, and therefore made it practicable. Having thought it, he did it. Or rather, *as* he thought it, he did it and taught others to do the same. He gave the lie to Yeats's poem:

> The fascination of what's difficult
> Has dried the sap out of my veins, and rent
> Spontaneous joy and natural content
> Out of my heart.*

The fascination keeps that sap in even the most weekend mountaineer flowing, swift and sweet.

* W. B. Yeats, 'The fascination of what's difficult' (Macmillan 1939), p. 104.

8 Sport, cash and technology—the book of numbers

THE PRIVATE SPORTS – for instance, climbing, fishing, bowls, canoeing, swimming – all have their public side, just as the public sports, the spectator and professional sports, have, so to speak, their private ones. As I have insisted, either kind of sport is woven into the texture of social relations, which means that in a society whose energy is provided by the market place, the sports also are places of busy economic activity.

I quoted earlier Marx's observation, 'Even the highest intellectual productions are only recognized and accepted by the bourgeois because they are presented as direct producers of material wealth and wrongly shown to be such'. As things are, this is clearly true of paintings, china and sculptures, as well as manuscripts and first editions, because these things can be seen and classified as objects. At a time when techniques of cheap reproduction soon make the rarity and novelty of rich men's possessions obsolete, the only objects which cannot be devalued by mass production are the originals: the real painting, the real teapot, the real chair or carpet. This is why the autograph is so important: it is not a copy; copies are cheap. The first implication of a bargain capture of some antique or other is that its value is assured because of its rarity. Rarity confers status, and status pays back in solid interest rates.

Such are the ways of a people whose habit of thought tends to turn everything into an object and when once made into an object ('reified') to call it a commodity on the more-or-less open market. Open, that is, if you have the money. It is easy to see how lethal such a frame of mind is, and how poisonous to human relations it is that a man's worth be also measured by the size of his market price. For its own sanity, however, this frame of mind keeps open certain areas where the commodity values do not apply, where artistic production is *not* 'presented as the direct producer of material wealth'. In these areas, the intellectual and artistic productions become not objects but practices. It is easy to see how sport is one such practice.

Take the distinction for a moment between commodity culture and culture-as-process. There is a traffic between the two. Thus, for a long time people use a pot or a settle; it is then part of process – of everyday domestic living. Then, by a shift in taste and by the simple passage of time, the pot or settle becomes a commodity on the market. An unusual teapot in its respectable old age acquires an exchange value of some hundreds of pounds (not that anyone puts tea in it). This change cannot happen to a novel (only to its manuscript). On the whole, it doesn't happen to photographs, because photographs are reproducible and casual. They remain part of social practice and process, not its production. Similarly, if Britain had, like France, a proper national gastronomy, the same would be true of that. Cuisine as art. Sport is exempt in the same way.

This is perhaps sport's simplest and certainly its most important social meaning: it is non-productive. As I put it before, it is good-for-nothing, except itself. You cannot use it. It inverts the dominant cultural drives which impel our social life.

This does not mean that there is no one ready to make a fortune or simply to earn a living out of his sport. Thousands earn their living, and the stars together with a few impresarios do make fortunes. But the economic structures of sport are, as I said, non-productive. Though football clubs are limited liability companies, hardly one of them pays a dividend, even the richest, and it is a paradox that many men are prepared to put a great deal of capital into sports clubs with little hope of any back. Nor is the hope the point. There is no intention to retrieve any capital. And it is in this way that much spectator sport proceeds in this country.

Let me summarize and illustrate the economics of sport. In the first place, the money transactions are those of the simplest model of the free market, supply-and-demand economy. People buy what they want after a due consideration of the competing commodities available; they are well informed by straightforward advertising. These are the transactions of weekend fishermen, climbers, bowlsmen, sailors.

In the second place, we can see the cultures of a primitive capitalism beginning to emerge. Professional clubs canvass for capital among potential shareholders. They sell their product (football, cricket, etc.) in competition with one another to a consumer market in which success can be measured quantitatively (large crowds) and is achieved by superior production (winning matches). Defeats result in poorer gates, and inefficiency of this sort is punished by reduced takings. This picture is complicated by the fact that the labour-force is at once the plant and the product. As we shall see, some football clubs survive economically by investing in good young players, bringing them to maturity, and selling them at a high profit. (This is only possible in football and baseball.) In this situation, the player is the product. He is also the plant – the machinery which represents his club's capital investment – and he depreciates accordingly. Lastly and obviously, he is the labour-force, and – again in football – as Jimmy Hill recognized when in the late 'fifties he led the movement to unionize the footballers, the sporting labour-force is immune to rationalization techniques. You are in a very strong bargaining position if your production systems cannot benefit from automation.

In the third place, however, this classically capitalist form to sporting economics changed with the advent of modern mass entertainment. One could say that up to about 1950 football and cricket, the two dominant types of mass spectator sport, retained the economic structures of nineteenth-century capitalism as I have described them: modest capital inflow calculated on limited share issue, fixed assets, free market competition, low growth rates, and (in football) ready liquidity made available by the transfer system. Since that date, these sports have changed structurally in many of the same ways as the more formal kinds of industry. So, clubs have found that share issues and ordinary revenue do not balance their books. In the manner of industrial firms in similar difficulties, they have diversified their activities, becoming in one place a large-scale, sporting, family and community centre, elsewhere promoting their own football pools, racing totes, sports shops, and hotels. At the same time, the enormous extension of the entertainment industry has changed the whole structure of sport, most obviously on television. In so far as the technology which made possible the distribution of news and pictures to private homes was the result of distinct *social* and not just technical forces, then we may say that television cut back the crowds who used to pay to watch and has been a powerful element in the structural change I mentioned. I shall go back to some of the details of this change – the sums of money paid by the communication industry to the sporting agencies, for instance. For now, it is enough to note that in the past twenty-five years, the forces of the entertainment and communication business have vastly complicated the economics of sport, as much as anything by strengthening and distributing the superstar system. To say this is to say again that sporting economics reflect a general economic (and therefore social) movement. Its successful agents, both at an individual and a club (or company) level have moved into a closer economic relationship with one another, like that of a cartel, in which their interests are best served by encouraging the interpenetration of their economics in such a way as better to resist, or compete successfully against, the same concentration of capital and resources in other sectors of the relevant industries.

Thus the superleague of football clubs like Leeds, Liverpool, Tottenham, Celtic, Rangers, and others, are interlocked not so much by rivalry as by the need to remain on the European circuit and in the contact which permits the easy movements of cash and players necessary for continued success. The imminent ending, in 1976, of the contract system speeds up this process. The flexible structure of top players, top managers, big, regular crowds, and ready capital precisely reflects the forms of such giant corporations as the British Steel Corporation, ITT, Chrysler or ICI, who are the models of modern economic planning. Their concentration of capital, restrictive pricing, high and minutely differentiated wage structure, mobility and, above all, their internationalism, all serve to bankrupt certain areas and leave them derelict, and to draw smaller organizations into a subordinate and wholly dependent position. So it is with the big football teams and their stars; so it is also with the international tennis and golf circuses; in a less specific way, the cadre of international cricketers operates to keep up differentials, although cricket has less of the closed hierarchies of international football, tennis and golf.

Mention, however, of the individual performers who make their fortunes from this system returns us to consider not simply the *reflection* of late capitalism to be seen in sporting economics, but also the penetration of those economics by its own, specific agencies. This penetration has been of two kinds. The first, of longer standing, has remained a fairly straightforward marketing exercise. Motor racing is its purest example, where the technology adapted the natural tendency of men to race their new toys against each other, in order to experiment with and develop new and more efficient models. Car manufacturers went into motor racing in order to compete in the most visible way for increased speed, manoeuvrability, control. As the car market began to stratify itself in terms of class, status and function, so new gradations of motor racing, the Formulas, began to appear, which in turn reflected and confirmed this process. Then not only the subsidiary competitors – the motor fuel firms and tyre manufacturers – entered the field, but the subtler demands of an industry, most of whose products were almost uniformly standardized to the point of no distinction, but which depended on the continuity of its relentless competition, required the introduction into its marketing of a novel symbolism which would parade distinction and achievement where no distinction was. Motor racing became an ideal arena for this advertising. It was and remains dangerous and attractive. It lent itself immediately to the manufacture of glamour and publicity; it served as focus for the most inflammable and booming sector of the consumer economy. No wonder, therefore, that motor racing became, on this analysis, the first and most successful capture by exploitative enterprise of a no doubt authentic expression of popular interest and feeling. The technological nature of motor racing, as well as its economic significance in the capitalism of the past forty or fifty years, meant that in the tension between exploitation and expression, which I have insisted on as the twistpoint of popular culture, exploitation would win.

Furthermore, motor racing is a new sport. Its absence of historical roots and a strong culture of its own such as horse racing and cricket have always shown, also made it much more open to this colonization. The sport and the commercial interests stood in a one-to-one relationship. The arrival of these interests in rather more oblique forms of patronage as sponsorship is a very much more recent development, of course, and I shall suggest later, rises from contradictory sources. For the moment, however, let us say that company sponsorship in golf, tennis, football and cricket – the John Player league, the Benson and Hedges and Rothman's competitions, the Gillette Cup, the Watney Cup – all these signal the more or less deep suffusion of sporting institutions and their economies in the terms of giant capitalist corporations and their morality. The extension of this process into minority and rich men's sports which transpires, for instance, in the *Sunday Times* long-distance yachting races, the *Daily Express* powerboat race and other such occasions for the fabrication of news for its own sake, is only to be expected. The dreadful 'It's a Knock-out' or 'Jeux Sans Frontières', television's ritual celebration of itself, is the apotheosis of the tendency.

We can distinguish, then, the following economic structures in sport. The first, the straight commodity and market economy; the second, the related capital and labour structure of a traditional kind; the third, a rescue structure of diversification and support, largely deriving from the gambling industry and extramural to the systems of sporting production; the fourth, a complex network of support, investment, and public relations in which the gambling and pools industries dominate and in which companies both in and out of sporting goods manufacture ally with the television companies and the BBC as interested parties. This is the structure of publicity, and hardly separable from the system of payments and revenue generated by the small galaxies of stars who form the most visible and glittering level of the whole giant edifice, but who provide a separate source of economic energy as fuel to its engine-house.

I have suggested a model of four interconnected structures for the economics of sport. To speak so confidently of smoothly functioning economies is these days obviously figurative. The convulsions of both capital and production which have impended in Britain since the early 'sixties increase in frequency and severity each year. Since 1973 it has become, for a season or so, impossible to read short-term economic behaviour along regular curves: its movement is violent and unpredictable. The only certainty is that, within its present provenance, capital will tend more and more to concentrate on the super-centres of production, leaving vacancy behind – unemployment and dead industry. National governments try to delay the flow away of investment by putting capital back into the abandoned areas, but are then faced with the irresolvable contradictions between replenishing an industry obsolescent in terms of the corporations who have gone elsewhere, and promoting a new industry for which there are no agencies to take up the offered capital. Short of wholesale socialist planning, a change of such immensity as is hardly imaginable short of an absolute, and wholly unlikely collapse in the economy of a member state of the EEC, this country at least will have to live with these contradictions.

Such a potted economics is necessary if we are to understand the ravellings of analysis before us. For the contradictions penetrate, as they must, the structures of sport as I have described them. In so far as sport itself is a non-productive activity, and further in that it at times *inverts* the received economic formulae – does not even replace let alone accumulate capital, is process not commodity, is immune to technological development, cannot rationalize its labour-force, etc. etc. – then the giant upheavals surging through economics hit it obliquely and variously.

Some events are simple: players will be turned off. Some events are larger, but at least intelligible: the vast topheaviness of British industry in which productive labour is so hugely outweighed by non-productive, an imbalance permanently funded by the public sector borrowing requirement, this topheaviness will feel the crisis as the shrinking of capital at its lower levels. Capital-earners will attract more capital and this will be true of, for example, either TV programme or sporting star. The rich and powerful will become more so. The lesser will earn less. But a great deal cannot be predicted at all. I would simply guess that although sponsorship is bound to become erratic, it will continue to sustain the sports its rich and powerful instigators care about. I would bet that betting will keep its important, inoffensive place in social life, and therefore continue to offer its indispensable aid. And I am certain that sport will maintain its necessary place, absorbing the grating abrasion of public upon private life, embodying in its negations and mirror-images the hope of non-commodity and non-productive values in the world.

High instability makes the latent structures of economy appear distorted, as though seen through water. I shall try to identify these structures in action; first, by considering the structures of two or three domestic economies in sport; second, by looking at the sponsorship system; third, by looking again at the star salariat.

II

Consider a representative county cricket club.* When we go far into its finances, it is clear that its assets and turnover are exceedingly modest. Although the new and shiny packaging of which Tony Lewis spoke in the last chapter has brought great financial harvests, the game makes little money. The county cricket club now in question showed an excess of expenditure over income of £11 700 in 1972, a loss made up by a share in the government grant paid after the cancellation of the 1970 South African tour (£2340) plus a transfer from a reserve fund. By comparison, they made a straight loss in 1975 of £10 000, already a figure reduced by £8500 by capital replacement. Apart from the considerable land and plant assets in the shape of the county cricket grounds, the club valued its investments at cost as a modest £123 500, and its season's expenditure on players' and officials' salaries, on travelling expenses and payments for running the side were nearly £54 000 in 1972, and £69 000 in 1975. The details of the club's income are worth looking at:

---

* For obvious reasons I shall not name this club, but of course I am grateful to its senior official who has given so generously of his time and information.

	1972 £	£	1975 £
By gates: County	3 643		3 817
Players' Sunday League	2 864		5 536
Tourists	772		4 834
Friendly	131		
Field membership	40		
	7 450		14 551
Less payment to tourists	550	less VAT	
		6 900	13 473
Members subscriptions	12 485		13 700
Vice-presidents	4 051		5 500
Affiliated clubs	209		
		16 745	19 199
Share of Test match profits, television and sound fees, etc.		4 601	26 000
Profit on sale of score cards, year books and brochures		199	220
Share of sponsorship		3 053	
Members' donations: catering	780		
cricket balls	415		
Supporters club		1 195	12 000
Catering rights		100	
Gillette Cup – share of profits		3 624	
BBC fees		4 400	4 160
Insurance claims		404	180
Sundry donations		255	
Cushion hire		39	
Bank interest		199	1 450
Profit on sale of members' ties		362	
		42 076	72 800
Excess of expenditure over income		11 759	10 000
		53 835	

In the present scales of international sport, this county club deals in peanuts. There is little comparison between these rates and transactions and those of the superleague footballers, golfers, and tennis stars. There is as there always has been a star system in cricket. The Yorkshire and Lancashire leagues in the 'thirties recruited West Indians, Indians and Australians who could play in their native country's winter time and achieve, if they were lucky, the social and personal success of a Learie Constantine as a result. More recently, the big international superstars have been able to sell their skills to the sponsor companies and the anonymous businessmen who have slid easily into place alongside the old seigneurs of the MCC. Barry Richards, for example, is reputedly paid

£5000 per season* (1973) with Hampshire, and counts among his sponsors the ice-cream company whose brandname he now bears among his peers as nickname. Richards is paid about £10 000 per year, which includes the two Hampshiremen's cheque which pays the first part, the Coca-Cola company who paid him an Australian dollar per run, and the Durban ice-cream merchant who offered four rand a run, and 'bought £2000 worth'.* Garfield Sobers was reported as being paid £3000 for his season's work with Nottinghamshire by a group of local businessmen acting privately, and as occasionally earning £10 000 a year from cricket.† Less exaltedly, a regular county player on a respectable season in 1975 would take home about £2500 before tax; a poorish season would lose him about £300 of that. The club prepares a breakdown of likely earnings to give to new players:

Wages arithmetic of capped player selected for all matches in all four competitions and tourists game 1973 and 1975

		1973	1975
Basic wage		£1242	£1830
20 County Championship without a win or gaining any bonus points	@ £6	120	
16 J.P.S.L. with no win	@ £10	160	unchanged
4 Benson Hedges no win	@ £10	40	£1588.00
1 Gillette Cup no win	@ £10	10	
1 Tourists game	@ £16	16	

This wage is guaranteed player over a period of 6 months
approx; even though not a single game is won.
Note other seasons may have two touring games and two friendlies. The taxable income for a top grade player will be about £2500.

Additional remuneration	1973	1975
Pension Gratuity	£40	5¼% of taxable basic salary
Kit allowance (the player is given 1 long and 1 short sleeve sweater, cap and player's tie)	40	50
	80	90

House loan
£2000 loan @ 1% for a period of 20 years or
until a benefit is granted, taking present
mortgage rates at 8% equals saving of £130.   £130.00

Possible wage without achieving any success   £1788.00

* *Sunday Times*, 18 August 1974.
† I should insist that these are well-attested reports, though I must respect the secrecy of my sources. In sport, as in anything else, people are touchy about how much they are paid, or pay out. But see *Daily Telegraph* magazine, 20 June 1975, p. 16.

Bonuses and extras

	1973	**1975**
County Championship	£8 first 100 points, £10 over 85	Basic £900 + 1st 3 wins £100 + 2nd 3 wins £150 + 3rd 3 wins £250
John Player	£5 per player per win £1000 shared for winning the competition £750 second £500 third £250 fourth	£7 per win, otherwise same
Benson Hedges	Players receive all sponsorship monies, i.e. 1st 4 games approx. £13 per man Losing quarter finalist £36 per man Losing semi finalist £56 per man Losing finalist £110 per man Winning finalist £220 per man	£69
Gillette Cup	1st win £5; 2nd win £10; 3rd win £40; final £80.	unchanged

Fringe benefits

£1.50 subsistence allowance i.e. evening meals, drinks, etc., when away from home: £2.50 in 1975

All hotel expenses paid by club

Benefit after 10 years £3500–£5000.   1975, £7000–10 000

At 7% annual-invested income £245–£350.

Matches played away – £2 per day subsistence.

   The full season is calculated as lasting twenty-two weeks; youngsters of sixteen or seventeen are taken on at between £15 and £18 per week, and a junior uncapped player who plays occasionally for the first team can expect to earn about £800 in his first season. The five-month season (often on a seven-day week) means, of course, that in theory players can have another job during the winter. In addition, the elaborate system of bonuses and incentives can add substantially to the salary of the players able to take advantage of it. The John Player League (Sunday afternoons, one match always televised) prize money in 1973 to 1975 was allocated in this way:

League champions will receive	£2000
League runners up will receive	£1000
League county placed third will receive	£ 500

The winning team in every match will receive	£ 50
Each time a batsman hits a six he will receive one share of	£1000
The batsman with the most sixes in a season will receive a bonus of	£ 150
Each time a bowler takes 4 wickets in an innings he will receive one share of	£1000
The bowler who has taken 4 or more wickets most times will receive a bonus of	£ 150
Fastest 50 on television	£ 250

A similar list of attractions is set out in prizes towards the Benson and Hedges cup, each of them conceived in terms of star performers and entertaining play which Lewis, along with many of his peers, notes as the defining but disabling characteristic of first-class cricket in the past decade.

Distribution of team prize money shall be as follows:

1st prize of	£2500
2nd prize of	£1250
Losing semi-finalists will each receive	£ 625
Losing quarter-finalists will each receive	£ 400

During the preliminary matches a 'Team of the Week' will be nominated for a prize of £250, during each of the 5 weeks in which the zonal part of the competition takes place.

The winners of individual matches in the regional stages of the competition will receive £150.

Individual awards shall be as follows:

To each 'Star of the Match' in each of 40 zonal matches	£ 25
To each 'Star of the Match' in the 4 quarter-final rounds	£ 50
To each 'Star of the Match' in the semi-final rounds	£ 75
To the 'Star of the Match' in the final	£100 *

The individual bonuses and prizes are pretty small when compared with the returns for star golfers, tennis players, and footballers, but these incentives have paid off not so much in the wage returns of the players as in the size of the crowds and the county-club takings.

The economic base of a county cricket club remained sufficiently wide and modest up to the years of inflation: the solid BBC contributions, the members' and vice-presidents' contributions, the doubling of gate-money by Sunday league play, the returns from the MCC shared out after Test matches and Gillette cup,† the sponsorship money – these revenues combined to provide a stable base for the small salaries they pay players and officials (themselves often past players). The rates of inflation since 1973 have hit such a delicately balanced economy very hard. The club secretary in one case writes to me, 'I anticipate a severe reduction in playing staff in the next two years – a cutting of second team cricket, etc.,

---

* All figures unchanged for 1975.

† Total distributed among counties in 1972 was £600000 (John Arlott, *Guardian*, 8 December 1972). In 1975 after 30 per cent inflation since 1972, the total rose only by 8 per cent (private communication from Mr Arlott).

and I suspect within ten years certain counties may have to amalgamate. We could not exist without sponsorship.' Here, too, are the centripetal tendencies of capital. And although richer and more successful county sides than this one exist,* they none of them vary on anything like the scale of football clubs, where poorer teams must remain in strictly client relationship to the bigtimers.

The bigtimers are, after all, few in number: a dozen or so clubs out of ninety-two every year make a profit.† The total losses for all league clubs in the decade 1964–74 was nearly eight million pounds. Take the third division club, Bury, whose discrepancy between expenditure on players' wages and staff salaries and total gate money in 1970 was £37 000. They recouped in this column of the ledger by selling a young player to Blackburn Rovers. Bury keeps going by selling young players; in the eight years 1963–71, these sales brought in a quarter of a million pounds. Such a policy has to be paid for, in the vice-chairman's words by 'producing from raw material a standard of professional footballers which will keep the club alive. That is the immediate concern, to keep the club alive. And, when necessary to balance the losses from lack of support, we transfer players that we produce through our own development nurseries.'‡ And although such a policy sells the team out of victory, it balances the books: when Bury does well, along come the buyers. As the manager says, 'You must know who's next for sale. It is heartbreaking, but what can you do? You see boys come in here, they come in at 14 and 15, you build them up for a couple of years and they start to show something and then you know very well that they are going to go. This is, you know, it's a dreadful thing.'‡

He cuts his staff – his labour force – to a bare minimum: 22 professionals, 8 apprentices (some clubs are down to a pool of 15 or 16 players), but always, 'We've got to have something in the stable, working it up and getting it ready for sale' (his pronouns) and the ungiving economic pressures make this vice-chairman look wistfully back at the days when there was a maximum wage, and the wealthy backers of third and fourth division clubs, who fund so much of that and non-league football, would not stand for restrictions which would mean the loss of better players who, as things are, stay for an exceptional wage in an unexceptional club.

Not that all clubs are so successful in effecting transfers. The Chester report of 1968 established that most transfers are *downwards*; the big clubs recruit their own people or transfer among themselves. Of 1488 transfers in the period under the Chester Committee's review, 848 went down the

---

* The transformation since the unrelieved gloom of the Clark reports published in 1966 is very striking. See *Wisden* 1967, pp. 101–14.

† See *Football League Review*, first number, 1972/3 season; also ITN *News at Ten*, 28 December 1975.

‡ Broadcast on 'The Football Business', BBC Radio 4, 4 September 1971, transcript by permission of BBC.

divisions, 206 upwards.* By and large, the money stays on the commanding heights.

In the circumstances, it is surprising that since 1960 only Accrington Stanley of the league clubs has gone bankrupt, although in 1975–76 several clubs announced that it was only the indulgence of their banks which kept them solvent. Many clubs keep going only because of the tireless efforts of supporters clubs and unofficial subventions from one or two individuals. (It is a remarkable fact that there are always people prepared to pay out large sums regularly not only to support the big clubs, but to keep afloat clubs who are always scraping along the bottom of the fourth division.) The gap between the financial world of Bury and that, for example, of Coventry City in the first division is very wide, for all that Coventry only balance their books and are not interested in making a profit. In this they are consistent with the economic climate of sport at large: individuals play sport and make fortunes. In some cases, no doubt, they play sport *to* make fortunes. But even those who commit large sums to sport are clear that its cultural meaning is non-productive. They may gain local power by their generosity, they may feed vanity, braggartry, they may have noble and disinterested motives. But the activity is still creative and self-sufficient. The money is for the life, and not the other way round.

Hence when Coventry's wealthy chairman, Derrick Robins, now alas emigrated, was asked whether the directors should support the club financially, he replied briskly:

> It's not their responsibility – but it's jolly nice if you can find a few clowns around the place who'll do so . . . when I took over as chairman, the directors paid up to give the club a new boardroom . . . we haven't had to do this sort of thing as a Board many more times, although it is obviously general knowledge that I personally have done quite a bit, but then I'm one of the clowns I spoke about before.†

In the five years 1966–71, Coventry spent £750 000 on club facilities, the same sum on players, and got back 'perhaps £400 000 to £450 000 on transfers'. An outlay of a million pounds in five years.

> The pool brings in £80 000 per annum. £140 000 from season tickets i.e. £220 000 per annum. It begins to balance. If the bank cuts down on the overdraft, you have to bide your time until something can be adjusted and invariably somebody comes along for the reserve player you don't want, so you sell him, that looks a little healthier and then you do a little bit of hire purchase on a player and so you spread it into the next, and so the thing goes on.†

The scale is vastly different to Bury's, and so is the lavishness and rather engaging swank with which Coventry City, true to its place on the one-

---

* See Peter Douglas, *The Football Industry* (Allen & Unwin, 1973), p. 87.
† 'The Football Business', Radio 4.

time booming waves in car manufacture, has spent on its bijou cocktail bars, butteries, and the executive suites built at the ground for rent by British Leyland.

> And then one begins to say – Well if you're 6th in the 1st Division, by jove, we really ought to be having at least the 6th best in the country – but being Coventry City you'll be saying – no, by this time we've got to have the best of everything. So I think we do go a bit fast at it, perhaps faster than other clubs might, but I don't think it's been unjustified.*

The swimming pools, the sky blue vans, the three club lounges, the restaurant, the Sky Blue local radio programme, the extravagant plans for 'badminton, squash, sauna baths, a really big club room where we might do the sort of Humperdink programme', are all tokens of a very different conception of what a football club is in its own community. It sorts well with a Coventry which will see out the recession and inflation, a town remade after the war by the push of a renovated capitalism thriving on cheap oil. Contrast the city bosses in Coventry of whom Robbins is such an amiable example with the more dour style of a Bob Lord† in Burnley, whose dogged continuity in the first division is the product of a depopulated cotton town overshadowed by Manchester. There you find a measure not so much of sums of money as of styles of sponsorship.

III

Those rough accounts give something of the feel of the economies of the two football clubs, and the county cricket club. Each account includes aspects of the structures I listed. I want now to pick up a few traces of the enormous and pervasive structure of revenue which is present at every level of professional sport (in itself a notoriously problematic category) but whose influence can only be guessed at from the brute totals dispersed or circulated in the balance sheets of individual companies.

The most obvious example of this process is gambling, which is, as you would expect, most seriously turned to for help by horse racing. The Horserace Levy Board levies a 1 per cent tax on the gross income from all money staked with both bookmakers and tote at race-meetings recognized by the Jockey Club. With total betting turnover at about £1285 million‡ per year in the UK, this levy brought in about nine million pounds in 1974, to be used for prize money and for the benefit of breeding and veterinary

---

* 'The Football Business', Radio 4.

† c.f. *Observer Magazine*, 19 August 1973.

‡ 'Sportsview – hard times for the racing men', *Times*, 23 December 1975. Lord George Wigg, now President of the Betting Office Licencees Association, points out that £97 million of this goes in tax. He asks for a lump sum of £50 million to be paid back from the £200 million revenue on all sporting stakes, to all sports. Racing, he calculates, would get about £7 million of any such grant. See *Pacemaker*, September 1974, and *Bloodstock and Racehorses Confederation* pamphlet, December 1975.

projects, jockey training and recruiting, and a variety of superannuation and grant schemes. The sum is vastly less generous than in any other EEC country.

Racing has always been a rich sport. The prize money is enough evidence of that. Average prize money per race was £1707 in 1974. An ordinary card at a small meeting like Chepstow or Uttoxeter shows prize money for winners ranging from £200 to £450; even a modest course like Redcar supports the Vaux Gold Tankard at £5800 (a brewery backing), Kempton Park runs from £600 or so to the Henry II stakes at £3500, and the classic courses provide prize money from £15 000 at Ascot for the Kings Standard Stakes and at Cheltenham for the Gold Cup, £25 000 at Aintree, Liverpool, for the Grand National, and £100 000 for the Derby. (It is hard to find out jockeys' earnings.. Top jockeys get up to £5000 as retainers from rich trainers, and may be asking up to 10 per cent of prize money. Jockeys like Piggott or Joe Mercer, racing in two or three countries in a week, are probably being paid £35 000 in a year, and taking 25 per cent of their wins.)*

These very large sums are intricately linked to racing's historical system of refined stud, breeding, and training, and the auction price of horses (which may vary between £2000 and £250 000 – the top forty sales at the December bloodstock sales in 1975 went from 96 000 to 16 000 guineas) † is much more part of a pattern of investment than ever it is in football. Racing has always been self-sufficient. It is the activity of a smallish number of very rich men who have kept the running of the sport to themselves and have possessed the land, the technology and the historical experience to run it well. As a consequence the sport is experienced almost entirely as spectacle. It is never an activity. Its symbolism is exclusive (as witness the graceful wrought iron gates at Ascot and Epsom). Its elite is drawn from the ruling class, and its economic structure, though in fine working order, has registered fewer of the changes of other sports.

It is now true that the racing owner is in deep trouble: with average prize money per horse in this country £750 in 1974‡ and training costs at £2820 per horse, once more capital moves into the hands of the big owners and consortia; the small owner is forced out. The big owner dominates as a function of capital, of power, and of style.

Football is the only other major sport to draw directly on gambling. Pools promoters' gross proceeds announced in 1973 were £168 million, and their association agreed with the football league to pay them two million pounds copyright fees,††which is 2 per cent of the promoters' gross income after the 33⅓ per cent deduction of betting tax. Several people, Derrick Robins most forcible among them, argued that 5 per cent would

* *Times*, 18 March 1975.
† *Pacemaker*, January 1976.
‡ *Guardian*, 16 April 1974.
††£3 million in 1975, same proportions (BBC *Radio 4* news, December 1976).

have looked more reasonable, and it is hard to believe that the pools promoters would really – as the rumour went – have moved to continental football if the squeeze had been put on them. In any case, gambling revenue stands in this direct relation to these two sports: neither could be sustained without the other.

The position of sponsorship is a good deal more ambiguous. Consider the table below drawn up for 1972–73.*

The top ten sponsoring industries		*The top ten sponsoring companies*	
	£		£
Tobacco (at least)	1 800 000	John Player & Son	750 000
Oil	800 000	Rothmans	330 000
Alcoholic drinks	550 000	W.D. & H.O. Wills	250 000
Tyres	400 000	Gallaher	250 000
Finance	220 000	Texaco	225 000
Food and confectionery	160 000	Marlborough	200 000
Press	150 000	Watney Mann	160 000
Bookmakers	125 000	Gulf Oil	(about) 100 000
Sports goods	70 000	Goodyear	(about) 100 000
Clothes	55 000	Firestone	(about) 100 000

The top eleven sponsored activities	
	£
Motor sports (more than)	3 000 000
Horse racing	700 000
Golf	500 000
Association Football	300 000
Cricket	260 000
Lawn tennis	230 000
Cycling	200 000
Equestrianism	200 000
Motor cycling	100 000
Powerboat racing	100 000
Sailing	100 000

The annual rise in such expenditure was estimated to be as large as another 25 per cent by the end of 1973, though nobody has as yet said how much these increases will be hit by the developing crisis of 1975–77. At any rate, tennis admitted to nearly double its 1972 figures of £230 000 as coming from sponsorship. Indirect costs are guessed as adding upwards of £10 000 000 to the 1972 figure.† But the future pattern of sponsorship is very obscure.

* Compiled by Raymond Palmer, *Observer Business News*, 5 August 1973.
† *Guardian*, special report, 7 August 1972.

Tackled for information about changes in their policy as inflation and stagnation hit the companies, very few of the now familiar names would commit themselves 'on confidential matters' and you cannot find the figures in the annual reports. But Gulf Oil have cut back 90 per cent in 1975, Benson and Hedges have quit squash rackets altogether, and it seems likely that these two are straws in a wind getting up among the sponsors. All the same, I am convinced that, for better and for worse, sponsorship emerged from complex cultural as well as economic origins, and will survive the present crisis.

The origins of these top ten sponsors are not far to seek. The fuel and tyre firms made theirs initially to car-racing, which pulls in overwhelmingly the largest sums. But with the legislation of 1966 against cigarette advertising on television, cigarette companies found biggish funds on their hands at a time when they feared that their names would be much less visible to the great smoking public. It now looks self-explanatory that these funds should go to these important but impoverished social activities, and thereby ensure that the famous names – Player's, Benson's, Piccadilly, Rothman's and the others – were regularly to be seen behind the bowler's arm and all along the touchlines.* At any rate, once the cigarette firms, together with Gillette, had made the first agreements, whole ranges of sport hitherto untouched by sponsorship, were opened up for colonization. It had always been there in horse and motor racing; in the past nine years, cricket, tennis, golf and football have all found a support whose returns for the sponsor are nothing like so explicable as they are in more technological or playboy sports like powerboats or sailing. Indeed it is my personal, strong conviction that tobacco sponsorship for cricket arose simply from the private passion of senior directors when they realized they had spare funds going and could justify far larger subventions than the generous vice-presidential cheques they had been writing for years. The justification had to remain at the exceedingly general level that the firms concerned built goodwill (that well-known purchasable commodity) by linking their names with the pleasures of sport. I am not persuaded by the argument. It seems far more likely that the senior executives able to authorize the sponsorship, found they could afford it and were delighted to do so. Sponsorship, for all the official dressing-up in terms of increased goodwill and popularity, television exposure and prominence of brand names, looks more like the result of that deep affection for sport as valuable in itself which remains its central cultural significance. These firms pay for sport because they like it and they want to. It is good to be able to pay such tribute in a book in which the whole push of the argument is to name and condemn the ugliness and human weakness their parent system, industrial capitalism, emphasizes at all its levels.

* John Arlott reported a rumour (*Guardian*, 3 May 1972) that the balcony railing at Lord's is let as a hoarding for £20 000 per year.

For one thing, the list of sponsors has itself begun to wear an increasingly arbitrary (not to say hilarious) look. Take a selection: Marks and Spencer gave £5000 in 'Walking-out dress' for international teams in 1975;* the Prudential Assurance Company spent £30 000 on tennis in 1973; Barclays Bank backed Guy Edwards and Lola cars for £15 000 per year; the Milk Board puts £45 000 per year into the tour of Britain cycle race; the Midland Bank backs cross-country horse trials; Wimpey International backs the European tug-of-war championships on Barry Island (it does, it does). It is hard to believe that these firms see much return on these payments and I·do not see why we should expect them to. Easier, perhaps, to understand the £1.5 million paid by firms for the right to use the Olympic Games symbol during 1972 (Esso coming out top), with another £4 million on free goods and services for use during the time at Munich.† The advertising return there is intelligible if unmeasurable. Yet even there, appearance seems to me to count for more than reality.

Sponsorship may be said to be lethal in so far as it signals the penetration of sporting virtues – the non-productive, essentially human and creative virtues – by manipulative, merely commercial values. The values of acquisition, of publicity, of the cynical deployment of human relations as commodities for profit. Thus far, to see the names of the giant corporations at Wembley, Lord's, Gleneagles or the Olympic stadium, is to be reminded of their vast omnipresence. It is to understand again their profound instinct and drive for domination, so that even the games we play take place beneath those large, imperial banners. More than that, sponsorship is part of a frame of mind, a state of consciousness in the culture. For when we in the West look for patrons, we turn naturally to industry rather than to the sources and resources of social wealth. What we provide for ourselves is called the welfare state. At best, it lives in perpetual rivalry with the central dynamos of the giant companies; at worst, the state is pushed out into a broad, dismal margin around the foreground which capital commands, and which is filled with the rich prizes commended to us by its advertising agents. It is worth noting that it is via ITV and its consortia that a good deal more company money flows into sport in payment for televised weekends. The *ITV Handbook* mentions a figure of £2 400 000 to pay for sport coverage; the BBC, however, lays out £6 500 000 per year. In 1976, for example, the BBC paid £550 000 to televise the Montreal Olympics to the UK (compare this with £95 000 for the 1975 Australian Test series).‡

But I do not want to end *on* these bleak and necessary recognitions. Sponsorship and the structure of its payments to sport signify, as I have emphasized, an official and ritual overturning of the sponsors' dominant

---

* Personal communication.
† *Guardian*, 7 August 1972.
‡ *Guardian*, 26 September 1975; *Daily Mail*, 20 January 1976; *Coverage of Sport on BBC Television*, BBC, December 1974.

principles. They pay for fun. They pay, in the words of an old but still stirring litany, for 'an association in which the free development of each is the condition for the free development of all.'

IV

The star system is the pinnacle structure of all these interlocking economies. It is also the least necessary, except in so far as it confers legendary status upon the stars and makes them part of the glittering world of what is rightly called show business – it being just that. A brief selection of incomes makes it clear just how fabulous this star status is:

*Some top world golfers**

1973

1st Arnold Weiskopf, USA	$349 645
2nd Jack Nicklaus, USA	$328 620
1st from UK, 39th Peter Oosterhuis	$ 81 691
2nd from UK, 46th Tony Jacklin	$ 73 982
3rd from UK, 105th Neil Coles	$ 36 870

1974

Johnny Miller, USA	$400 255
Lee Trevino, USA	$268 168
1st from UK, 24th Peter Oosterhuis	$111 098
2nd from UK, 47th Tony Jacklin	$ 68 868
3rd from UK, 63rd Peter Townsend	$ 56 717

Some top tennis players †

A.T.P. prize money earnings 1975

American Arthur Ashe is the first player in the history of professional tennis to break the $300 000 barrier in tournament prize winnings for a single season.

Winner of 10 tournaments, including Wimbledon and the WCT Dallas final, Ashe's 1975 yearly total of $326 750 also enabled him to become the second player in tournament history to break the one million dollar mark in lifetime earnings. Rod Laver was the first.

The release of the final 1975 prize money figures shows an increased depth in earning power all the way down the board. Fourteen players earned over $100 000 in 1975, in comparison with 13 in 1974 and eight in 1973. Thirty-eight players earned over $50 000 on the 1975 international circuit compared with 31 in 1974 and 19 in 1973.

1.	Arthur Ashe (USA)	$326 750
2.	Manuel Orantes (Spain)	269 785
3.	Guillermo Vilas (Arg)	249 287
4.	Bjorn Borg (Swed)	221 088

* Mark McCormack, *Golf Annual 1974* and *Golf Annual 1975* (Collins).

† J. Kramer and M. Robertson, eds., *Encyclopedia of Tennis* (Allen & Unwin, 1974), and J. Barratt, ed., *PP Book of Tennis* (Queen Anne Press, 1974).

5.	Raul Ramirez (Mexico)	211 385
6.	Ilie Nastase (Rum)	180 536
7.	Brian Gottfried (USA)	167 960
8.	Jimmy Connors (USA)	163 165
9.	Roscoe Tanner (USA)	150 459
10.	John Alexander (Aust)	138 050
11.	Harold Solomon (USA)	137 625
12.	Rod Laver (Aust)	120 416
13.	Adriano Panatta (Italy)	109 000
14.	Ross Case (Aust)	104 900
15.	Juan Gisbert (Spain)	98 105
16.	Jaime Fillol (Chile)	96 835
17.	Stan Smith (USA)	90 624
18.	Tom Okker (Holl)	89 082
19.	Bob Lutz (USA)	87 050
20.	Jan Kodes (Czech)	86 190
	and	
24.	Mark Cox (GB)	77 700
29.	Roger Taylor (GB)	59 105
40.	Chris Mottram (GB)	45 575

quoted from *Tennis World*, 7, 10, 10 March 1976.

Note: The ATP Prize Money Board reflects money earned from recognized prize money events and does not include income derived from contracts, exhibitions, challenge matches, team competitions or personal guarantees.

Tennis is the only sport in which women can be paid as much as men.* In 1973, playing on a single professional circuit (not always the same one) in the USA, the higher salariat included the following names even before they began at Wimbledon,† where the men's singles winner take in 1977 £15 000 and the women's £13 500 out of total prize money of £160 000.

Margaret Court	$75 000
Rosemary Casals	$59 550
Chris Evert	$41 000 (total winnings for year over $200 000)
Kerry Melville	$34 075
Evonne Goolagong	$23 000
Virginia Wade	$22 650

NB compare any of these earnings with Barry Richard's, described earlier.

Jackie Stewart, the then world motor-racing champion, was paid 'within reach of £200 000' in 1973,‡ but it is of course professional

---

* Becoming less true. In 1973–74 Laura Baugh, aged 19, is said to have collected $200 000 for her golf by way of advertising. Kathy Whitworth is rumoured to have made half a million dollars from her golf in the past three years (*Times*, 11 August 1974).

† Kramer and Robertson.

‡ B. Gill, ed., *John Player Motorsport Yearbook* (Queen Anne Press, 1974).

heavyweight boxing where the prizes are most completely fairytale, and which top off the superstar tall stories. When Joe Frazier beat Muhammed Ali for the world crown in 1972, they each took home one million dollars. When Ali won the return in 1975 he took home two and a quarter million dollars.

The star system is the point at which the sporting and entertainment worlds intersect. The stars make fortunes inasmuch as other people make fortunes out of them. And stars have become the success heroes of their time. The sporting stars sit easily beside the film and pop stars. They are all young, and they are all classless. Once upon a time, old footballers just faded away:* Jimmy Logie sold papers on a street corner, Wilf Mannion went back to the steel shop floor, Hughie Gallacher threw himself under a train. At fifty-two, an unemployed, bankrupt Tommy Lawton nearly did the same,† and was only rescued by a spontaneous testimonial match. In 1973 Bobby Moore and Bobby Charlton were taking home £10 000 per year from football alone, and the legendary Best with his boutiques and discotheques far surpassed that. In 1973, Billy Bremner of Leeds made £80 000 gross income.‡ The regular player in a successful First Division club was paid in 1973 a basic income of £5000 to £6000††before internationals or championships, and together with the glamour and celebrity, these men are grouped in the popular imagination as stars of the same kind as the much wealthier golfers, jockeys, and tennis players. Below the stars, sporting rates of pay are unremarkable – about thirty six quid a week in the Second Division, forty five quid for a seven-day week in county cricket.

The stars are like a combination of travelling gunslinger and the people's hero. The vast payments instil not envy or resentment, but hope. The stars look down, and many others look up and say, this man, this woman, is ours.

---

* Such a tale is very well told of a cricketer's rise and fall to a seedy suicide, in *Pro* by Bruce Hamilton (Cresset, 1946).
† See *Guardian*, 4 November 1972.
‡ *Daily Telegraph* magazine, 20 June 1975.
††See Peter Douglas, *The Football Industry* (Allen & Unwin 1973), pp. 113–15.

9 The world on the move

Herbert Marcuse once wrote:

> By affirmative culture is meant that culture of the bourgeois epoch which led
> in the course of its own development to the segregation from civilization of the
> mental and spiritual world as an independent realm of value that is considered
> superior to civilization. Its decisive characteristic is the assertion of a universally
> obligatory, eternally better and more valuable world that must be uncon-
> ditionally affirmed: a world essentially different from the factual world of the
> daily struggle for existence, yet realizable by every individual for himself 'from
> within' without any transformation of the state of fact.*

In the summer of 1948, a small boy of eleven sprawled all over a
comfortable floor, well-carpeted and warm. The sun shone down through
tall, plate-glass windows. He was listening to a big radiogram in a walnut
case, the pattern cut in the veneer front revealing the wide woven texture
of coarse thread through which the mysterious sound came. In front of him
was a big, official, cricket score book and as the voices, the legendary,
disembodied voices of John Arlott, Rex Alston, Alan MacGillivray, went
through the leisurely details of the Test Match, the small boy solemnly
wrote them in the score book, ball at a time, run at a time. The great names
whose doing he listened to were those of gods and heroes: Miller, Lindwall,
Harvey, and most unsurpassable, Bradman. And the names of his own
heroes: Hutton, Compton, Edrich, Bedser, for all their English magic,
proved all too weak before the Australian titans. Later that year, on a wet
Northern promenade beneath a warm, soft rain slowly darkening the sand
and the sea, his father handed him an evening paper which told of
England's final disgrace and humiliation at Australian hands when,
rattled out at the Oval for 52, they had only managed a score his school
would think of as pitiful. He burst into tears, and felt his father's hand
heavy upon his shoulder in consolation. Not long before, he had listened to
the jumbled slapping of runners' feet in the rain coming over the radio;
and drowning the commentator's excited voice, the unforgettable chant of
the great crowd in the London Olympic stadium, 'Zat-O-Pek, Zat-O-Pek'.

---

* Herbert Marcuse, *Negations: Essays in Critical Theory*, trans. J. Schapiro (Allen
Lane, 1969), p. 95.

A German cultural critic, friend and associate of Marcuse's, wanted to write an essay consisting only of quotations from other books. In this manner, he thought, he could get his personal and subjective experience out of the way, and act simply as a conduit for the richness and resonance of the social experience round him. All writing expresses objective cultural tendencies unintended by their authors. Walter Benjamin wanted to let these tendencies come through more clearly, unmuffled by the peculiarities of his own voice. He would still be there, of course, because he chose the quotations, but there would be no pretence in such an essay that it was all the writer's own work (as though it were his private property). The single voice could not then imply a false communality and unity of elements. Contradictions could speak for themselves.

This book is written in a single voice. But it is with Benjamin's idea in mind that I have quoted so widely. Now, as far as possible, I want to paste together a series of remarks and memories and pieces of information which may also render the way a culture lives in the life of an individual; the way millions of individuals acting separately none the less create discernible patterns in their actions, and these patterns can sometimes seem to have an inflexible strength, as though an individual is merely an adjunct of society, and incapable of his own spontaneous, free life.

Jean Paul Sartre once wrote:

> An emotion is a transformation of the world. When the paths become too difficult or we cannot see our way . . . all ways are barred and nevertheless we must act. So then we try to change the world, that is to live in it as though the relations between things and their potentialities were not governed by determinist processes, but by magic. Our effort is not conscious of what it is, for then it would be an object of reflection. It is, above all, an apprehension of new relationships and new demands. The apprehension of the object being impossible or giving rise to unbearable tension, the consciousness apprehends it, or *tries* to apprehend it otherwise. That is, tries to transform itself in order to transform the object.*

Genuine art keeps alive the idea of Utopia. It is an expression of men's proper interest in their future happiness. Stendhal said that art holds out the promise of happiness.

A rugby team is playing, one beautiful April day in 1963, in front of its own crowd. The team is a good one, and has had its best season – a record total of 616 points (this team, like any other, is obsessed by the statistics of its sport). Its opponents today are not strong, and because the grass is thick and green, and the soft sunshine is on their backs, the home team falls into a purple passage of football. They are winning by 20 points, and they suddenly will win by 60. The team breaks into the rippling flowers of its imagination, every man of them running across and back and across again, weaving an intricate pattern of movement, caught for a moment longer on

* Jean-Paul Sartre, *Sketch for a Theory of the Emotions* (Methuen, 1962), p. 68.

the retina of eye and imagination than is really there on the grass, so that spectators can use the words 'weaving patterns' and 'spells'. The team is marvellously fit, the beautiful, hard bodies colliding with solid, audible thuds, and moving fluidly and lambently on. Except one player, a bit of a card, and a favourite with the crowd. He is heavy and for a lad of twenty-five, portly, with a round, neat little belly which protrudes over his shorts. He runs with a sort of strut, that way of running a player will promote who is in comfortable circumstances with himself and handing the ball on to team-mates who have run up a record total and do not look like stopping. Over a few yards, he is glitteringly fast, the short legs suddenly pistoning him away, and giving the next player, shouting for the ball, all the room in the world.

But he is blown. He watches the scorer run in under the posts with his hands on his hips, bending over, blowing hard. Gradually and infectiously the other players realize this, and time and again the ball is switched back to the fat lad until his ruddy cheeks go pale and his blowing turns to strained, grinding gasps. A movement starts in a flutter. The crowd is laughing now, with the players. A long, elegant player runs diagonally across the field and the tired opposition falls raggedly back. A giant of a man, hugely chested, curly haired, the captain, shouts from behind, 'Laurie, get it to Mike', and the crowd roars with laughter again. 'Now then big Dave', they call. The passes whisk rapidly through three pairs of hands to the now exhausted, stationary, fat player. He raises one brief spurt to clear him from an uncertain defender, and as his team drop laughingly away from him and leave him to run in his 40-yard try, he spins in a single, complete circle in order to shift the ball to his kicking foot, and from way out on the touchline, drop kicks it, in a sweet, sure, swinging curve, right between the posts.

> A successful work of art . . . is not one which resolves contradictions in a spurious harmony, but one which expresses the idea of harmony negatively by embodying the contradictions, pure and uncompromised, in its innermost structure . . . Art . . . always was, and is, a force of protest of the humane against the pressure of domineering institutions, . . . no less than it reflects their substance. (Theodor W. Adorno).

'No less than it reflects their substance.' But it *does* so reflect it. So art, and sport, are political. In Britain, politics is almost equated with class. Not that it is easy to say what class means. Say, for now, it is what *The Directory of Occupations* says it is. These quotations come from an unpublished survey of sporting interests, conducted by the Opinion Research Centre* (but my commentary).

* *Sports Sponsorship, General Report* (Opinion Research Centre, 1972). I am very grateful to Mr Nigel Speakman for showing me this report. The sample was a stratified random sample taken at fixed intervals: 30 names in 120 constituencies of the electoral role, probability proportionate to size. The survey was conducted during September and October 1972.

SUMMARY OF MAIN FINDINGS

Interest in sports
Respondents were asked which sports they were 'at all interested in nowadays' and, later, which they 'followed with interest'. The same broad pattern of preferences emerges from the results of both questions. Clearly the most popular sports are:

	All Adults	
	Interested in at all	*Follow with interest*
	%	%
Association football	53	40
Athletics	41	24
Show jumping	39	24
Tennis	33	21
Cricket	28	19
Competitive swimming	28	14
Horse racing (flat)	25	17
Motor racing	21	10

Of less interest to adults as a whole are autocross, car rallies, darts, golf, powerboat racing, snooker and speedway. Between 10% and 20% of adults say they are 'at all interested in' each of these. Below 10%, respondents were interested in bowls, cycling, rowing, sailing.

Women's interest in sports
Behind this general order of popularity, however, lie significant differences in the preferences of men and of women. Most of the eight most popular sports listed above were mentioned much more often by men than by women. But athletics appears to be followed by almost as many women as men, while competitive swimming, show jumping and tennis are rather more popular among women – the factor which is partly responsible for their perhaps surprisingly high place in the popularity order:

	Follow with interest	
	Men	*Women*
	%	%
Athletics	28	21
Show jumping	18	30
Tennis	17	25
Competitive swimming	13	16

Other demographic differences
Interest in sport does not vary very greatly by age. All the sports covered in the survey, with the exception of bowls, are marginally more popular among the younger age groups, but this factor discriminates less than sex or socio-economic class. A lot of the sports have a class bias, usually of the kind that one might expect. Tennis, cricket and golf are most popular among members of the AB and C1 classes, while association football, darts and horse-racing are followed most frequently by the C2 and DE classes. (In raw totals.)

Sport	Interested at all Social Class					Follow with interest Social Class			
	AB	C1	C2	DE		AB	C1	C2	DE
	Totals					Totals			
Association football	283	505	748	672					
	131	260	417	357	M	96	179	318	289
	46	51	56	53	F	34	35	42	43
Athletics	122	234	332	212	M	74	145	190	127
	43	46	44	31	F	26	29	25	19
Autocross	28	50	87	52	M	11	17	38	23
	10	10	12	8	F	4	3	5	3
Bowls (flat green)	22	29	49	56	M	7	9	28	31
	8	6	6	8	F	3	2	4	5
Bowls (crown green)	17	20	42	36	M	9	9	17	19
	6	4	6	5	F	3	2	2	3
Car rallies	42	78	122	80	M	18	27	56	34
	15	15	16	12	F	6	5	7	5
Competitive swimming	73	147	230	168	M	34	76	113	96
	26	29	31	25	F	12	15	15	14
Cricket	101	154	190	173	M	73	100	113	124
	36	30	25	26	F	26	20	15	18
Cycling	19	50	71	63	M	7	22	22	32
	7	10	10	9	F	3	4	3	5
Darts	27	58	131	107	M	11	25	64	60
	10	12	18	16	F	4	5	9	9
Golf	70	107	131	90	M	41	62	76	49
	25	21	18	13	F	14	12	10	7
Greyhound racing	9	30	47	58	M	2	15	10	28
	3	6	6	9	F	1	3	1	4
Horse racing (flat)	53	98	187	218	M	28	60	119	158
	19	19	25	32	F	10	12	16	24
Motor racing	62	117	180	107	M	34	46	86	56
	22	23	24	16	F	12	9	11	8
Powerboat racing	22	57	90	51	M	8	16	35	25
	8	11	12	8	F	3	3	5	4
Rowing	23	48	44	40	M	9	18	13	19
	8	9	6	6	F	3	4	2	3
Sailing	38	59	60	41	M	15	27	29	16
	14	12	8	6	F	5	5	4	2
Show jumping	124	204	295	246	M	79	122	171	166
	44	40	39	37	F	28	24	23	25
Snooker	34	92	126	117	M	18	43	52	63
	12	18	17	17	F	6	8	7	9
Speedway	9	61	120	96	M	4	26	63	41
	3	12	16	14	F	2	5	8	6
Tennis	148	201	235	149	M	103	121	146	96
	52	40	31	22	F	36	24	19	14
None/don't know/ no answer	28	59	94	138	M	63	133	174	196
	10	12	13	21	F	22	26	23	29

Key: AB social class — professional and managerial
C1 — skilled clerical
C2 — skilled manual
DE — unskilled

the other players realize this, and time and again the ball is switched

There are obvious omissions in this sort of survey. It only provides a huge grid upon which to lay the closer kinds of analysis, speculation and thought. A questionnaire of this kind depends so much on what is presented by the questioner. On the context of the questions. Think, for instance, of those sports not mentioned in the list. Or of those which were thought of first because they are regularly televised.

When people were asked how they followed sport, this is how they replied:

	Follow on television	
	Men	Women
	%	%
Association football	53	22
Athletics	27	20
Show jumping	17	29
Tennis	16	23
Cricket	27	8
Competitive swimming	12	15
Horse racing (flat)	19	12
Motor racing	13	5

And when asked what sports they ever played, obviously the highest proportion of players came between the ages of 16 and 34. For instance, 18 per cent play football between these ages (it is not known how often), $5\frac{1}{2}$ per cent take part in athletics, 11 per cent in cricket, $16\frac{1}{2}$ per cent (remarkably) in tennis, $5\frac{1}{2}$ per cent in competitive swimming. Four per cent of the over-55s play bowls, 4 per cent of the whole population (16 to 65+) play golf, and 9 per cent of the whole population play darts. (Nobody was asked about fishing.)

Minority interests, as they say. But how large is a majority? If, for example, you take only men in these percentages – and men, according to the questionnaire, are by a very long way the more active participants – then the percentages go up to nearly double.

So nearly a third of able-bodied males between 16 and 34 play some football? And one in five plays cricket? Every twelfth time you pass an elderly man – or rather, a man over 55 – he probably plays bowls. Imagine, as the globe turns slowly towards the dark and moves among the stars, five and a half million people are playing darts.

Minorities, then. A man lives in many minorities. These are the close minorities whose denser networks make up the texture of British private and popular culture. For the mistake about mass culture is, largely, to call it mass culture. There are few masses and there are many minorities. What we all fear in our lives, we are right to fear: the invasion of our senses by the deadly, invasive forces not of a blind technology but a culture equipped with a purposeful, subtle technology whose every intention is to corral and subordinate life to its greater profits. What we counterpoise to this process is, precisely, the fact of our various minority. The irreducible stubbornness of human particularity. It is this which is amazing about culture.

What is your favourite sporting memory? I think mine might be Rex Alston's commentary on the 1954 Vancouver Commonwealth Games when Roger Bannister followed John Landy round the mile until the last 80 yards. I was in the bath at about half past ten at night, and listened gloomily as Landy opened his lead. And then that amazing, beautiful triumph as Bannister swept into the splendour of his finish, and Landy glanced inwards, leftwards to check on his rival's position as Bannister strode gloriously past on his right. But there are so many memories. And memory is the action of the past in the present.

> And here face down beneath the sun
> And here upon earth's noonward height
> To feel the always coming on
> The always rising of the night:
>
> To feel creep up the curving east
> The earthy chill of dusk and slow
> Upon those under lands the vast
> And ever climbing shadow grow
>
> And strange at Ecbatan the trees
> Take leaf by leaf the evening strange
> The flooding dark about their knees
> The mountains over Persia change
>
> And now at Kermanshah the gate
> Dark empty and the withered grass
> And through the twilight now the late
> Few travellers in the westward pass
> .   .   .   .   .
>
> And over Sicily the air
> Still flashing with the landward gulls
> And loom and slowly disappear
> The sails above the shadowy hulls
>
> And Spain go under and the shore
> Of Africa the gilded sand
> And evening vanish and no more
> The low pale light across that land
>
> Nor now the long light on the sea;
> And here face downward in the sun
> To feel how swift how secretly
> The shadow of the night comes on . . .*

* Archibald Macleish, 'You, Andrew Marvell' in *Collected Poems*, Bodley Head, 1948.

The world moves, and the sports move with it. Men are paid by their nations to run for their nation's political honour. Well, why not? I do not think this means that sport is a sort of surrogate warfare, as George Orwell seemed to think. It means that sport is internationally understood at a time when intense local feeling, localism rather than nationalism, is the only world ideology. It is natural to feel this nationalism about sport. One important connexion between sport and nationalism is that this book is written in English. World sporting culture is one consequence of British power: the sports have been the cultural export of the British industrial revolutions. Not winter sports, no doubt; but apart from volleyball and the dreary beach substitute for bowls which Frenchmen play – boring games both – there is no sport of international currency but it started in Britain during the nineteenth century. (All this tarradiddle about medieval football is so much history-hunting, like saying that the Saxon Witenagemot is a primitive House of Commons).

But the distortions in world sport as well as domestic sport are hateful. The anabolic steroids and the pharmaceutic aids to endurance, the buying and selling which has come near to destroying the Olympic Games (300 Mexican students were shot during riots a mile from the 1968 Olympic village). There is the meanness, the rancour and nastiness of World Cup football, and of the domestic game if it comes to that. One of the best home football reporters told me he was packing up as a football reporter, he found the game so repellent these days.

Jeremiah's gradient is always smoothly downhill. From the bullying and petulance of players to fights on the terraces. From these to a generalized notion that violence of some inexpressible kind threatens social life in all its communal forms.

> Changes in football have been traumatic for members of the working-class football 'subculture', especially for those who have been left out of the increasing affluence of our time by virtue of the fact that they are unemployed, unemployable or downwardly socially mobile. Such people constitute what he calls a kind of 'subcultural rump'. It is they, he argues, who principally engage in behaviour which the authorities designate as 'hooliganism'. Their response to current changes is ambivalent. They welcome competition with foreign teams because it offers the chance to vindicate the values of their subculture in a wider field of competition. But they resent the highly paid, sports-car driving, 'jet-setting' modern player, because he appears to have severed his links with the working classes. Above all, they resent the fact that the game is changing in ways beyond their control. The decision to internationalise and 'bourgeoisify' football was taken without their consent. Much of their so-called 'hooliganism', Taylor suggests, is a more or less rational attempt on their part to reassert the control which they believed they could formerly assert in helping their side to achieve victory. Shouting, chanting, singing, throwing stones, bottles and beer cans at opposing players are more or less rational ways, he argues, of attempting to put them off their game and to increase their own side's chance of winning. Running

on to the pitch when a goal has been disallowed, may be a'way, he suggests, not only of expressing disapproval but of magically attempting to persuade the referee to reverse his decision. Being caught and escorted from the ground by the police is a way of telling players and managers who the *really genuine* supporters are and that they have abandoned them by introducing undesirable changes into the game.*

It is not hard to see where the sociologist's reported sympathies are, whatever official protestations of objectivity may be made. The supporters have been divested of their own and have to reclaim it.

The problem raises again the question, the lived human question, what is sport for?

Imagine a teacher and his pupil. They are on a mountain, roped, and the teacher is going through the techniques of belaying. He opens the grain of the rope with his finger and thumb, pushing his thumbnail in to show the white, clean fibre inside. Imagine a father and his ten-year-old daughter. He is teaching her to play croquet. They bend over their mallets and he taps his through the hoop, with a soft click. She taps hers too hard and it rolls hard up against the metal strut. She stamps her foot, and then hits the mallet clumsily into the turf. Her father glances at her with amused reproof. Imagine, finally, a schoolteacher in a gymnasium. She is young and pretty, and the line of pushing, elbowing, fourteen-year-old boys are all shapes and sizes – wobblingly obese, gangling and skinny, all angles and bones, grubby, noisy, raucous. She only just has them under her twenty-two-year-old control. She shows them, in her own clean, crisp style, how to vault a low vaulting-horse, her long legs in tracksuit and plimsolls pointing accurately out in a wide vee as she goes over, her long thick hair tossed up in a perfectly straight line by the vault.

What is being taught? The thumbnail in the rope, the unspoken reproof of the father on the croquet lawn, the pretty P.E. teacher's uneasiness with her class. They are teaching a tradition. They invoke the understanding of honourable men and women acting in concert, disinterestedly, to experience certain moments of pure style. The honour is a function of trust: they must act together in terms of the tradition (which they can modify) in order for it to take place at all. They enter tradition, and teach others to enter, much as a swimmer enters a stretch of water or a swimming bath when he has no need to cross it. The conventions are what keep him afloat. The long caressing movement with which a cricketer feels the white blade of a new bat. The rapid, dextrous flicking of his racket as the squash player walks towards the courts.

Death establishes an uncanny, necessary relation between genius and convention. The relation is not fixed. This is obvious in all sport.

* E. Dunning, summarizing Ian Taylor, in *Readings in the Sociology of Sport* (F. Cass, 1971), pp. 341–2.

Football crowds and vandalism. Murder even.* It is not a simple coincidence. Football has to contain too much. In this, its spectators are more like the provisional IRA than like spectators of other sports. That is, football matches and IRA ritual murder and destruction are occasions which can be used to justify randomly and blindly malignant actions. They are forms of non-ideological (i.e. non-rational) behaviour for most of their agents. They are occasions which invite the expression of blindly hating feelings.

That is what I meant by saying that, in our times, sport has to contain too much. It is the container into which people pour so much unnamed, nameless ideas, feelings, impulses. If that is all there is, no wonder that for the poorest, most anarchic and also energetic and forceful of a people's children, ritual spectator sport is the place where that great mass of human energy boils up and out.

Consider the links between these figures and that suggested explanation. Local authority expenditure on sport in Britain:

1965–66   £16.4 million
1970–71   £14   ,,
1971–72   £19   ,,
1972–73   £20.5   ,,
1973–74   £13   ,,
1974–75   £14.8   ,,

Hamburg's population, like Bristol and its environs, is 1½ million; Hamburg has 280 sports centres where Bristol has one.†

What other governments spend on sport per head of population (1973):

Great Britain   47p
West Germany   £1.27
France   £1.35
Holland   £1.78

Trends in selected sports:

	1961	1966	1971	1975
Football Association (clubs in membership in 1000s)	23	25	38	39

* A boy was stabbed to death at a match early in the 1974 season.
† Central and Local Government grants to Sports Council:

	1974	1975
D of E	£5 m	£6.5 m
Local Authorities	£162 000	£193 000

see *Sports Council Annual Report* 1974–5 (Sports Council, 70 Brompton Road, London, SW3 1EX) and *General Statistics of New District Councils*, Chartered Institute of Public Finance, 1975.

Trends in selected sports: (continued)

	1961	1966	1971	1975
Badminton Association of England (clubs in membership in 100s)	26	30	34	84
Amateur Swimming Association (teaching certificates awarded)	472	2308	1507	1434
British Sub-Aqua Club (membership in 1000s)	5	8	16	19 (1973)
British Gliding Association (flying hours in 1000)	31	37	77(1970)	
Rugby Football Union (clubs in membership in 100s)	9	10	16	17
Amateur Fencing Association (clubs in membership)	425	510	670	
Squash Rackets Association (nos of courts in 100s)	6	7.5	11.5	14.5 (1973)

The following prices are paid at the moment for private participation in field sports:

Double-barrelled shotgun	£80–£40 000
5 days grouse-shooting with Lord Seafield's Sporting and Country Club	£1000
10 days rough shooting range (see *The Field*, for details)	£150–£1500 person
Split-cane salmon rod	£85
One week's salmon fishing on the Dee (Sporting Services International)	£400
Fishing stretch rights, River Test	£700/year*

Sport holds out 'the promise of happiness'. Its very detailed and elaborate rules and conventions, its beliefs and forms of knowledge impose form and style upon life by their timing and arbitrariness.

Two lines upon a piece of white paper resist the blankness round them. They give meaning (a very limited one to begin with) to the space. They define shape and distance.

A tree in a landscape gives a very much more complicated meaning to what surrounds it. It grows and changes, it alters the possible definitions of space and distance. Its boundaries flow in and out of its surroundings. Both adapt to the other.

A machine, a bridge, say, or a lorry, moves through space differently again. Think of a big old truck jolting and whining up a bumpy road.

* Sources for all foregoing figures: *Guardian*, 30 September 1972, Sports Council pamphlet *Sport for All* (Sports Council, 1973), *Sports Development Bulletin* (also Sports Council), *Sunday Times*, Colour Magazine, December 1973, also private communications from Sports Council, and *Holidays in Britain*, 1976, *TV Times* November 1976.

Think of the long sweep of a bridge's suspension cables. They are definite but limited. They command their immediate vacancy and they depend upon its laws. They have purpose but no possibility.

A runner has both. So has a fisherman. Their movements, properly executed (this is not a matter simply of moving gracefully: I am talking physics rather than aesthetics) are both form and content of their sport. Their opposition to space, their *resistance*, promotes continuity. They pit themselves against time and space. Their mobility is both victory and defeat: they do not continue and last for ever, but they are not victims of time either. They decide what they can do. The paradox is something like the one expressed in Andrew Marvell's famous couplet,

> Thus, though we cannot make our sun
> Stand still, yet we will make him run.

In this way, sports are moral monuments.

I think this may be the reason so many people use them as signs of duration and of continuity. They can commemorate our present activities in the future.

Sportsmen come home tired, even exhausted. They are often muddy, bruised, soaked through, sleepy. The end of every proper sporting occasion is a huge meal. They remember the game, and reconstruct the perfect works of art which they made out of its possibilities. Their accounts of what happened become trophies which they hand over to their friends, their sweethearts, and their families. The exhilaration, the intimate, impenetrable talk, the famous names they have and the famous names they have played with or have seen. These are the trophies and the commemorations. They are their guarantees and their bequests to the future. They are acts of faith and hope that those the players love, and those who follow them will *have* a future.

Bibliography

As I noted in my introduction, this list is not inclusive, indeed it is so short on the academic side because so much writing in that area is stone dead. I list, by and large, books which I have read and which contribute both vitality and intellectual clarity to the effort to understand and value sport and sporting lives. In the case of primary sources—biographies and the like—I name a few of what I've found to be the best written, but, of course, my reading is tiny out of so vast a list of books. I have included no single articles, nor periodicals, but most of the books naturally include detailed bibliographies themselves.

I SPORT AND THE CULTURAL SCIENCES
Barthes, R., *Mythologies*, Jonathan Cape 1972, Paladin 1973.
Beisser, A. R., *The Madness in Sports*, Appleton, Century, Crofts, 1967.
Berger, J., *A Painter of our Time*, Penguin 1965, Writers' Collective 1976.
    The Look of Things, Penguin 1972.
    G: A Novel, Weidenfeld & Nicolson, 1972, Penguin 1974.
Berger, P. and B., *The Homeless Mind*, Penguin 1974.
Burke, K., *Permanence and Change*, Bobbs Merrill 1955.
Caillois, R., *Man, Play, Games*, Plon 1960, Thames & Hudson 1962.
Centre for Contemporary Cultural Studies, *Working Papers in Cultural Studies 1–8*, University of Birmingham 1972–6.
Clayre, A., *Work and Play*, Weidenfeld & Nicolson 1974.
Dubord, G., *La Société du Spectacle*, Le Seuil, Paris 1967.
Dunning, E. (ed.), *The Sociology of Sport: A Selection of Readings*, Frank Cass 1971.
Erikson, E., *Identity: Youth and the Social Crisis*, Faber & Faber 1950.
Geertz, C., *The Interpretation of Cultures*, Hutchinson 1975.
Gerber, E. W. (ed.), *Sport and the Body*, Lea & Febiger 1971.
Goffmann, E., *The Presentation of Self in Everyday Life*, Doubleday and Penguin 1969.
Hoggart, R. *The Uses of Literacy*, Chatto & Windus 1957, Penguin 1958.
    Speaking to Each Other, 2 volumes, Chatto & Windus 1970.
Huizinga, J., *Homo Ludens: A Study of the Play Elements in Culture*, Routledge & Kegan Paul 1949, Paladin 1970.
Inglis, F., *Ideology and the Imagination*, Cambridge 1975.

Jay, M., *The Dialectical Imagination: The Frankfurt Institute for Social Research 1923–1950*, Heinemann Educational Books 1973.
Jackson, B., *Working Class Community*, Routledge & Kegan Paul 1968.
Leavis, F. R., *The Living Principle*, Chatto & Windus 1975.
Loy, J. W., and Kenyon, G. S., *Sport, Culture and Society*, Collier-Macmillan 1969.
MacIntyre, A. C., *Against the Self-Images of the Age*, Duckworth 1971.
Marcuse, H., *One-Dimensional Man*, Doubleday 1964, Abacus 1970.
    Negations: Essays in Critical Theory, Allen Lane 1969.
Merleau-Ponty, M., *The Phenomenology of Perception*, Routledge & Kegan Paul 1955.
Mills, C. Wright, *The Power Elite*, Oxford 1955.
Riesman, D., *Individualism Reconsidered*, Glencoe Free Press 1954.
Rosenberg, B., and White, D. M., (eds.), *Mass Culture*, Glencoe Free Press 1960.
Sartre, J.-P., *Sketch for a Theory of the Emotions*, Methuen 1962.
    The Psychology of Imagination, Methuen 1972.
Slovenko, R., and Knight, J. H. (eds.), *Play, Games, and Motivation in Sports*, Bobbs Merrill 1967.
Slusher, H., *Man, Sport and Existence*, Lea & Febiger 1967.
Vanderzwaag, H. J., *Towards a Philosophy of Sport*, Addison Wesley 1972.
Weiss, P., *Sport: a Philosophic Inquiry*, Carbondale, S. Illinois University 1971.
Winnicott, D. W., *Playing and Reality*, Tavistock 1971, Penguin 1974.
Williams, R., *The Long Revolution*, Chatto & Windus 1961, Penguin 1962.
Wittgenstein, L. L., *Philosophical Investigations*, Basil Blackwell 1953.
    Conversations about Aesthetics, C. Barratt (ed.), Basil Blackwell 1967.

2. SPORT, LEISURE AND MASS COMMUNICATIONS
Ball, D. W., and Loy, J. W., *Sport and the Social Order*, Addison Wesley 1975.
Barker, P., (ed.), *Arts in Society*, Fontana 1977.
BBC, *Coverage of Sport on BBC TV*, BBC, 1974.
British Film Institute, *Football on TV*, BFI Monographs 1975.
Boorstin, J., *The Image*, Weidenfeld & Nicolson 1962, Penguin 1964.
Cheek, N. H., Field, D. R., and Burdge, R. J., *Leisure and Recreation Places*, Wiley 1976.
Douglas, P., *The Football Industry*, Allen & Unwin 1973.
Downes, D. M., Davies, B. P., David, M. E., and Stone, P., *Gambling, Work and Leisure—A Study across three Areas*, Routledge & Kegan Paul 1976.
Enzensberger, H., *Raids and Reconstructions*, Pluto Press 1977.
Dumazedier, J., *Sociology of Leisure*, Elsevier 1974.
Glanville, B., *People in Sport*, Collins 1970.
Halloran, J. D. (ed.), *The Effects of Television*, Panther 1970.
Halloran, J. D., and Murdock, G., *Demonstrations and Communications: A Case Study*, Penguin 1970.

Landers, D. M. (ed.), *Social Problems in Athletics*, Illinois 1976.
Larrabee, E., and Meyerson, E., *Mass Culture*, Glencoe Free Press 1958.
McLuhan, H. M., *Understanding Media*, Sphere 1965.
McQuail, D., *The Sociology of Mass Communications*, Penguin 1972.
Parker, S., *The Sociology of Leisure*, Allen & Unwin 1976.
Rapoport, R. and R., *Leisure and the Family Life Cycle*, Routledge & Kegan
    Paul 1975.
Williams, R., *Television—Technology and Cultural Form*, Fontana 1974.
    Communications, Penguin, revised edition 1976.

3. PHYSICAL EDUCATION
This is a very brief list from a large but very modest crowd of contenders.
Best, D., *Expression in Movement and the Arts*, Lepus Books 1975.
Brooke, J. D., and Whiting, H. T. A. (eds.), *Human Movement: a Field of
    Study*, Kimpton 1973.
Fraysinnet, P., *Le Sport parmi les Beaux Arts*, Dargaud S.A. 1960.
I.C.S.P.E., *Declaration on Sport*, UNESCO 1964.
Jokl, E., and Simon, E., *International Research in Sport and Physical Education*,
    Springfield: Thomas 1964.
Haworth, J. T., and Smith, M. A., *Work and Leisure: An Interdisciplinary
    Study in Theory, Education and Planning*, Lepus Books 1975.
Kane, J., *Physical Education in Secondary Schools*, Macmillan, for the Schools
    Council, 1974.
    Curriculum Development in Physical Education, Crosby, Lockwood, Staples,
    1976.
Knapp, B. N., *Skill in Sport*, Routledge & Kegan Paul 1964.
McIntosh, P. C., *Sport and Society*, Watts: Thinkers Library 1963.
    Physical Education in England Since 1800, Bell 1970.
Metheny, E., *Movement and Meaning*, McGraw Hill 1968.
Van Dalen, D. B., and Bennett, B. L., *A World History of Physical Education,
    Cultural, Philosophical, Comparative*, Prentice Hall, 2nd edition, 1971.
Whiting, H. T. A., and Masterson, D. W., *Readings in the Aesthetics of Sport*,
    Lepus Books 1974.

4. HISTORY, BIOGRAPHY, NOVELS
This last list is very uneven. In some sports I have, over the years, read a
large amount of what has come out. In others, I have simply picked books
which I have come across which give some insight into the workings of a
particular sport, or sportsman. In this process I have been an inevitably
random chooser, victim alike of newspaper selection and of my own
interest and tastes. The quality as *between* sports is extremely marked:
mountaineers seem all to be spirited writers and talkers, rugby players
rarely get far beyond the verbal limits of James Thurber's famous college

footballer, a sort of cross between King Kong and a long-distance lorry. I have picked what I take to be a few of the absolute best—cricket has, not surprisingly in view of its importance in the oldest seats of learning and power, the best literature—and a sample more of those books which I have found the best in those particular sports. There are bound to be serious omissions, of both authors and sports, and I apologise to their supporters. The standards I use to choose the best, I try to show at work in Chapter 6.

Andreano, J., *No Joy in Mudville*, Schenkmann 1965.
Arlott, J., *Fred: Portrait of a Fast Bowler*, Eyre & Spottiswoode 1971.
  Vintage Summer: 1947, Eyre & Spottiswoode 1967.
Bannister, R., *First Four Minutes*, Putnam 1958.
Blanchflower, D., *The Double and After*, Cassell 1963.
Bonington, C., *Annapurna*, Cassell 1971, Penguin 1973.
  Everest, South West Face, Cassell 1973, Penguin 1974.
Boyle, R. H., *Sport: Mirror of American Life*, Boston 1963.
Brown, J., *The Hard Years*, Victor Gollancz 1967, Penguin (revised edition) 1976.
Cardus, Sir N., *Autobiography*, Collins 1947.
  Second Innings, Collins 1952.
  Full Score, Cassell 1970.
Chataway, C., and Goodhart, P., *War without Weapons*, W. H. Allen 1965.
Constantine, Sir L., *Cricketers' Carnival*, Hutchinson 1948.
Cooper, H., *An Autobiography*, Cassell 1972.
Cotton, H., *This Game of Golf*, Collins 1948.
Darwin, B., *A Bernard Darwin Anthology*, P. Ryde (ed.), Black 1976.
Davies, H., *The Glory Game*, Weidenfeld & Nicolson 1972, Sphere 1973.
Dougan, D., *The Sash He Never Wore*, Allison & Busby 1973.
Ehrmann, J. (ed.), *Games, Play, Literature*, Beacon Press 1968.
Francis, D., *The Sport of Queens*, Michael Joseph 1957, revised edition Pan 1974.
  Odds Against, Michael Joseph 1965.
  Bonecrack, Michael Joseph 1972.
Glanville, B., *King of Hackney Marshes*, Secker & Warburg 1965.
  The Olympian, Secker & Warburg 1967, Pan 1968.
  The Dying of the Light, Secker & Warburg 1976.
Green, M., *The Art of Coarse Rugby*, Hutchinson 1969.
  The Art of Coarse Golf, Hutchinson 1972.
  The Art of Coarse Cruising, Hutchinson 1976.
Hamilton, B., *Pro*, Cresset Press 1946.
Haston, D., *The Eiger*, Cassell 1974.
Heath, E., *Sailing: A Course of my Life*, Sidgwick & Jackson 1975.
Hemingway, E., *The Sun Also Rises*, Jonathan Cape 1927, Pan 1949.
  Death in the Afternoon, Scribners 1945.
Hillary, Sir E., *Nothing Venture, Nothing Win*, Hodder & Stoughton 1975.

Hopcraft, A., *Football Man: People and Passions in Soccer*, Collins 1968, Penguin (revised edition) 1971.
Hunt, Sir J., *The Ascent of Everest*, Hodder & Stoughton 1954.
Hunter, J., *The Flame*, Faber & Faber 1966.
Insole, D., *Cricket from the Middle*, Heinemann 1960.
James, C. L. R., *Beyond a Boundary*, Hutchinson 1963.
John, B., *The Barry John Story*, Collins 1973.
Keeler, O. B., and Rice, G., *The Bobby Jones Story*, Fireside Press 1972.
Laidlaw, C., *Mud in Your Eye*, Pelham 1973.
Lawton, T., *When the Cheering Stopped*, Golden Eagle 1973.
Lewis, Tony, *Summer of Cricket: 1975*, Pelham 1976.
Longhurst, H., *Only on Sundays*, Cassell 1964.
Macdonnell, A. G., *England, Their England*, Macmillan 1933, Pan 1949.
Mailer, N., *The Fight*, Hart-Davis MacGibbon 1976.
Malamud, B., *The Natural*, Farrar Strauss Giroux 1952, Dell 1971.
Michener, J. A., *Michener on Sport*, Secker & Warburg 1976.
Moffatt, G., *On my Home Ground*, Hodder & Stoughton 1968.
Nagler, B., *James Norris and the Decline of Boxing*, Bobbs Merrill 1964.
Peters, M., with Wooldridge, I., *Mary P: Autobiography*, Stanley Paul 1974.
Robertson, D., *George Mallory*, Faber & Faber 1969.
Robertson–Glasgow, R. C., *Crusoe on Cricket*, A. Ross 1966.
Sassoon, S., *Memoirs of a Fox–Hunting Man*, Faber & Faber 1949.
Snow, J., *Cricket Rebel*, Hamlyn 1976.
Storey, D., *This Sporting Life*, Longman 1960, Penguin 1962.
   The Changing Room, Heinemann Educational Books, 1977.
Swanton, E., *A Sort of Cricket Person*, Collins & Fontana 1972.
   (ed.), *Best Cricket Stories*, Collins 1950.
Whillans, D., and Ormerod, A., *Don Whillans: Portrait of a Mountaineer*, Heinemann 1971, Penguin 1976.
Whiting, G., *Great Fights of the Sixties*, Frewin 1967.
Wodehouse, P. G., *Mike*, Herbert Jenkins, re-issued 1961.
   The Clicking of Cuthbert, Herbert Jenkins 1953.
   Golf Omnibus, Barrie & Jenkins 1973.
Worsley, T. C., *Flannelled Fool: a Slice of Life in the Thirties*, A. Ross 1967.

List of Photographs

(copyright holders are gratefully acknowledged)

Jacket (front)

Top left: spectator at Lord's, England v. West Indies (photo, Sport and General)

Top right: Queen's Park Rangers v. Manchester United (photo, Chris Smith, Camera Press)

Bottom right: Grand Prix at Silverstone, 1975 (photo, Camera Press)

Jacket (back)

from top to bottom, left to right

E. Arzhanov (USSR) falls in second place in the 800 m final, won by D. Wottle (USA) and 3rd M. Boit (Kenya), Munich Olympics 1972 (photo, E. D. Lacey)

England and Wales v. Scotland and Ireland, Twickenham, 3 October 1970 (photo, E. D. Lacey)

Mark Spitz, Great Britain v. USA at Crystal Palace, 1967 (photo, E. D. Lacey)

The Goodwood Cup 1972 (photo, Sport and General)

Fishing (photo, Keystone Press)

Ilie Nastase at the International Tennis Games at Monte Carlo (photo, Naccache, Camera Press)

Cricket (photo, Anil Konar, Camera Press)

p. viii Netball (photo, E. D. Lacey)
   1 Rugby (photo, S. N. Priestman)
   2 Rugby Group (photo, S. N. Priestman)
   3 Olga Korbut (photo, E. D. Lacey)
 4–5 World Cup 1966 (photos, Sport and General)
   6 (left) Victor Trumper (photo, Sport and General)
   6 (right) Bobby Jones (photo, Sport and General)
   7 Suzanne Lenglen (photo, Sport and General)
   8 Ascot 1973 (photo, E. D. Lacey)
   9 Brigadier Gerard, Newmarket 1973 (photo, E. D. Lacey)
  10 Bobby Charlton, 1968 (photo, E. D. Lacey)

12 (from left to right) Christopher Brasher, Roger Bannister and
    Christopher Chataway (photo, Sport and General)
13–14 Kip Keino (photos, E. D. Lacey)
  15 Ben Jipko (photo, E. D. Lacey)
  16 Emil Zatopek (photo, E. D. Lacey)
  17 and 19 Girl divers (photos, E. D. Lacey)
  18 Sailing boat (photo, David Hornbrook)
  20 Mary Peters (photo, E. D. Lacey)
  21 D. Aaron (photo, E. D. Lacey)
  22 Lee Trevino (photo, E. D. Lacey)
  23 Tamara Press (photo, E. D. Lacey)
  24 Virginia Wade (photo, E. D. Lacey)
  25 K.O.'d boxer (photo, Sport and General)
  26 Terry McGowan (photo, E. D. Lacey)
27–8 Joe Brown (photos, BBC Copyright)
  29 Bowls (photo, E. D. Lacey)
  30 Tony Jacklin (photo, E. D. Lacey)
31–2 Lyn Davies (photos, E. D. Lacey)
  33 Cricket, England v. Australia (photo, E. D. Lacey)
  33 Cross-country race (photo, E. D. Lacey)

Index

Adorno, T. W., 192
Ali, Muhammed, 71, 118, 159, 189, 162–6, 170–1
Alston, R., 190, 196
anthropology, 47, 69–72
Arlott, J., 79, 85–9, 90, 95, 113, 120, 132, 134, 141, 179, 185, 190, 192
art, and sport, 11, 16, 19, 25–6, 35–9, 42, 53, 59, 66–70, 77–80, 128–9, 150–2, 201
Ashe, A., 48, 187
Atkinson, H. (*The Games*), 143–4

Bannister, R., 12, 83, 131, 162–3, 196
Baugh, F., 97, 105
beauty, and sport, 16–17, 22, 24, 25, 26, 39, 55, 77–8, 106, 128, 147–52
Beaverbrook Press, 92, 111
Benaud, R., 95, 113
Benjamin, W., 191
Benson and Hedges, 173–9, 185
Bentham, J., 49
Berger, J., 75, 85, 128
Best, G., 121–9, 139, 189
Blanchflower, D., 99, 118, 129–30, 132, 156
bowls, 29, 193–5
Brasher, C., 12, 19, 113, 130–2, 134
Brown, J., 27–8, 133, 166–9
bull-fighting, 150–2
Burke, K., 49
Bury, F.C., 180
Butler, F., 92

Caillois, R., 64–6
Cardus, N., 79–83, 84, 85, 86, 90, 113

Charlton, B., 10–11, 113, 118, 122, 133, 160, 189
Charlton, J., 159–161
Chataway, C., 12, 16, 125, 131
Chester report, 180
children and development, 36, 37–40, 42–3, 44–5
Clark report, 180
class in sport, 58, 60–1, 79–89, 93, 106–10, 134–43, 161–9
climbing, 25–8, 139, 149, 161–9, 198
Clough, B., 104
cognition, and physical activity, 25–6, 45, 46, 64, 71–2, 70–3, 153
Coleman, D., 95–6, 97–9, 114
Collingwood, R. G., 92
Conrad, J.
    The Shadow Line, 50–7
    Lord Jim, 57
conviviality and friendship, 1–30, 46–7, 56–7, 59, 133–42, 147–52, 191–2
Cooke, A., 83–4
Cooper, H., 113
Cotton, H., 120–1
Coventry City F.C., 181–2
cricket, 33, 35, 59, 79–89, 154, 172–9, 193–5
crowd behaviour, 121–2, 197–8

dance, 16, 17, 31, 70–1, 105, 200–1
Dartmouth, 49–50, 52–9
Davie, M., 130–2
Day, R., 95, 97
Delderfield, R. F., 141
D'Oliveira, B., 48
Dougan, D., 155–7, 160
Drury, R., 92

economics and sport, structures of, 20, 108, 149, 170–89, 199–200
Eliot, T. S., 2, 36, 166
emotions, and sport, 34–8, 42–3, 51–2, 53–5, 64, 191
Erikson, E., 44–5

fact/value distinction, 41–2, 45–6, 51, 153
femininity in sport, 23–4, 75
fishing, 35, 60, 114–15, 147–50, 194
Fitzgerald, F. Scott, 89
football, 6, 10, 11, 34–40, 43, 120–9, 152, 154–61, 172–3, 180–3, 193–5, 197–9
Foreman, G., 71
Francis, D., 144
Frost, D., 96–7

Geertz, C., 71–2
genius, the idea of, 76–7
gentleman, as ideal in sport, 16, 66–7, 72, 80–4, 85, 118, 128, 161–6
Gillette Cup, 173–9, 185
Glanville, B., 78, 90, 121–2, 144, 149
Goffman, E., 123
golf, 19–30, 83–4
Graham, F., 92

Hackett, D., 92, 93, 100, 101, 110, 114
Halloran, J. D., 94
happiness, in sport, 129, 133–8, 141–2, 147–50, 191–2
Harding, D. W., 142
Hay, I., 141, 142
Hemingway, E., 147–52, 154, 155
heroes and heroism, 15, 18, 35, 55, 56, 59, 74, 76–85, 88–9, 115–29, 139, 190–1
Hill, J., 95, 104, 113, 171
Hillary, E., 83
Hoby, A., 92, 101
Hopcraft, A., 112–3, 129
Huizinga, J., 52, 66–7, 72
Hunt, J., 158
Hunter, J., 145–7

hunting, 60

identity, social and personal, 34, 37–40, 44, 45, 51, 52, 58, 63–73, 75, 88–9, 122–9
image (as created by media) of celebrities, 1–30, 85–9, 94–5, 104, 105, 114–21, 122–9, 150–2, 155–61, 187–9

Jacklin, T., 30, 119, 187
James, H., 80
Jipko, B., 14, 159
John, B., 123–4
Jones, B., 5, 65, 83–4

Keino, K., 13–14, 159
Korbut, O., 3, 99
Kramer, J., 95, 187

Laker, P., 109–10
Landy, J., 12, 196
language as rule-system and as gesture, 42–3, 45–6, 62–9, 70–3, 113, 153
Larkin, P., 8–9, 42
Lawrence, D. H., 158
Leavis, F. R., 69
Lenglen, S., 6
Lewis, T., 104, 113, 132, 160–1, 175
Luther, 56

Macdonell, A. G., 141–3
Macintyre, A. C., 54, 148–9
MacLaren, A. C., 80–2
MacLeish, A., 196
Malamud, B., 143
Mallory, G., 161–6
manliness as ideal, 56, 138, 149–52, 156, 161–9
Manning, J. L., 110, 112
Marcuse, H., 190
Marx, K., 21, 153, 170
Maskell, D., 114
May, P., 83

McGhee, F., 92, 101, 112, 127
McLuhan, H. M., 95–6, 99, 105
meaning, in sports, 18, 19, 26, 37, 39, 41, 45–6, 49–52, 53–4, 57, 66–74, 76, 134
Miller, K., 113
Moore, B., 122, 124, 189
moral values, in sport, 36–7, 38–9, 40–4, 51–2, 52–3, 54, 128–9, 133–52, 185–7

nationalism, 13–14, 34–5, 150–2
newspapers and the press, 72, 78, 90–101, 105–15
  Daily Express, 92, 93, 94, 100, 102, 105–6
  Daily Mail, 92, 93, 102, 129
  Daily Mirror, 91, 100, 101, 102, 105–6, 107–10, 126
  Daily Telegraph, 102, 105–10, 113
  Guardian, 102, 105–6, 127–8
  Observer, 110–11, 130, 184
  People, 113
  Sun, 102, 125–7
  Sunday Times, 177, 200
  Times, 102, 182, 183
Northcliffe, 92, 93

Odell, N., 164–5
Orwell, G., 78
O'Sullivan, P., 92, 106

Palmer, A., 84, 120
Perry, F., 120–1
Peters, M., 18, 120
photography, 1–30
Plato, 55
play and playfulness, 43, 44, 47, 52, 66–7
Player (John Player league), 173–9, 184, 185
politics and culture, 14, 23, 35–9, 40–1, 42–3, 48, 60–4, 94–5, 97–8, 104, 116–29, 134–41, 153, 157–61, 190–2, 199, 200

popular culture, 22, 35–6, 40, 48, 90, 94, 96–100, 190–201
puritanism and will, 34, 43, 56, 74, 131

racing, as sport, prize money, 7, 106–8, 182–3, 193–5
Ramsey, A., 116–17
Raphael, 133
Rattigan, T., 141
Riefenstahl, L., 132, 141
Richards, B., 176–7
Robins, D., 181, 183
Rothmans, 173–9, 185
rugby, football, 2, 3, 60, 134–41, 191–2
running, 12–16, 19, 31, 32, 42, 43, 130–2, 162–3, 193–5

sailing, 16, 18, 49–59, 193–5
salaries in sport, 121–9, 172–89, 197–9
Sartre, J.-P., 191
Shakespeare, 38, 75, 78
skipping, 71
snooker, 105
Sobers, G., 177
social science, 47, 51, 57, 67–73, 85–6
Somervell, P., 164–5
sponsorship, sport and no capital accumulation, 21–2, 46, 52–3, 55, 58, 182–7
Sports Council, 200–1
Storey, D., 64, 134–141, 144, 145, 147, 154, 157
Swanton, E. W., 108–10, 112, 113

Taylor, A. J. P., 93
Taylor, C., 53
television, 34, 35, 72, 90, 95–100, 102–5, 115–21, 134, 145–6, 172–5, 186
tennis, 45, 193–5
theory of sport and games, 49, 51, 64–6, 67–9, 153–4
Thomas, E., 78
Tolstoy, 133–4
tradition in sport, 5–8, 40, 43–5, 51, 55,

56, 57, 59, 60, 74–8, 141–3, 163–5,
169, 198
Trueman, F. S., 85–9, 113, 120
Trumper, V., 5
Tudor, A., 97

Wade, V., 23–4, 120, 154, 188
Walker, J., 67
Waring, E., 92, 119
Wellings, E. M., 92
Whicker, A., 98–9
Whillans, D., 166–7
White, C., 92, 113

Whiting, G., 110, 111–12, 113
Wilson, P., 91–2, 100, 101–2, 110
Wittgenstein, L. L., 58, 67–9, 70, 153–4
work in modern culture, 35–6, 53–9,
134–41, 150–2, 154–5, 157–61
Wodehouse, P. G., 141
World Cup 1966, 1970, 4–5, 34

Yeats, W. B., 16–18, 46, 48, 76, 169

Zatopek, E., 16, 159, 190